An excellent introduction t  fully guides readers through Hebrew Bible and the most c

No background knowledge is presumed, and no other introduction to the Old Testament is as readable. Students and teachers alike will appreciate Strawn's jargon-free and undogmatic discussion of debates among scholars, his humor and literary sensitivity with biblical prose and poetry, as well as his attention throughout to the diversity and complexity of issues that face all readers of biblical literature.

— **Davis Hankins**, Appalachian State
University, USA

Brent A. Strawn's *The Old Testament: A Concise Introduction* is a *tour-de-force* that provides an exceptional orientation to the "lay of the land" stretching before students as they set out to explore the texts of the Hebrew Bible. Strawn overviews the content of the Old Testament with a balance of detail, clarity, and wit, while also presenting an outstanding up-to-date primer to the long history of biblical interpretation that students will meet in the classroom. Strawn is an expert field guide who welcomes readers with unrivaled sensitivity and care for detail, and his book will inspire thoughtful, critical engagement with the biblical text for years to come, in both undergraduate and seminary settings.

— **Kelly J. Murphy**, Central Michigan
University, USA

Aimed at first-time readers of the Old Testament, Brent Strawn's *Concise Introduction* is a highly readable, accessible, and reliable guide to the rich anthology of literatures that make up the Old Testament. Readers will come away from this book with a much deeper appreciation of the complexity, the sophistication, and the compelling nature of the Old Testament as an ancient but timeless word that proves timely for each new context and generation. Strawn helps us see how the Old Testament may be read paradoxically "as if" it were a grand, coherent story *and* "as if" it were unsettled, open-ended poetry, constantly sparking new questions and avenues of interpretation.

— **Dennis Olson**, Princeton Theological
Seminary, USA

THE OLD TESTAMENT

This concise volume introduces readers to the three main sections of the Hebrew Bible (*Tanakh*) and to the biblical books found in each. It is organized around two primary "stories": the story that scholars tell about the Old Testament and the story the literature itself tells. Concluding with a reconsideration of the Old Testament as more like poetry than a story, three main chapters cover:

- The Pentateuch (*Torah*)
- The Prophets (*Nevi'im*)
- The Writings (*Ketuvim*)

With key summaries of what the parts of the Old Testament "are all about," and including suggestions for further reading, this volume is an ideal introduction for students of and newcomers to the Old Testament.

Brent A. Strawn is Professor of Old Testament at Duke University, USA. He has edited more than 20 volumes to date, including the award-winning *The Oxford Encyclopedia of the Bible and Law* (2015). His most recent book is *The Old Testament Is Dying: A Diagnosis and Recommended Treatment* (2017). He was a member of the translation team and editorial board for *The Common English Bible*.

THE OLD TESTAMENT

A CONCISE INTRODUCTION

Brent A. Strawn

Routledge
Taylor & Francis Group

NEW YORK AND LONDON

First published 2020
by Routledge

52 Vanderbilt Avenue, New York, NY 10017
and by Routledge
2 Park Square, Milton Park, Abingdon, Oxon, OX14 4RN

Routledge is an imprint of the Taylor & Francis Group, an informa business

© 2020 Taylor & Francis

Library of Congress Cataloging-in-Publication Data
Title: The Old Testament: a concise introduction / Brent A. Strawn.
Description: New York, NY: Routledge, 2019. | Includes bibliographical references and index.
Identifiers: LCCN 2019036234 (print) | LCCN 2019036235 (ebook) |
Subjects: LCSH: Bible. Old Testament—Introductions.
Classification: LCC BS1140.3 .S77 2019 (print) | LCC BS1140.3 (ebook) |
DDC 221.6/1—dc23
LC record available at https://lccn.loc.gov/2019036234
LC ebook record available at https://lccn.loc.gov/2019036235

ISBN: 978-0-415-64299-6 (hbk)
ISBN: 978-0-415-64300-9 (pbk)
ISBN: 978-0-203-07569-2 (ebk)

Typeset in Bembo
by codeMantra

For Walter Brueggemann—

early inspiration and, much later, treasured
colleague and dear friend who remains mentor,
example, paragon

CONTENTS

CHARTS, BOXES, MAPS, AND FIGURES

CHARTS

BOXES

MAP

FIGURES

A NOTE ON TRANSLITERATION

This book occasionally brings Hebrew and Greek words into English script, which is called *transliteration*. For the sake of English-only readers, I have opted for a simplified transliteration so as to approximate what the words sound like if pronounced today.

PREFACE

The present volume is intended to serve as an introduction—a *concise* one, as the title indicates—to the Old Testament, also known as the Hebrew Bible. I have tried to write the book that I have desired for my own students ever since I began teaching: a succinct treatment that covers the entire sweep of the Old Testament in relatively brief compass, a book that is more about the forest than the trees, that would orient students to the lay of the land, and that they could read in a sitting or two before they came face to face in subsequent lectures with larger vistas or the specific foliage in intimate and sometimes exhausting detail. I've been searching for that book for over 20 years now and have yet to find it exactly, though there are certainly a number of honorable mentions. While I am conscious that the present volume has limitations and is not quite as concise as I originally intended, I nevertheless hope it performs the purposes that I have envisioned. Most of all I hope that readers, especially those new to the Old Testament, will agree, since this book is written for them.

Although the focus here is very much on the big picture painted with broad strokes, that larger portrait is made up of many, much smaller pieces—different types and colors of paint, to continue the metaphor. These smaller pieces include not only the various books and blocks of literature within the Old Testament but also key moments in the history of modern scholarship that has been devoted to the Old Testament for several centuries now. And so, while the main goal of this book is to overview the *content* of the Old Testament, that cannot be done without at least some discussion of the *scholarship* that has cast important light on that content. The most detailed points of biblical scholarship are rarely on display here, certainly not extensively, since this is not the place for that given the goals and size of the volume. Even so, while the fullest scope of scholarly theory is usually not explicit in what follows, it is nevertheless operative everywhere—even if only under the surface. But readers should take special note of the fact that there is hardly a nook or cranny in biblical scholarship that is not marked by a wide diversity of opinion—sometimes sharp. The scholarship that is utilized here, then, is just a selection from a vast and deep sea.

To maximize the book's readability, I have not included any notes—a painful discipline since I love few things more than a perfectly crafted footnote! As a coping mechanism, and to give some indication of the scholarship that I have drawn upon and to give readers a few ideas about where to go from here, each chapter contains suggestions for further reading. These suggestions are not always as concise as they might have been; I occasionally include specialized and detailed studies. If nothing else, this underscores that even a concise introduction is rooted in the long history of biblical interpretation.

The reader that I have had in mind while writing this book is one who has never read the Old Testament, or at least not the entirety, majority, or even large swaths of it. My wish for these readers is simply this: that this little introduction might begin to open up the Old Testament for them so that they will never be bored by it and that they will return to it, reading in it all the days of their life (see Deut 17:19). If that happens, its author will have achieved far more than is his right to hope, let alone his ability to achieve. I can personally testify that a little book by Hans Walter Wolff, *The Old Testament: A Guide to Its Writings*, played such a role in my own life as an undergraduate. I believe I am a biblical scholar today in part because of that short volume and its author, whom, sadly, I never got the chance to meet.

As a freshman in college I encountered another influential book, *The Prophetic Imagination* by Walter Brueggemann. My debts to Brueggemann outweigh, by megatons, my debts to Wolff, and his influence is quite obvious, I'm sure, to all those who know me personally or have read some of my other writings. It is a great pleasure, therefore, to dedicate this book to him with *endless* gratitude (and, yes, Walter, with two more sets of threes!) for his influence and for the unexpected and astonishing gift of our treasured friendship.

It remains to register a few important words of thanks: Andy Beck was present at the creation of this volume years ago. I am thankful for his help and wisdom way back when, and I was delighted that, when he moved to Routledge, my book eventually followed suit. Steve Wiggins got the book under contract and, more recently, Sarah Gore, Gabrielle Coakeley, Rebecca Shillabeer, and Jack Boothroyd have proven exceedingly helpful, supportive, and patient despite several unfortunate delays. Some dear colleagues and friends took time to read all or parts of the book and offer feedback: James K. Mead, Patrick D. Miller, David L. Petersen, and my research assistant, Evan Bassett, who checked references and offered other significant assistance. Special thanks go to a trio of devoted readers: Ryan P. Bonfiglio, T. Collin R. P. Cornell, and Joel M. LeMon, with whom I'd trust anything I write (and much more besides). I am also grateful to my wife, Holly, who read bits along the way but, more than that, deserves extra credit for listening to countless (mostly sad) oral reports about it, and to my in-laws, Reese and Beverly Verner, who gave feedback at the very start of the idea—and others I'm sure to have left unmentioned to my embarrassment. All of the above individuals should be congratulated for anything good in the book; any guilt they bear for what isn't decent is only because they stubbornly continue to associate with me. But, even if I should reflect poorly on them, I am confident of the precise opposite in my case. These friends and family members have made me a better person in numerous ways, and the same holds true for the three greatest gifts of all—my children: Caleb (who also read and offered helpful comments on several chapters), Annie, and Micah. Perhaps I shouldn't neglect to mention our new puppy Finley Isaiah. The book would've been finished much sooner had he not made such a meteoric entrance into the family last Fall.

bas
Spring 2019

ABBREVIATIONS

AD	*Anno Domini* (same as CE)
b.	Precedes references to the Babylonian Talmud
BC	Before Christ (same as BCE)
BCE	Before Common Era (same as BC)
ca.	*Circa*, approximately
CE	Common Era (same as AD)
CEB	Common English Bible
cf.	Compare
ChrH	The Chronicler's History
D	The D Source or Deuteronomy (or parts thereof)
DH	The Deuteronomistic History (same as DtrH)
Dtr	The Deuteronomist (responsible for the DH/DtrH)
DtrH	The Deuteronomistic History (same as DH)
E	The Elohistic Source
e.g.	For example
H	The Holiness Code or Collection
HS	Holiness School
i.e.	That is
J	The J or Yahwistic Source
LXX	The Septuagint, the Greek translation of the Old Testament
m.	Precedes references to the Mishnah
MSG	The Message
MT	The Masoretic Text, the traditional version of the Hebrew Bible
NAB	New American Bible

NASB   New American Standard Bible
NIV   New International Version
NJPSV   New Jewish Publication Society Version
NRSV   New Revised Standard Version
P   The Priestly Source

THE STORY *OF* THE OLD TESTAMENT AND THE OLD TESTAMENT *AS* STORY

At some point in history—when, exactly, we do not know—the Bible as it now is, or something very much like it, came into existence. The reasons why we don't know exactly when this happened is because the evidence at our disposal is limited and fragmentary. It is also because the Bible is a complex document, or rather set of documents, which means that some parts came to their present form at different times than others.

It seems clear that two developments facilitated the Bible's coming-to-be as we now have it. The first might be called *ideological*: various decisions were made by various people to establish a discrete "canon" of Scripture, including the processes by which some books were admitted into that official collection and others were not. That is, in fact, what *canon* means: a set list of authoritative texts. But here, too, much remains unclear: exactly when these kinds of decisions were finalized, and by whom, is not entirely certain and likely varies from one biblical composition to another. Discussions on some of these matters, and some of these books, went on for a very long time. The final ordering of the biblical books, or even parts within some books, went on even longer—well into the early centuries of the Common Era, and in some cases even later. (A traditional perspective, that the ultimate moment was a Jewish council held in Jamnia ca. 90 CE, is almost certainly erroneous; most scholars place the finished Hebrew Bible later than that, though the first steps were in some ways and at certain points considerably earlier.)

The second development was *technological*—to be specific, the rise of the codex in the Roman world allowed compositions that had previously existed as separate documents (manuscripts, scrolls, etc.) to be bound together in one collection between two covers. The codex, while not a Christian invention, nevertheless caught on quickly in Christian circles where it was widely used. And, while Jews also adopted the codex form, it did not have quite the same appeal within Judaism, perhaps in part due to Christian fascination with the codex. And so, to this day, what one finds in a synagogue is a Torah *scroll* not a Torah codex. In fact, it should be noted that the earliest complete codex of the Hebrew Bible in existence (the Leningrad Codex from St. Petersburg) dates only as far back as 1008 or 1009 CE. The earliest codex, that is, dates to roughly 2,000 years *after* the time of David, 1,800 years *after* the prophet Isaiah, and 1,500 years *after* the priest Ezra.

Whatever the fine details of these two developments—some of which are known but many of which remain elusive—they helped the Bible-as-one-collection eventually come into being. When it did, the biblical writings achieved "literary simultaneity": the Bible could be read together as a unit, synchronically, as if it were one book. In the codex form, of course, it *really was* one book.

While many people find the ins-and-outs of developments like these fascinating, the fine details are, at least to some degree, unimportant—at least for the purposes of the present book. That is because, despite the many steps that led to the Bible's current form, it is in *this* form that we now have it today: it is now a book, bound between two covers—sometimes quite expensive leather covers with gilded pages. The Bible is now a unified collection, even if that unity is historically secondary, the result of a long developmental process, one that is due in part to its book-like form. However it happened, the Bible is now received as a whole despite its many subparts (the various "books of the Bible"), not unlike so many other books (with their various "chapters" or "parts"). If the Bible is ever given as a gift, it is given as a whole; one doesn't give or receive Isaiah or Exodus or Amos all by themselves.

The Bible-as-one-collection or book solves some problems, like keeping many different compositions together in one place, but it also raises a number of questions. Is the Bible-as-a-book like any other? And what kind of book is the Bible-as-a-book? There are, after all, many different types of literature. Is the Bible's one book form akin to the novel—whether non-fiction, historical fiction, or fiction—such that it ought to be read accordingly, with the standard elements that are typically present in those kinds of narratives: characters, character development, rising action, climax, denouement, and all the rest? Or is the Bible best related to some other genre, whatever that might be, with a different set of conventions that affect reading and interpretation? One can easily imagine other literary genres to which the Old Testament as a collection might be compared, at least analogously, if only because the Bible itself is comprised of many different genres: different stories, yes, but also different poems and prophecies and wise sayings and so on and so forth. This suggests that *literary anthology* could be a good candidate for how to understand the Bible. Reading an anthology is quite different from reading a straightforward novel. Narrative, then, is just one possibility—even if an important one—among several possibilities when considering what kind of book the Bible might be.

Whatever the case, it is important to observe that readers often make decisions about *what* they are reading *even before* they read it. Those kinds of decisions make a difference as to *how* people read what they are reading. The very form of what one reads—a book, say, containing 15 prophets (and more), as opposed to a scroll containing only one—will affect how it is read. Readers don't usually confuse Tweets with the most careful and considered prose, nor advertisements with verified statements of fact.

THE STORY *OF* THE OLD TESTAMENT

Another curiosity about the Bible-as-a-book is found in the title "the Bible" itself. That title derives from Greek *ta biblia*, which is grammatically *plural*: "the books." In its very name, then, *The Bible*—"The Books"—actually resists the unified impression that is created by its singular, one-book-like form. So, is the Bible one singular book or many discrete books? The form of the Bible suggests the former, but the content of the Bible, and its name, suggests the latter. At this point, we seem to have returned to where we began: yes, the Bible at some point emerged in its current form as a collection made up of preexisting compositions, and, yes, we have it that way now, *but what about before now?*

Septuagint (LXX)	Roman Catholic	Orthodox
Genesis	Genesis	Genesis
Exodus	Exodus	Exodus
Leviticus	Leviticus	Leviticus
Numbers	Numbers	Numbers
Deuteronomy	Deuteronomy	Deuteronomy
Joshua	Joshua	Joshua
Judges	Judges	Judges
Ruth	Ruth	Ruth
1 Reigns	1 Samuel	1 Kingdoms
2 Reigns	2 Samuel	2 Kingdoms
3 Reigns	1 Kings	3 Kingdoms
4 Reigns	2 Kings	4 Kingdoms
1 Chronicles	1 Chronicles	1 Chronicles
2 Chronicles	2 Chronicles	2 Chronicles + Prayer of Manasseh
*1 Esdras		1 Esdras
*2 Esdras	Ezra-Nehemiah	2 Esdras (Ezra-Nehemiah)
*(Greek) Esther	Tobit	Tobit
*Judith	Judith	Judith
*Tobit	Greek Esther	Greek Esther
*1 Maccabees	1 Maccabees	1 Maccabees
*2 Maccabees	2 Maccabees	2 Maccabees
*3 Maccabees		*3 Maccabees
*4 Maccabees		
	Job	
Psalms	Psalms	Psalms
*Psalm 151		Psalm 151
		Job
*Prayer of Manasseh		(see 2 Chronicles above)
Proverbs	Proverbs	Proverbs
Ecclesiastes	Ecclesiastes	Ecclesiastes
Song of Songs	Song of Songs	Song of Songs
Job	(see above)	(see above)
*Wisdom	Wisdom	Wisdom
*Sirach	Sirach	Sirach
*Psalms of Solomon		
	Isaiah	
	Jeremiah	
	Lamentations	
	Baruch + Letter of Jeremiah	
	Ezekiel	
	Susannah	
	Greek Daniel	
	Bel and the Dragon	
Hosea	Hosea	Hosea
Amos	Joel	Amos
Micah	Amos	Micah
Joel	Obadiah	Joel
Obadiah	Jonah	Obadiah
Jonah	Micah	Jonah
Nahum	Nahum	Nahum
Habakkuk	Habakkuk	Habakkuk
Zephaniah	Zephaniah	Zephaniah
Haggai	Haggai	Haggai
Zechariah	Zechariah	Zechariah
Malachi	Malachi	Malachi

Chart 1.1 Some Different Canons of Scripture

Isaiah	(see above)	Isaiah
Jeremiah	(see above)	Jeremiah
*Baruch	(see above)	Baruch
Lamentations	(see above)	Lamentations
*Letter of Jeremiah	(see Baruch above)	Letter of Jeremiah
Ezekiel	(see above)	Ezekiel
*Susanna	(see above)	Susannah
*(Greek) Daniel	(see above)	(Greek) Daniel
*Bel and the Dragon	(see above)	Bel and the Dragon

For the Hebrew ordering, see Chart 1.2. To highlight the differences, the Septuagint sequence is given first, following the presentation found in Albert Pietersma and Benjamin G. Wright, eds., *A New English Translation of the Septuagint* (New York: Oxford University Press, 2007). Different manuscripts (as well as traditional lists) can vary, particularly for the books after Chronicles (see Henry Barclay Swete, *An Introduction to the Old Testament in Greek* [Peabody: Hendrickson,1989], 197-230). Asterisks indicate compositions not found in the Masoretic Text of the Hebrew Bible. The Catholic sequence follows the NAB. The Orthodox ordering follows *The Orthodox Study Bible* (Nashville: Thomas Nelson, 2008). Some (not all) of the more significant differences in sequencing among the columns are boxed and, together with the standard Protestant ordering (see Chart 1.2), reveal that the three main Christian traditions vary among themselves on in how closely they follow the Greek tradition. See also the lists provided in Lee Martin McDonald, *The Biblical Canon: Its Origin, Transmission, and Authority* (Grand Rapids: Baker Academic, 2006), 439-44; and Lee Martin McDonald and James A. Sanders, eds., *The Canon Debate* (Peabody: Hendrickson, 2002), 585-90.

Chart 1.1 (Continued)

A great deal of modern biblical scholarship, which extends back to at least the eighteenth century with even earlier roots, has been devoted to that very question: "What was the Bible like before the Bible?" For centuries, scholars have pursued what might be called the story *of* the Bible or, put differently, the *history* of the Bible. How did it come to be? How did its various parts—not just its books but also its subparts: the parts of the parts of a book—come together in the shapes and forms we now have? This is to ask, for example, not only how the 39 books of the Old Testament came to be and how they came to be joined together with the 27 books of the New Testament to form the 66 books of the Protestant Christian canon of Scripture (cf. Chart 1.1), but also to ask, how did the various psalms come together in what is now the Book of Psalms? Or how did the various sayings attributed to the eighth-century prophet Isaiah, the son of Amoz, come together to form what is now the Book of Isaiah?

The history of biblical interpretation repeatedly shows that scholars have not remained content with the *formation* of a biblical book as it now stands (or the whole Bible as it now exists) but have been very interested in questions of *pre*-formation. What lies *behind* or *prior to* this particular saying of Isaiah or that specific psalm? When was it said or written? By whom? What real-life situation lies behind it? These are very different questions than asking about how or when a particular saying was joined to other sayings in order to make a larger unit, chapter, or book. Of course, the two types of questions are related, at least at times, as, for example, in terms of chronological development: "part A was first said by so-and-so, in such-and-such a period, for this-or-that reason; subsequently, part A was joined to part B, and parts A+B to C," and so on and so forth.

The story of the Bible, then, according to modern biblical scholarship, is a very *long* story. It is a rather drawn out history that begins before the words of the Bible itself, asking after origins, influences, and possible relationships with antecedent material (whether from Israel or from its neighbors throughout the ancient Near East). It then extends all the way through the specific biblical utterances in question, to their subsequent life as they were remembered, passed on, collected, collated, put into writing (if originally oral), and finally gathered up into larger units, traditions, compositions, books, and, ultimately, the canon of Holy Scripture. The present introduction cannot cover this long story of the Old Testament's development in great detail, though some of that story is recounted in each of the chapters that follow. For present purposes, it is enough to know that the Old Testament itself *has* a story, which is to say the Bible has an origin, a history, a development, and a reception that continues up to the present day. In truth, each of these items—origin, history, development, and reception—is not singular but a plurality because *the Bible* is, after all, *ta biblia*, "The Books." Each of the Bible's books, then, along with those book's constituent subparts, has its own story to tell, resulting in *multiple* origins, histories, developments, and receptions. So, if the Old Testament can be said to have a story, it is a long and highly complicated one that is made up of countless other stories. That is to be expected, of course, whenever we consider something like the Bible in historical perspective, since it is both ancient and complex.

THE OLD TESTAMENT *AS* STORY

But if it can be said that the Old Testament *has a story* in the sense that it has a history reflecting its growth, development, and the like, it can also be said that the Old Testament *contains and conveys* a story. Put differently, we can say that the Old Testament *tells* a story or at least that it is possible to read the Old Testament *as if* it were a story. (This "as if" is actually quite important.)

The Old Testament, as also the larger Christian Bible of which it is the first major part, is many things to many people, whether religious or not. But whatever one's personal inclinations may be, the Old Testament is, irrefutably, a piece of literature. Or, better, in light of what was said earlier, the Old Testament is *pieces* of literature, a *collection* of *literatures*: an anthology or library. This point granted, a decent-sized bit of biblical literature is in story form. It is partly the dominance of narrative, on the one hand, and, on the other, our familiarity with that kind of genre—its dominance in contemporary society—that leads many readers to construe the Old Testament or entire Bible as one giant narrative. It is not uncommon to hear of the Bible described as (or even published in some form as) the great "story of God." Such a construal of the Bible makes a certain degree of sense and is not entirely without merit. For example, biblical scholars sometimes call the Books of Genesis through Kings the Primary History since this extended block of material can be read as telling a single story, with a unified (though long and complex) plot that runs from the creation of the world to the end of the southern kingdom of Judah, when Jerusalem falls to the Babylonians (see further Chapter 3). The order of the Old Testament books found in most English Bibles, which is largely derived from Greek orderings (see Chart 1.1), further reinforces this story-like impression by:

- placing Ruth immediately after Judges, since it claims to come from "the days when the Judges judged" (Ruth 1:1);
- putting Chronicles after Samuel-Kings, since it repeats a good bit of that material though it adds some new information as well; and
- setting Ezra-Nehemiah and Esther after Chronicles, as these books continue the story in, around, and after the Persian rule mentioned at the end of 2 Chronicles 36.

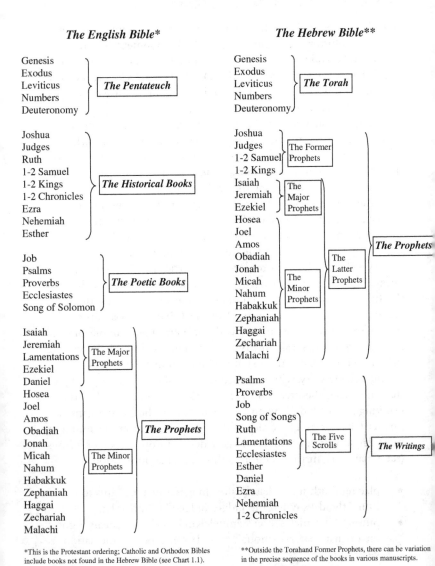

The English Bible*

Genesis
Exodus
Leviticus   **The Pentateuch**
Numbers
Deuteronomy

Joshua
Judges
Ruth
1-2 Samuel
1-2 Kings   **The Historical Books**
1-2 Chronicles
Ezra
Nehemiah
Esther

Job
Psalms
Proverbs   **The Poetic Books**
Ecclesiastes
Song of Solomon

Isaiah
Jeremiah
Lamentations   The Major
Ezekiel   Prophets
Daniel

Hosea
Joel
Amos
Obadiah
Jonah   **The Prophets**
Micah
Nahum   The Minor
Habakkuk   Prophets
Zephaniah
Haggai
Zechariah
Malachi

The Hebrew Bible**

Genesis
Exodus
Leviticus   **The Torah**
Numbers
Deuteronomy

Joshua
Judges   The Former
1-2 Samuel   Prophets
1-2 Kings

Isaiah   The
Jeremiah   Major
Ezekiel   Prophets

Hosea
Joel
Amos
Obadiah   **The Prophets**
Jonah   The
Micah   Minor   The
Nahum   Prophets   Latter
Habakkuk   Prophets
Zephaniah
Haggai
Zechariah
Malachi

Psalms
Proverbs
Job
Song of Songs
Ruth
Lamentations   The Five   **The Writings**
Ecclesiastes   Scrolls
Esther
Daniel
Ezra
Nehemiah
1-2 Chronicles

*This is the Protestant ordering; Catholic and Orthodox Bibles include books not found in the Hebrew Bible (see Chart 1.1).

**Outside the Torah and Former Prophets, there can be variation in the precise sequence of the books in various manuscripts.

Chart 1.2 The Contents and Order of the English and Hebrew Bibles Compared

Two problems face this Bible-as-one-big-story understanding, however. The first is that the order of the Hebrew Bible is actually quite different from that found in most English Bibles (see Chart 1.2). That means the straightforward narrative "flow" isn't quite the same in Hebrew vs. English editions (see Chapters 3–4). The second, more substantial problem is that, even in the "plot" described above from Genesis through Kings (or Esther), a linear reading eventually breaks down. It turns out that the straightforward narrative isn't nearly so straightforward, especially outside the Primary History. Where, for example, does the Book of Job fit into this "story"? Many early biblical interpreters wondered the same thing, though they answered the question in different ways. In some circles, Job was identified with the "Jobab" mentioned in Gen 10:29. By means of that identification, Job could be placed in the period of Israel's ancestors alongside Abraham, Sarah, Isaac, Rebekah, and the rest. The Peshitta, an ancient translation of the Old Testament into Syriac, goes so far as to situate the Book of Job immediately after the first five books of the Bible, making this connection between Job and the ancestral period as explicit—and as physical—as possible. The community that composed the Dead Sea Scrolls seems to have felt similarly, though they made the connection between Job and the ancestors in a different way. They did not do so by means of the ordering of biblical books in a codex (which they didn't use), but by the special handwriting they used when copying Job. Among the many Dead Sea Scrolls that have been recovered, only texts from the Pentateuch (Genesis–Deuteronomy) and Job are occasionally written in an archaic form of the Hebrew script known as paleo-Hebrew. It may be that, by writing these texts in paleo-Hebrew, the scribes were signaling their belief that the Pentateuch and Job were equally ancient compositions that somehow belonged together.

But, despite Gen 10:29, the Peshitta, and the Dead Sea Scrolls, there are really no explicit clues in the Book of Job itself that would warrant its placement within the timeframe of the Pentateuch. The subject matter of Job is quite removed from the driving "plot" of the Primary History along with Chronicles, Ezra-Nehemiah, and Esther. Of course, one *could* stick Job in there somewhere, but it would be a parallel storyline at best, not at all necessary for nor directly contributing to the primary plot. And that means that one *could* stick Job somewhere else entirely, which is exactly what both English and Hebrew Bibles do (Chart 1.2).

The problem seen with the Book of Job is only worsened with something like the Book of Psalms. Some of the psalms are connected to King David by occasional references to moments in his life or by means of a phrase used in many superscriptions in the Psalms, *le-David*. This phrase could mean "of David," as in "(written) by David," but it could also mean something else entirely: "for David," as in "dedicated to David," for example, or "in Davidic mode" or the like (see further Chapter 4). Whatever the case, an even larger number of psalms do neither of these things as they lack any references to David. These psalms *might* still be attributed to David in some fashion, but they do nothing to encourage such attribution and certainly do not require it. The significance of these psalms, in other words, does not depend on their placement within the "story of David." David's story, at any rate, is not told in the Book of Psalms at all—which is a collection of poems, not stories— but preserved, instead, in Samuel and Chronicles.

Beyond Job and Psalms we might consider the Books of Proverbs, Ecclesiastes, and the Song of Songs, all of which are traditionally attributed to David's son and heir, King Solomon, but which, again, cannot be assigned in toto (if at all) to "Solomon's wisdom" (see further Chapter 4). Regardless of that, the larger issue is that none of these three books advance the plot found in Genesis–Kings + Chronicles, Ezra-Nehemiah, and Esther. Even more pointedly, it is hard to see how these three "wisdom books" relate to those other texts at all.

Finally, what about the prophetic books? Through introductory superscriptions, many of the prophets are tied to the reigns of specific kings (see, e.g., Isa 1:1; 6:1; Jer 1:1–3; Ezek 1:1–3; Hos 1:1; Amos 1:1; etc.). These books can thus be placed, at least roughly, into the history of Israel and its monarchy as recounted in Samuel–Kings (also Chronicles), as well as, in a few select cases, into the period *after* the monarchy. But biblical scholars have long believed that the prophetic books are themselves anthologies: pastiches of different oracles that are rarely, if ever, put in chronological order and that often collect material from periods far removed from those of the superscriptions proper (see further Chapter 3). Once again, therefore, the prophetic books simply do not easily fit into the grand narrative of Genesis–Kings (or Genesis–Esther); neither do they contribute straightforwardly to its plot. Instead, the prophetic books are a collection of voices that were active during a 300- or 400-year period within the latter part of Israel's monarchic history. They do not seem to advance the storyline begun in Genesis. Instead, they must be somehow peppered back into the narratives about Israel's history. And yet, even when that is done, the prophets do and say a good bit more than merely "contribute" to that "story."

Telling the Old Testament's own "story" is even more difficult if one follows, as the present volume does, the order of the Hebrew Bible (see Chart 1.2). The point of all this is simply to say that, while the Old Testament (and the Christian Bible as a whole) includes many narratives, it is not exclusively or primarily one coherent, linear story. That simple fact is precisely what complicates much reading of the Bible since most people expect to find a narrative—something akin to a novel—most of the time when they pick up a book. The problem with such an expectation is that the Bible fails to meet it, and this can frustrate readers' experience and interpretation. Even at the level of specific biblical books, the preceding discussion shows that many of the biblical compositions are also not "stories." Books like the Psalms, most of the prophets, Proverbs, Job, and Ecclesiastes—to name a few—often lie at considerable remove from even the most disjointed or downright odd novels. Probably for these very reasons, books like these are rarely on the average person's "favorite Bible book" list simply because they are hard to read. And they are hard to read precisely because they are *not* stories.

Despite and in spite of all that, many people continue to understand the Bible as a kind of grand narrative, "the story of God." Though such an approach doesn't do full justice to the specific contents of the Bible, there is nevertheless something that remains helpful about the language of story, and this is undoubtedly why so many people continue to use it. So, while it is not quite right to say that the Old Testament *is* a story or even that the Torah, the Prophets, or the Writings contain *a* story, it is nevertheless helpful to speak—even if only metaphorically—of the "stories" that these larger units or the specific books tell. So, alongside the story scholars tell *of* or *about* the Old Testament, we can also consider the Old Testament's *own* story—that is, what the content of the Old Testament is about. This latter story, no less than the former, will likely need to be fairly long and detailed if it is to be accurate. And it won't be accurate at all if we reduce everything to narrative. Even so, the two types of story—the one relating to scholarship and the one relating to content—are useful points of entry, especially when approaching the Old Testament for the first time.

THE *REST* OF THE STORY ... AND THIS BOOK

Given its utility, this two-fold understanding of the Old Testament's story will be used throughout the present volume. The three main divisions of the Hebrew Bible—Torah, Prophets, and Writings—are treated sequentially in the three chapters that follow. In each one, the "story" *of* or *about* that particular division and its constituent books will be discussed. This story is primarily an academic one, recounting the origin, development, and history of these sections and books of the Old Testament: how, to the best of our knowledge (and centuries of research), they came to be in the form we now have them. After this, each chapter offers an account of the "story" that these three large divisions and representative books *tell*—as far as that is possible. If the first story is primarily about history and composition, the second is largely literary, introducing readers to the main content that is found in the material. If there is any imbalance in telling these two stories about the Old Testament, it is the second, literary one that is favored. In both cases, "story" should (once again) not be taken too strictly; it is meant only as a helpful way to categorize the material at hand.

Much of what we know, or think we know, of the "story" *about* the Old Testament—the origins, history, and development of the canonical divisions and biblical books—depends on much speculation and so much remains uncertain. Another way to put this would be to say that if scholarly investigations and reconstructions really do constitute a story, that story might well end up being fictional (!)—at least in some ways and at some points because scholars are constantly refining if not overturning prior theories. In the case of the story that the Old Testament itself tells, the goal of the present volume is to provide readers with a useful but concise overview of content. Toward that end, each chapter concludes by highlighting two things that are crucial to that division of the Hebrew Bible. To boil the Torah, Prophets, and Writings down to only two items is certainly an exercise in fantastic reduction. Even so, the focus on two significant aspects begins to capture, especially for those new to the Old Testament, what the larger division is about and what it contributes to the Hebrew Bible as a whole.

Before moving on, two final items must be mentioned:

First, as already indicated, this book follows the ordering of the Hebrew Bible, which is often called by the acronym *Tanakh*, created from the first letters of the three major divisions:

- *T* is for *Torah*—Hebrew for "Law" or "Instruction," the first five books of the Bible;
- *N* is for *Nevi'im*—Hebrew for "Prophets," divided into "Former" (*Rishonim*) and "Latter" (*Acharonim*) prophets; and
- *K* is for *Ketuvim*—Hebrew for "Writings," something of a hodge-podge or catch-all for what did not fit into *Torah* or *Nevi'im* and/or that was written too late to be incorporated therein.

The specific content of the *Tanakh* is as follows (cf. Chart 1.2):

- *Torah: Genesis*, Exodus, Leviticus, Numbers, Deuteronomy
- *Nevi'im*
  - *Nevi'im Rishonim*: Joshua, Judges, Samuel, Kings
  - *Nevi'im Acharonim*: Isaiah, Jeremiah, Ezekiel, Hosea, Joel, Amos, Obadiah, Jonah, Micah, Nahum, Habakkuk, Zephaniah, Haggai, Zechariah, Malachi
- *Ketuvim*: Psalms, Job, Proverbs, Ruth, Song of Songs, Ecclesiastes, Lamentations, Esther, Daniel, Ezra, Nehemiah, Chronicles.

As noted earlier, the Hebrew order differs in important respects from the order found in most English Bibles, which depends on the Greek translation of the Hebrew Bible known as the Septuagint (LXX). The Septuagint also contains a number of books that are not present in the Hebrew Bible—the so-called Apocrypha or deutero-canonical books (see Chart 1.1).

I have decided to follow the order of the *Tanakh* for a number of reasons. Primary among these is my desire to present the Old Testament in its native literary habitat. Even English Bibles that follow the Greek order are almost always translated from editions of the Hebrew Bible that utilize the *Tanakh*-structure. Truth be told, the orderings of the books of the Bible—whether in Hebrew,

Greek, English, or other languages—have often varied widely over the centuries. But some sections of the Bible have been more secure than others in terms of a set order; it may be that these parts were finalized before the others. The Torah, for instance, is preeminent in this regard: its order is well attested from early periods and seems to have never suffered any variation in the manuscript tradition. So, among other reasons that might be mentioned, the *Tanakh*-structure is helpful in that it highlights the primacy of the Torah; the secondary, commentary-like nature of the Prophets, who speak and preach after the Torah; and, finally, the tertiary nature of the Writings. While many readers of the Bible would in principle *resist* privileging one part over another, the hierarchy just described, with Torah at the top, remains operative—explicitly or implicitly—in many circles, especially within contemporary Judaism. Almost no one would quibble with the fact that books like Genesis or Deuteronomy are at least a tad bit more important than, say, Obadiah or Haggai, if for no other reason than that the former are found in the Torah. Of course, that just proves the point about the preeminence of Torah!

Second, if I have deliberately decided to follow the order of the Hebrew Bible, it may legitimately be asked why I so often employ the title "Old Testament." There can be no doubt that "Old Testament" is a Christian designation, implying, as it obviously does, a *New* Testament that, together with the Old, comprises the Christian Bible. The title "Hebrew Bible" seems more neutral, on the face of it, and is perhaps to be preferred for just that reason. But there are problems with this latter term, no less than the former. Not all of the "Hebrew Bible" is, in fact, actually written in Hebrew. A few sections exist only in Aramaic (portions of Daniel and Ezra, a verse in Jeremiah, a phrase in Genesis). Alternatively, if one wishes to use a term that is more congenial to contemporary Jewish usage, then one would probably adopt, not "Hebrew Bible," but something like *Tanakh* or *Mikra* (Hebrew for "Scripture") or simply "the Bible"— with all due respect to Christians who would want to include the 27 books of the New Testament in the latter designation. Another point is that, historically, versions of the Bible in languages other than Hebrew (especially the Greek Septuagint, the Latin Vulgate, the Aramaic Targums, and the Syriac Peshitta) have been exceedingly important for both Jews and Christians—indeed, at some points and in certain circles, *more* important than the Hebrew text itself.

For reasons like these I have opted to use "Old Testament" throughout this book, partly out of habit and partly as a matter of confession. I am a Christian, an ordained minister in fact, and cannot pretend to be otherwise. I certainly cannot pretend that I am Jewish, which I am not, as much as I love and respect Judaism, its history, its practice, and its texts—my lifelong devotion to the Hebrew Bible (and here I use the term quite intentionally) is at least partial proof of this latter point. But, despite my personal religious commitments, when I use "Old Testament" in this book, I rarely— actually, I think, never—mean to imply let alone require recourse to the New Testament, though in my own life, practice, and teaching I often do make such recourse. When I do mean to include the New Testament, I will thus speak of the "Christian Bible." In what follows, then, I use both "Old Testament" and "Hebrew Bible" (the latter especially when speaking about a point evident only in Hebrew [or Aramaic!]) and do so interchangeably, signifying by the former, especially, that I am a Christian reader, and by the latter, especially, that I care about the Hebrew original which retains its vitality, significance, importance, and authority quite apart from what happens later in the histories of Judaism and Christianity.

To these two items let me amend one additional suggestion, and that is that one should have a good Bible handy whenever reading a book about the Bible. There are numerous excellent translations to choose from, but I recommend the following four above all others: NRSV, NJPSV, NIV, and CEB. This specific presentation of these four runs from translations that are more formal (or wooden) to more dynamic (or free), though this categorization is something of a moving target and varies from book to book within these translations, sometimes even from verse to verse! This categorization is also value-neutral on my part. After participating in several translation projects (including the CEB and the revision of the NRSV), the word "literal" is, in my judgment, an altogether unhelpful and inaccurate category when it comes to translation! The best translation is often one that is dynamic and free enough to capture the overall sense better than one that is excessively mechanical.

Readers may also benefit from having a copy of their preferred translation (or even two—it can be helpful to compare more than one given the various options of bringing the original into English) in a study Bible edition, replete with notes and introductory essays of various kinds. I especially recommend the following four: *The Jewish Study Bible* (2nd ed.) with NJPSV; *The New Oxford Annotated Bible* (5th ed.) and *The Harper Collins Study Bible* (rev. ed.), both with NRSV; and *The CEB Study Bible with Apocrypha.*

SUGGESTIONS FOR FURTHER READING

The most important book to read about the Old Testament is the Old Testament itself which, as noted above, can be found in a number of excellent English translations. NRSV is often used among English-speaking biblical scholars, but all readers will find NIV and CEB more accessible. NJPSV is another excellent translation, which has the added benefit of following the Hebrew Bible in book-order and versification. Ecumenical Bibles of various sorts will include the Apocrypha or deuterocanonical books which are deemed scriptural by Catholic and Orthodox Christians but not by Protestants.

Helpful overviews of the Bible in English translation can be found in Steven M. Sheeley and Robert N. Nash Jr., *The Bible in English Translation: An Essential Guide* (Nashville: Abingdon, 1997); and Gordon D. Fee and Mark L. Strauss, *How to Choose a Translation for All Its Worth: A Guide to Understanding and Using Bible Versions* (Grand Rapids: Zondervan, 2007). A fascinating treatment of the Bible in its various published forms is found in Timothy Beal, *The Rise and Fall of the Bible: The Unexpected History of an Accidental Book* (Boston: Houghton Mifflin Harcourt, 2011).

For the Bible in "novel" or "book" form, see Walter Wangerin, Jr., *The Book of God: The Bible as a Novel* (Grand Rapids: Zondervan, 1996); and the version of the NIV issued as *The Story: The Bible as One Continuing Story of God and His People* (Grand Rapids: Zondervan, 2011). Note also the recent, high-quality production of the entire Christian Bible in five novel-like volumes by Bibliotheca, created by Adam Lewis Greene (www.bibliotheca.co). For recent discussions of the Bible as a coherent story (of sorts), see Sandra L. Richter, *The Epic of Eden: A Christian Entry into the Old Testament* (Downers Grove: IVP Academic, 2010); and Brad E. Kelle, *Telling the Old Testament Story: God's Mission and God's People* (Nashville: Abingdon, 2017).

Recommended reading on the composition history of the Old Testament, its parts and specific books, can be found in Chapters 2–4. A list of useful introductions and state-of-the-art overviews is found at the end of the present volume. The history of biblical interpretation is a massive subject, but a readable introduction with very intriguing case studies may be found in John L. Thompson, *Reading the Bible with the Dead: What You Can Learn from the History of Exegesis that You Can't Learn from Exegesis Alone* (Grand Rapids: Eerdmans, 2007).

For orientations to the different scholarly methods currently used in biblical studies, some of which are touched on in Chapters 2–4, see John Barton, *Reading the Old Testament: Method in Biblical Study* (rev. ed.; Louisville: Westminster John Knox, 1996); Susan E. Gillingham, *One Bible, Many Voices: Different Approaches to Biblical Studies* (Grand Rapids: Eerdmans, 1999); Joel M. LeMon and Kent Harold Richards, eds., *Method Matters: Essays on the Interpretation of the Hebrew Bible in Honor of David L. Petersen* (Atlanta: Society of Biblical Literature, 2009); and William P. Brown, *A Handbook to Old Testament Exegesis* (Louisville: Westminster John Knox, 2017).

Finally, for the notion of "literary simultaneity," see Jon D. Levenson, "The Eighth Principle of Judaism and the Literary Simultaneity of Scripture," in idem, *The Hebrew Bible, the Old Testament, and Historical Criticism: Jews and Christians in Biblical Studies* (Louisville: Westminster John Knox, 1993), 62–81.

THE PENTATEUCH (TORAH)

The first five books of the Old Testament are commonly referred to as the Pentateuch, a term that comes into English via Latin and, earlier and more originally, from a Greek word for a five-book collection (*pentateuchos*). In Hebrew, these books are traditionally called *Torah*, the Hebrew word for "law," "instruction," or "teaching." Both terms, Pentateuch and Torah, are useful because this unit is comprised of five discrete "books" (initially scrolls, see Chapter 1) and because the collection does contain a good bit of "law" in the more technical and narrow understanding of the term *Torah*. But this collection also contains different kinds of instruction—not just law properly so called—including teaching by means of storytelling or by means of poetry and song. That is why words like "instruction" and "teaching" are fully appropriate translations and understandings of *Torah*. Indeed, if these first five books are anything, it is clear that they are not just one, singular thing, and that is a very important point to grasp from the very beginning. These five books are not of one piece, they cover much ground (chronologically, literarily, and historically), and they are a complex mixture of material, incorporating several different kinds of literature. Despite this important, initial point, the first five books of the Bible have traditionally been ascribed or somehow attributed to Moses—the primary human protagonist in the Pentateuch. This explains the common practice in some circles to refer to the "Five Books of Moses" or to speak of Genesis, for example, as "the first book of Moses," even though Moses does not arrive on the scene until the second chapter of Exodus.

It is possible to see this attribution to Moses as emerging from the Old Testament itself. There are a few texts that speak of Moses writing things down, including things like laws (Exod 24:4; 34:27–28), narratives (Exod 17:14; Num 33:2), some combination of both (Deut 31: 9, 24)—even a poem (Deut 31:19, 22). Moses, in the Torah, is clearly a literate individual, which was extremely rare in the ancient world. Even so, these texts about Moses as a kind of scribe are actually few and far between, scattered across vast stretches of the Pentateuch, and it is often not entirely clear, even in these references, what, exactly, Moses wrote. It seems extremely doubtful that these texts are suggesting that Moses wrote the *entire* Pentateuch in its current form all by himself during his lifetime. Such a perspective would be especially tricky with Genesis since Moses isn't alive during the periods it covers. The idea that God dictated the Book of Genesis to Moses while he was on Sinai (see Exod 24:18; 34:28; Deut 9:9–10; 10:10) is a possible inference—even a reasonable one according to some religious traditions—but it is hardly an obvious or necessary one. Nothing said in the Bible about Moses' time on Sinai indicates that he was taking dictation. Moreover, the account of Moses' death seems sufficient by itself to disprove his authorship—of that portion of the Pentateuch at least (Deut 34:1–12). It is hard, after all, to write accurately about your own death and burial spot, especially when the latter remains unknown (Deut 34:6)!

For reasons like these, scholars have come to very different conclusions when it comes to the question of the authorship of the Pentateuch. The traditional attribution of the Torah to Moses—a tradition that isn't fully developed until later in the Greco-Roman period—probably has as much to do with how large Moses looms in the Pentateuch as it does with those few verses that portray him as some sort of literate scribe. Moses is far and away the most important human character mentioned in the Torah, second only to God in significance. In later periods, it was common to refer to portions of the Old Testament by their most important characters or "patron saints": David for the Psalms, Solomon for texts that deal with wisdom, and Moses for the Torah. This practice explains the references to "Moses" and "David" that occur in subsequent books of the Old Testament (e.g., 2 Chr 25:4; Ezra 6:18; Neh 13:1; cf. Josh 1:7–8), and also in the New (e.g., Matt 19:7; 22:24; Mark 7:10; 12:26; John 1:17; 5:46; 7:23), without requiring one to see these references as somehow proving or asserting authorship, especially as we understand that concept today. Indeed, since it is clear from many psalms and portions of the wisdom books that they were *not* authored exclusively by David and Solomon (see Chapter 4), it seems safe to say that the Torah, too, was *not* authored solely by Moses—with all due respect for traditional perspectives and ways of speaking about the Pentateuch. In sum, references to "the books of Moses" are best taken as a shorthand way to refer not to authorship per se but to the significance of Moses for (and in) the Torah. What this means is that, for the Torah, no less than many other parts of the Old Testament, the authorship of the five books of the Pentateuch is unknown, anonymous.

That conclusion is one that scholars have reached after centuries of careful study—it is part of the story they tell *about* the Old Testament. But this conclusion is also the beginning of that scholarly story, as biblical interpreters have done their best to find out more about the authorship of the Pentateuch and perhaps eliminate any anonymity. I will discuss the scholarly story *about* the Torah before turning to the story the Torah itself tells. Readers could, if they desire, reverse this order so as to start with the content of the Torah before hearing about the scholarly theories about the Torah (they could pursue a similar tactic in Chapters 3 and 4). The present chapter begins, however, with a brief case study from the opening chapters of Genesis that demonstrates how these two stories relate to one another and why, in the end, they deserve to be told together.

THE BEGINNING OF TWO—OR RATHER THREE—DIFFERENT STORIES

"In the beginning God created the heavens and the earth."

This is how the Bible begins, at least in the venerable King James Version of the Bible (KJV), first published in 1611. In the Hebrew Bible, however, the Bible begins as follows:

בְּרֵאשִׁית בָּרָא אֱלֹהִים אֵת הַשָּׁמַיִם וְאֵת הָאָרֶץ

The words here are flush with the right-hand margin because Hebrew is read right to left. For native English readers that is instantaneous, almost visceral, proof that the Bible comes from a very different culture, place, and time than King James' England, let alone the modern, twenty-first century world. Even stranger for English speakers is the fact that Hebrew was originally written without vowel markings (the small dots and lines placed above or below the letters). It isn't hard to imagine that a language written without vowels would be open to more than its fair share of ambiguity, though the ambiguity is reduced with more language expertise. The point, regardless, is that the way the Hebrew Book of Genesis begins is a far cry from the good ole' KJV!

To complicate matters further: the KJV's translation could be challenged as the beginning of the Bible not only because it is an English rendering of the Hebrew original but also because its formulation isn't the only possible way to translate the Hebrew into English. Other translations diverge from the KJV in notable ways. Consider the following three options:

"In the beginning when God created the heavens and the earth,"
   (NRSV);
"When God began to create heaven and earth—" (NJPSV); and
"When God began to create the heavens and the earth—" (CEB).

None of these alternative translations understand the first verse of Genesis to form a complete, self-standing sentence (as the KJV does). Instead, each takes Gen 1:1 as a circumstantial clause that is grammatically subordinate to what follows. That is why these versions end not with periods but with commas or dashes, and why all three translations include the word "when."

While NRSV, NJPSV, and CEB all agree that the first verse of the Bible is a subordinate clause, they do not agree on where the first sentence of the Bible finally ends. They also disagree over what the main verb of that sentence is, and where it comes, as can be seen by comparing them more fully (the main verb in each is italicized):

> In the beginning when God created the heavens and the earth, the earth *was* a formless void and darkness covered the face of the deep, while a wind from God swept over the face of the waters. (Gen 1:1–2; NRSV)
>
> When God began to create heaven and earth—the earth being unformed and void, with darkness over the surface of the deep and a wind from God sweeping over the water—God *said*, "Let there be light"; and there was light. (Gen 1:1–3; NJPSV)

> When God began to create the heavens and the earth—the earth was without shape or form, it was dark over the deep sea, and God's wind swept over the waters—God *said*, "Let there be light." And so light appeared. (Gen 1:1–3; CEB)

There are quite a number of differences between these translations when examined closely. And these are just three translations. Many more could be added, whether English or otherwise, recent or ancient, and still more differences would become apparent. And this is just the first sentence of the Bible! Small wonder that much is debated when it comes to the Old Testament.

Two important points can be taken from this brief discussion of Gen 1:1: First, the Bible was originally written in a different language, in a different culture, and in a far distant past. This fact complicates a vast number of things, including the translation of the Bible into different languages like English. Second, there is more than one way to adequately and accurately render the Old Testament's original language into another language like English. That is in part because of ongoing discussion among experts about the meaning of words, the proper understanding of grammar, and so forth, when it comes to the original language; but it is also due to the nature of the other language, which never corresponds exactly to the source—if it did no translation would be necessary! Still further, languages like English are constantly changing: no one speaks King James' English these days and contemporary editions of the KJV differ from the 1611 version. *Every* translation depends, therefore, on an immense number of interpretive decisions. Indeed, as we've seen, not even the first verse of the Bible gets translated without significant difference of opinion. In no small way, the different translations and interpretations of Gen 1:1 stem from difficulties inherent in the very first Hebrew word. So, again, one can't get very far in the Old Testament—not even one word in!—before running into the kind of difficulties that lead to debates over meaning. Put simply: when it comes to the Bible, interpretation is inescapable.

However Gen 1:1 is translated, it is how the Old Testament and the Book of Genesis begins. The first chapter of Genesis tells of God's creation of the world in a high literary style that borders on the poetic. There are numerous repetitions of key formulas (e.g., "God saw that it was good") and a kind of mirrored structure for creation that is couched in a one-week, seven-day structure. God creates light on the first day (Gen 1:3–5), sky and the division of sea and earth on the second day (1:6–8), and land and vegetation on the third day (1:9–13). These acts are paralleled, in Days 4 through 6, by the creation of other things that somehow correspond to what was created in Days 1 through 3:

Day 1: Light ←————————→ Day 4: Sun, moon, stars (1:14–19)
Day 2: Sky and water ←————→ Day 5: Marine animals and birds (1:20–23)
Day 3: Land and vegetation ←——→ Day 6: Land animals (1:24–25)

This tightly designed structure comes to a climax in two ways. First, at the end of the sixth day, God decides to create human beings. This act is highlighted by its extended treatment (1:26–30), inclusion of some poetry (1:27), and the fact that the humans are said to be made in God's image and likeness (1:26–27). The second and ultimate climax is located in the first few verses of the next chapter (2:1–3), which report how God rested on the seventh day and blessed it accordingly.

The fact that the opening story about the creation of the world runs from Gen 1:1–2:3 is proof that chapter and verse divisions are not always helpful when reading the Bible. In point of fact, chapters and verses were only added much later to the Bible—in some instances, not until the sixteenth century CE/AD. While dividing the text up into chapters and verses can be useful, contemporary readers should remember those divisions are secondary and not definitive.

Any feeling of oddity about how the opening story of creation runs from Gen 1:1 into the first few verses of chapter 2 pales in comparison to the strangeness one experiences when reading the very next story found in Gen 2:4–3:24. Here is another, *second* account of God's creation, which, upon closer inspection, appears to be at *significant odds* with the first one. In the first story, the land brings forth vegetation on Day 3 *before* animals are created, and land animals are made on Day 6 before humans. In the second story, we hear of a time *before* any vegetation (2:5), and it is during this pre-plant period that a human being is formed (2:7). Only *after* the creation of a human being is there mention of a garden for the human being to tend (2:8). While the first story spoke of the creation of both male and female (Gen 1:27), the second speaks initially of a non-descript earth creature (*'adam*) made from the earth (*'adamah*). As one scholar has put it, this is "a human from the fertile *humus*" or "a human 'soul' from the soil." It is only later in the second account that we read of a clear division of this initial human being into two sexes: the "woman" is formed from the "man" after God performs the first surgical procedure recorded in the Bible (2:21–25).

Another difference between these two accounts is that, unlike the goodness that was a repeated mark of God's creation in Genesis 1 (vv. 10, 12, 18, 21, 25, 31), the human being's isolation at the start of Genesis 2 is said to be "*not* good" (2:18). This negative judgment is what leads God to create all of the animals—once again, *after* the creation of the human being, in a precise reversal of Day 6 in Genesis 1—to see if one might be a suitable companion. When the animals fail to fit the bill, God decides that surgery is in order. The procedure is quite successful according to the poetic outburst uttered by the man about the woman (2:23). In this way, the creation of woman, not man, is the ultimate climax of Genesis 2.

What follows next, in Genesis 3, recounts what happened in the Garden of Eden to this first man and first woman, who are eventually called "Adam" and "Eve" (see 3:20; 4:1, 25; 5:1–4). For present purposes, this very brief retelling of the two different creation stories in the opening chapters of Genesis suffices to demonstrate that another, third story needs to be told: the story of how these two creation accounts relate to each other. Some explanation seems required since the two versions appear to report very different and distinct stories. The order of creation in the two accounts differs notably, and the same holds true for several specific details within these two versions. There is also a palpable difference in style: Gen 1:1–2:3 is tightly structured, regular, almost poetic. Genesis 2:4–3:24 is also artful, but far more prosaic—it is a well-crafted narrative, but not poetry. And there is still one more important difference that should be mentioned: different names are used of God in these two accounts (see Box 2.1). In the first story, we hear of "God" (*Elohim*) creating, but in the second, it is "the LORD God" (*Yhwh Elohim*) who performs the various duties of creation. Factors like these indicate that we have two rather different accounts of creation in the opening chapters of Genesis. Why these versions should differ and how two varying accounts came to reside side by side in the first book of the Bible leads directly into the story scholars tell about the Torah.

BOX 2.1. THE DIVINE NAME *YHWH* ("THE LORD")

God goes by several different names in the Hebrew Bible, but by far the most important one is *Yhwh*, traditionally translated in English Bibles as "the LORD" (cf. MSG: "GOD"). The use of all capital letters for the word "LORD" is a way to signal readers that the underlying Hebrew word is *Yhwh* and not a common noun that means "lord." *Yhwh*, that is, is not a title, which is what the word "lord" is. *Yhwh* is a proper name.

This name is revealed to Moses in Exodus 3, when Moses asks for God's identity and receives a very enigmatic response: "I am who I am" (*'ehyeh 'asher 'ehyeh*; 3:14). This sentence can be translated in other ways as well, including "I will be who I will be." God immediately tells Moses that *Yhwh* "is my name forever" (3:15). The enigmatic "I am who I am" appears to connect the proper name *Yhwh* to the Hebrew verb "to be" (*h-y-h*, the verb used in *'ehyeh*). If so, the name *Yhwh* might mean something like "he who is," which is exactly how the Septuagint translated Hebrew *'ehyeh 'asher 'ehyeh*. Another possibility is that *Yhwh* means something like "he who creates," especially when conjoined with the Hebrew word *tzebaoth*, a term that refers to God's heavenly "armies" or "forces."

The divine name is given again, a second time, in Exod 6:2–3. This, then, is a doublet—the kind of evidence used in source-critical approaches to the Pentateuch. What is particularly interesting about Exodus 6 is that it states that Abraham, Isaac, and Jacob did *not* know the divine name *Yhwh*. This would appear to be in direct conflict with Gen 4:26, which says people began to call on the name *Yhwh* as early as the third generation of humankind, well before the period of Israel's ancestors. Exodus 6 also seems to conflict with Genesis 2, which uses the compound name *Yhwh Elohim* ("LORD God"). This does not yet mention the conflict between Exodus 6 and Gen 15:7 where God explicitly tells Abram: "I am *Yhwh*." How then, can Exodus 6 say that Abraham didn't know the name *Yhwh*?

Source criticism is one way to answer that question. Scholars often attribute the Genesis passages to the J (Yahwistic) source, the Exodus 3 text to the E (Elohistic) source, and the Exodus 6 account to the P (Priestly) source. Each of these sources, from different authors, were presumably independent at some point. It is understandable, in this light, that they might have different understandings of when the divine name *Yhwh* came to be known and used.

For various reasons, including evidence from various individuals' names that utilize the divine name, or short forms that use only the first syllable of it (*Yah*), many scholars believe that *Yhwh* was originally pronounced something like "Yahweh." At some point prior to the turn of the eras, it was thought improper to pronounce God's personal name. So a substitute term, *'adonay*, "my lord"—a title, not a name—was used instead of *Yhwh*. Eventually, in later editions of the Hebrew Bible, the vowels of the word *'adonay* were added to the consonants of *Yhwh* so as to avoid pronouncing the divine name and as a reminder to say "my lord" instead. It is this combination— the vowels of one word used with the consonants of another—that led to the curious hybrid word "Jehovah." Jehovah, however, is most certainly *not* how the divine name *Yhwh* was ever pronounced. Many Jews continue to show utmost respect for the divine name to this day, substituting *Ha-Shem* ("the Name") instead of *'adonay*, and often de-vocalizing references to the Deity in any and every written form (e.g., "G-d" for God).

THE SCHOLARLY STORY OF THE TORAH

Observations like the ones just made about the two creation accounts of Genesis 1–3 lie very close to the beginning of critical analysis of the Bible, with "critical" here meaning "academic" or "scholarly" without any negative connotations. In fact, it would not be going too far to say that modern biblical scholarship was born from and cut its teeth on the questions of the authorship and formation of the Pentateuch. Observations about textual conundrums like the two adjacent creation accounts in Genesis were occasionally offered in pre-modern times. Already in the twelfth century, for example, the great Jewish scholar Abraham ben Meir ibn Ezra wondered how Moses could have written about his own death. Centuries before ibn Ezra, the Babylonian Talmud—a massive repository of Jewish rabbinical thinking—indicated that the account of Moses' death must have been written by Joshua (*b. Men.* 30a). This is a sensible solution, but there are other problems for the idea of Moses' authorship of the Pentateuch. For example, the Book of Numbers states that "Moses was very humble, more so than anyone else on the face of the earth" (Num 12:3; NRSV). Interpreters—both ancient and modern—have understandably wondered how Moses, if he was indeed the author of the Pentateuch and truly that humble, could write such a statement about himself. It seems the exact opposite of humility! Or, as yet another example, there is the problem of *anachronism*: textual details that come from a much later period than the time they are purporting to report. A famous instance is Gen 12:6, which states that, "the Canaanites lived in the land at that time" (CEB). That remark reveals that the author who made it was familiar with, and thus writing from, a later time when the Canaanites were *not* living in the land. That is not the situation, however, that faced Moses according to Numbers and Deuteronomy, let alone the generations after Moses in Joshua–Judges. Whatever their subject matter, anachronisms make it hard to sustain the idea of just one author for the entire Pentateuch.

Again, details like these have been noticed by attentive readers for thousands of years. But it was these kinds of observations, and especially the presence of doublets and triplets—multiple versions of what appears to be the same story—that helped modern scholars begin to reconstruct how the Torah came to be in its current form. There are a handful of *triplet* accounts: the story of a patriarch endangering his wife by pretending he isn't married to her (Gen 12:10–20; 20:1–19; 26:6–14), the three versions of the Ten Commandments (Exod 20:1–17; 34:10–28; Deut 5:6–18), or variations on certain slavery laws (Exod 21:1–6; Lev 25:39–46; Deut 15:12–18), for example. There is an even larger number of *doublets* like the creation stories in Genesis 1–3, the genealogy from Adam (Gen 4:17–26; 5:1–32), the covenant with Abraham (Genesis 15 and 17), the prophecy of Isaac's birth (Gen 17:16–19; 18:10–14), the revelation of God's special name (Exod 3:14–15; 6:2–3), and so forth.

The existence of doublets and triplets was combined with other evidence, above all else the use of different divine names, in order to sort passages into groups that seemed to be related. This process has come to be called *source criticism*. Source criticism seeks to separate the biblical texts into distinct sources, even documents, that likely trace back to different authors. This is one reasonable (though admittedly modern) way to account for differences like those found in Genesis 1–3: different accounts differ because they were written by different people, likely at different times, perhaps without awareness of any other source.

Although there were predecessors, an eighteenth-century French physician named Jean Astruc is usually credited with inaugurating modern, source-critical study of the Pentateuch. Astruc believed Moses didn't compose the Pentateuch but compiled it on the basis of preexisting sources. Astruc used the different divine names *Elohim* and *Yhwh* as his basic criterion for distinguishing these different sources.

The source-critical approach reached a mature stage in the late nineteenth century in the work of the German scholar Julius Wellhausen (1844–1918). In a now classic book, Wellhausen combined previous work with his own insights to produce what is now called the Documentary Hypothesis. According to this theory, the Torah is made up of four distinct documents (sources) that can be differentiated by textual details like varying names for God, but also by distinctive content and other considerations. A crucial, though controversial, element of Wellhausen's work was his arrangement of these four sources into a scheme that specified which source was earlier and which later. The four sources, along with their respective dates and some additional details—as refined by scholars working after Wellhausen—are as follows (cf. Map 2.1 and Chart 2.1):

- J is the Yahwistic source because it favors the divine name *Yhwh* (spelled *Jahwe* in German). J is the earliest source and comes from the south, from Judah, perhaps even Jerusalem itself, during the time of the United Monarchy in the tenth century BCE. In the Pentateuch, the J source begins in Gen 2:4.

- E is the Elohistic source. The E source prefers the divine name *Elohim* and comes from the ninth century BCE. It appears to be originally at home in the northern kingdom of Israel, which existed independently of Judah after the United Monarchy split (922 BCE). Perhaps E was something of a rival account to the south's J source. The E source is not as extensive or as easily identified as the others, with some recent scholars doubting its existence altogether. Others find its first occurrence in parts of

Genesis 15, with others believing it begins in earnest only in Gen 20:1–18. Some scholars believe J and E were combined in the eighth century, sometime after the fall of the northern kingdom of Israel to the Assyrians (722 BCE). Such an editorial combination (or "redaction") of JE would help to explain why there is less E than might otherwise be the case. In part it would be because the combination of J and E would have taken place in the south, where J was already well established.

- D is the Deuteronomic source, named after the Book of Deuteronomy. Deuteronomy has a very distinctive style that is easily distinguished from J and E. The D source is mostly limited to Deuteronomy proper, though scholars have sometimes wondered if other parts of the Pentateuch (and even beyond) have been edited by the person(s) responsible for D or by people within its sphere of influence. Conversely, it seems likely that parts of Deuteronomy were edited by still later hands (e.g., Deut 4:25–31; 34:1–4, 7–9). In the early 1800s, a scholar named W. M. L. de Wette argued that the D source was to be located in 622 BCE, the time of Josiah's reform (see 2 Kings 22) because the account of that reform lines up remarkably with Deuteronomy 12. Once de Wette fixed the D source in a specific period, it became an "Archimedean point" for the Pentateuch: the other sources could be dated relative to D, whether earlier or later.

- P is the Priestly source. It is concerned with priestly matters and so it comes as no surprise that the cultic and legal material in Exodus–Numbers is typically ascribed to P. One of the most controversial aspects of Wellhausen's work was that, in contrast to earlier scholars, he argued that P was the latest of the four sources, dating to the postexilic period (after 586 BCE). In Wellhausen's opinion, the priestly law postdated the prophets. Many scholars have deemed this a critical mistake, even if it was the result of some rather brilliant deduction. Other scholars have worried that Wellhausen's late dating of P was due to his anti-Semitic and anti-Catholic biases. Whatever the case, much recent scholarship has disagreed with Wellhausen on the date of the P source, arguing that it may belong to the late preexilic period (late seventh or early sixth century). In the Pentateuch, the P source begins with Gen 1:1.

1250 BCE	**Moses and the Exodus**
1200 BCE	**Conquest, Settlement, Period of the Judges**
1000 BCE	**United Monarchy: David and Solomon**
922 BCE	**Division of the Kingdom**

Period of the Divided Monarchies: the North (Israel), with its capital city in Samaria, and the South (Judah), with capital city in Jerusalem

[883-612 BCE   Assyrian Period]

722 BCE   **Fall of the Northern Kingdom (Samaria) to the Assyrians**—exile of northern Israelites to Mesopotamia, forced resettlement

[622 BCE   "The Book of the Law" recovered in the Temple]

[612-539 BCE   Babylonian Period]

587 BCE   **Fall of the Southern Kingdom (Jerusalem) to the Babylonians**—destruction of Jerusalem and second deportation of southern Judeans to Babylon (an earlier deportation took place in 597)

Exilic period

[539-332 BCE   Persian Period]

538 BCE   **Edict of Cyrus** allowing Judean exiles to return to Judah
515 BCE   **Completion of Second Temple**
458 BCE   **Ezra reads the Torah in Jerusalem** (see Neh 8:1-12)

[332-63 BCE   Hellenistic Period]

All dates are approximate with the earlier ones the most sharply contested. Note that the chronology found within the biblical texts often suggests different and earlier dates (e.g., an exodus in the 1500s BCE). Note also that some scholars would doubt the historical nature of some of the events listed above, especially as those are presently recounted in biblical texts that come from much later time periods.

Chart 2.1 Key Dates in the History of Israel and Judah

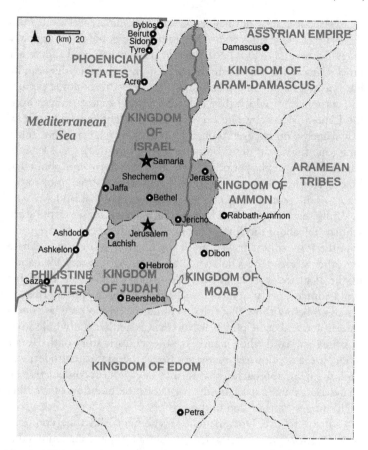

Map 2.1 The Kingdoms of Israel and Judah with Neighboring Regions.
Amended from Richardprins/FinnWikiNo, Wikimedia, CC BY-SA
3.0: https://creativecommons.org/licenses/by-sa/3.0/

Scholars committed to a source-critical understanding of the origins of the Pentateuch have been working at it now for more than 200 years. The Documentary Hypothesis is thus venerable; it is also helpful. It emerged from the careful analysis of various curiosities found in the Pentateuch: doublets and triplets, inconsistent content, different literary styles, and so on and so forth. To its great merit, the Documentary Hypothesis helps to explain all of these—at least to some degree.

Its explanation, in a nutshell, is that all such differences stem from the fact that the various texts manifesting them come from originally discrete sources, and thus from different authors who lived at different times. Once these sources are separated from each other, they can be interrogated for any information they might reveal about the periods and authors from which they come. So, if the J source really is from the United Monarchy, one can read it for insights into the time of David and Solomon, even though J says nothing explicit about either king (one must wait until Samuel and Kings for that). Or if P really comes from the exilic period, it can be read for information about that time, even though its specific content concerns the time prior to the taking of the promised land, let alone the losing of that land.

While the Documentary Hypothesis makes good sense, the story scholars tell about the Torah does not end with it because it remains hypothetical—and it has come in for revision and critique. There are other stories that scholars tell about the origin and formation of the Pentateuch that are not "documentarian," some of which avoid source-critical approaches altogether. The major alternatives discussed below show that the Documentary Hypothesis, as venerable as it is and as helpful as it has been, is neither the whole story nor the final word when it comes to the scholarly story of the Torah. There are, first, alternative compositional theories to consider; second, there are approaches that do not engage in reconstruction or analysis of sources at all, quite apart from the question of whether such sources even existed in the first place.

1. Prior to the Documentary Hypothesis, different compositional theories were entertained. In contrast to just four sources that spanned the Pentateuch, *fragmentary hypotheses* posited that numerous blocks of tradition were brought together later by an editor or editors. In the twentieth century, several scholars renewed this kind of approach in direct criticism of the Documentary Hypothesis. In their judgment, large and preexisting chunks of material like the primeval history (Genesis 2–11), the story of the exodus (Exodus 1–15), and the Sinai materials (Exodus 19–24) were joined together, end to end, to create the Pentateuch as we now have it.

Alongside fragmentary hypotheses, *supplementary theories* should also be mentioned. Supplementary theories posited that some source (or two), of some significance if not also size, served as the first building block of the Torah. Other sources were then added to this first, major unit, supplementing it in various ways. In recent times, some scholars have drastically reorganized the order of the sources established by Wellhausen, placing D as the earliest source and basis for the rest of the Torah, with the other sources supplementing D in various ways.

Fragmentary, supplementary, and documentary theories can be schematically visualized (see Figures 2.1–2.3).

The differences of opinion do not lie solely between these three source-critical camps, however. Even those who subscribe to some version of the Documentary Hypothesis rarely follow Wellhausen's specific iteration of it. The brief description of the four sources offered above employed different dates than Wellhausen and also acknowledged debate about certain details (e.g., the placement of P) that Wellhausen thought secure. In truth, the debate on all of these matters—and many others—is rather robust. Many disagreements center on the precise demarcation of the sources: where one leaves

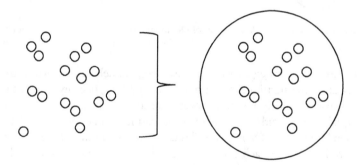

Figure 2.1 Schematic Presentation of Fragmentary Theories of the Pentateuch

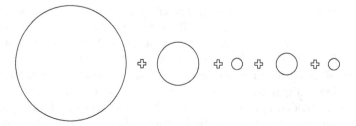

Figure 2.2 Schematic Presentation of Supplementary Theories of the Pentateuch

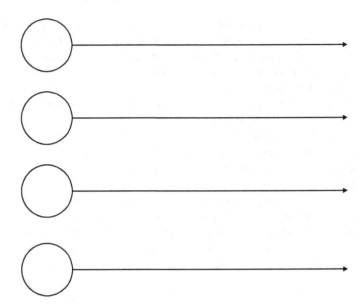

Figure 2.3 Schematic Presentation of Documentary Theories of the Pentateuch

off and another begins. In some instances, the debate concerns if the "source" in question ever existed (this has been especially true of the E source). Exactly where to locate the sources in time and space is equally vexed with recent scholarship dating them considerably later than Wellhausen. There is also discussion as to whether these sources have integrity. Is each source a singular, coherent entity? Or are the sources actually complex collections of tradition, which means that each might be further filleted into multiple sub-strands? One doesn't read very far in Pentateuchal theory these days before encountering a great deal of such "filleting." The talk, and the sub-strands, borders on the mathematical: not just P, for example, but also P^g ("g" for the Priestly base text, *Grundschrift* in German), P^s ("s" for secondary additions to P), and R^P (the final redactor, "R," of the Priestly material). Scholarly investigation of the composition of the Pentateuch is thus a highly technical discussion where even a single verse can be subdivided into two or more different sources or editors. One treatment of the Tower of Babel story in Genesis 11 identified no less than four distinct stages in the composition and redaction of its nine verses! Other scholars feel that only the D and P sources are identifiable and so term all other material "non-P" or "non-D."

For those unaccustomed to this kind of pursuit, the whole endeavor may see seem silly. Is it even possible to conduct this kind of granular analysis on a piece of literature? Though the results that have been offered in the case of the Pentateuch vary widely among themselves, the answer to that question seems positive, at least in theory. In recent years, the field of literary forensics has investigated things like handwriting, but also authorial style more generally, and this has led to famous cases where analysts have correctly identified previously anonymous authors. Or, with reference to deceased authors, English professors have conducted investigations of the life of William Shakespeare based mostly, if not exclusively, on his literary works. Such studies obviously involve a decent amount of imagination, even speculation. As a result, it is certain that these studies will not be entirely accurate. But it is equally certain that they are not entirely wrong; neither are they completely fabricated because they depend on evidence—*textual* evidence. Now we know from the very first verse of the Bible that textual evidence must be interpreted and that not all people interpret the same way. The same holds true for literary forensics and studies of English literature. In any event, investigations in fields like these demonstrate that source-critical analysis of the Torah is at least feasible, even as they also reveal why debates over the composition of the Pentateuch are likely to endure for a long time.

2. There is a completely different perspective on the composition of the Torah. This perspective thinks that not only is the source-critical approach not the only game in town, it's probably the wrong game to play when it comes to interpreting the Pentateuch. Even if compositional theories (in whatever form) aren't entirely inaccurate or a total waste of time, this alternative perspective thinks that those types of approaches nevertheless miss the point. The point in question is the meaning and function of the literature in the Torah as it now stands.

Scholarly attempts to attend to the Pentateuch in its present form, with little or no interest in preexisting sources, appear in more than one iteration. In general, however, this kind of approach differs from the others described thus far on some foundational points. Source-critical analyses are concerned with a biblical composition like Genesis, but also, and even more, with the author(s) or school(s) that lie *behind* the text of Genesis as we now have it: P, for instance, or J, or JE. The alternative, more literary perspective insists to the contrary that all we have at our disposal is the Book of Genesis. What we do *not* have is J-Genesis, E-Genesis, and P-Genesis. If those ever existed (along with any other strands or sub-strands), they are recoverable now—if at all—only through reconstruction, some of which is highly speculative. The Book of Genesis, however, exists regardless of scholarly reconstruction and no speculation is required in reading it whole, in contrast to filleting it into numerous sources. Similarly, we don't have an "Abraham Cycle" that exists independently of a self-standing "Joseph Novella." Instead, the now complete Book of Genesis includes materials about Abraham and Joseph, as well as Isaac, Jacob, and others. Scholarly theories about the possible independence of various accounts or sources all depend on a stage in time or a state of the text *antecedent* to what we now have—not Genesis per se, that is, but some *hypothetical*, presumably earlier, form of Genesis. Or part of Genesis.

While hypothetical analyses are possible, the Book of Genesis is patently *there*. It seems reasonable enough to suggest that the book as a whole, as it now stands, should be the proper subject of investigation. But to return to the two creation accounts, we have to admit that it is the text itself, as it currently stands, that raises a number of interpretive questions—questions like why there are two creation accounts in the first place. And then there are the many other doublets and triplets that are found in the Pentateuch. But there are ways to account for such "problems" besides simply chalking them up to different authors writing at different times. That kind of approach is an historical one—a diachronic explanation about the text's development *through time*. But there are literary understandings of these issues that are synchronic (*without respect to change through time*) which are, at least in some cases, equally plausible explanations.

Take the thrice-told story of the endangered wife as an example. On two different occasions, Abraham pawns his wife Sarah off as his sister, rather than his spouse (Gen 12:10–20; 20:1–18). In both cases, the truth is eventually discovered with the stories making clear that Abraham's deception was not good: it caused real problems for the other males involved (the Egyptian Pharaoh and Abimelech, the king of Gerar), who would have Sarah as their own. As if Abraham's two mistakes aren't bad enough, Isaac does the very same thing with his wife Rebekah just a few chapters later (Gen 26:1–11). Like father, like son, as the old saying goes!

That may, in fact, be the point of this repetition. "Like father, like son" is a pithy little proverb that nevertheless captures something true about humanity: children tend to be a good bit like their parents, whether for good or ill (or both). The phrase "like father, like son" captures that truism in a short, memorable way. The thrice-repeated story of the endangered wife captures it in a more extended literary form. The third installment shows that Isaac is not above making the same mistakes as his dad. And then there is poor Abimelech: he's the unwitting dolt who falls for this ruse not once but twice! That fact certainly says something about him, but he's not the only one to come off looking bad in this repetition. Isaac does, too. Readers of Genesis could plausibly deduce that Isaac should've known better, even if his dad's mistakes took place before he was even born. At the very least readers of Genesis know that Isaac's just-like-dad move with his own wife is going to end up badly, just as it did for his dad and mom. And then there is Abraham: he comes off looking more than a bit foolish by making the same mistake twice. Readers of Genesis might plausibly deduce that he should've learned from the first situation with Pharaoh and so not repeated the deception with Abimelech. Even further, readers might wonder if Isaac's later faux pas might be the result of poor parenting: Abraham not teaching Isaac to learn from the mistakes he himself had made.

These kinds of observations are literary in nature. They treat the story of an ancestor who endangers his wife as *a type scene*: a narrative employing a pattern of certain key elements that, when repeated, communicates a great deal of information about the character—including that character's character!—without extensive commentary or explicit moralizing.

Now, these sorts of observations about the Genesis materials may not be accurate: they depend not only on what seems evident in the texts but also on what is patently *not* evident in the texts (literary gaps). But the same judgment holds true for source-critical analyses. Literary interpretations, that is, are no less secure nor more speculative than composition-critical reconstructions. And vice versa. What is crucial to note is that a literary approach to this particular triplet comes to drastically different conclusions than a source-critical assessment. The reason that the story is told more than once, in source-critical perspective, is because different authors are at work: Gen 12:10–20 is traditionally ascribed to J, Gen 20:1–18 to E, and Gen 26:1–11 to J. According to source criticism, there are three stories because they come from two different sources.

This explanation has some holes in it, however. The doublet involving Abraham making the same mistake (Gen 12:10–20; 20:1–18) has played an important role in positing an E source that is distinct from J. But a consideration of J alone, which has accounts of both Abraham and Isaac endangering their wives, shows that one author could tell the same (or very similar) story twice. Perhaps the account in Gen 20:1–18 needn't be attributed to a different author after all, therefore. But even if that story does come from another source, the repetition of the story twice in J may still function as a type scene along the lines suggested above.

Whatever the case, the most important point to make is that good sense can be made of doublets and triplets in literary mode without any recourse to hypothetical sources. Not every doublet or triplet—and certainly not every little tension or contradiction—should or must be explained by positing multiple authors, strands, or schools of thought. The texts in question can be assessed as wholes: read and interpreted as such. There can be no doubt that literary approaches face their fair share of interpretive problems, but interpretive problems face any approach to any biblical text since every text requires interpretation. The problems facing literary approaches are no more numerous or serious than other, more diachronic approaches.

Neither should literary approaches be written off as simple-minded attempts to harmonize texts that cannot and must not be harmonized. It is worth underscoring at this point that source-critical theories for the Torah were not fully developed until the eighteenth century. That was not because readers prior to that century were stupid, naïve, or otherwise blind to tensions and distinctions. It is, rather, because the textual differences that were observed were not assessed via modern understandings of individual authorship. At its best, premodern or pre-critical interpretation was just as attuned to the warp and woof of the text as modern biblical scholarship. To be sure, early interpreters sometimes harmonized texts in ways that contemporary scholars would dismiss, but the ultimate point is simply that the present form of the text must be reckoned with.

Once again, the Book of Genesis is *there*, with its doublets and triplets and all the rest, and its current form—not just its constituent parts—suggests an integrity that deserves to be read and accounted for in some fashion.

One recent approach that has tried to do just that is called the canonical approach. In this approach, the Pentateuch is assumed to be a complex hybrid of various sources and traditions, however well those are and can be known. And yet, despite that historical, composition-critical knowledge—perhaps even in spite of it—the canonical approach makes the current, final form of the text the ultimate object of study. So, for example, a purely literary approach to the endangered wife stories might not care much about, or even consider at all, theories of different sources underlying the three versions. A canonical approach, however, would likely assume the source-critical results but nevertheless still press on to investigate the function of the current form of the text. This isn't just a matter of saying something about *how* the discrete pieces ended up together—which is a technical question about editorial processes—but is instead to ask *why* they were put together in this way and *what* the effect of that combination is. To return to Genesis 1–3, source criticism would be happy to differentiate the sources (classically P and J, respectively) and leave it at that. A canonical approach would ask after the significance of placing the P account prior to the J account, even and perhaps especially if the J account is truly the chronologically earlier of the two sources. What is the effect of beginning with the P version as opposed to J's? And how does their present juxtaposition function within the Book of Genesis? Even this brief example shows that a canonical approach will be uninterested in simplistically harmonizing textual differences, but it will nevertheless pursue larger meanings produced by textual differences and the combination of preexisting sources.

In the end, literary and canonical approaches reflect a different sensibility about the nature of the Torah than diachronic ones like source criticism. Among other things, the more holistic approaches to the Pentateuch seem more tolerant of tension than historical ones. Textual tension, in source-critical mode, is usually seen as a seam where different sources or traditions have been patched together; the task is then to carefully separate one from the other. Literary and canonical approaches recognize tension not as something to be explained away by positing distinct originating authors in different time periods and leaving things there but as something to be accounted for at the literary level of the text itself: how it means, what it is saying. Of course the fact that the Torah has more than its fair share of tensions is itself an historical fact. Quite apart from what contemporary readers think about sources, authorship, contradictions, tensions, and so forth, the Torah preserves more than just one perspective on a whole host of subjects. That fact says something about its origins and development, to be sure, but it also says something about its current form if not also its final editor(s). Something important may be learned from the Torah's "tension tolerance": perhaps the Pentateuch knows that the big issues it addresses must be spoken of in more than one way because no one way or voice can get it all said quite right, because the most important truths are multicolored, polyvalent. Of course, since the Torah is inanimate, perhaps we should make such predications not of the Pentateuchal text but of its final editor(s)/redactor(s), often abbreviated "R." The Jewish scholar Franz Rosenzweig (1886–1929) suggested that R stood not for "redactor," but for *rabbenu* (Hebrew for "our teacher") precisely because the redactor/*rabbenu* gave us a many-splendored Torah.

To sum up the story scholars tell about the Torah, one thing is certain: it is a complicated account. After more than two centuries of research on the Pentateuch, we can say that we know precious little, on the one hand, and, on the other hand, that we know quite a lot about the Torah's origin, composition, and development. We know precious little because what we have is the Torah as it has come down to us—in various manuscripts and ancient translations, many of which do not line up perfectly. We do *not* have countless discrete pieces, units, and so forth that served as the building blocks for the Torah as we now have it. Scholarly reconstructions of these various bits are carefully considered inferences and deductions that remain, at the end of the day, far from certain. It is very hard to know—and certainly not absolutely—if they are correct. Most of them are *not* correct because there are so many different scholarly proposals on these matters and they are often irreconcilable: they can't all be right! Put another way, the problem the Torah presents in its current form is very difficult to reverse engineer. It may be *impossible* to reverse engineer. Because of that fact, the scholarly story about the Torah's origin, history, and development will likely continue on indefinitely, perhaps with increased success and accuracy along the way, but maybe not. Assured results will likely elude us given the nature and extent of the data at hand. That is why, on the one hand, we know precious little about these matters.

On the other hand, we know quite a lot about these matters. Even if certainty on many specifics remains elusive, the story scholars tell about the Torah is univocal on a number of important points. Most obvious among these is that the Torah is complex. It is not one singular thing—one book, for example—but many things now combined and conjoined, united even if not fully unified (and certainly not uniform!). It is also clear that this complex Torah comes to us not from just one author and therefore not by means of just one process, whether historical or compositional. Instead, the Torah is the complex end result of a complex set of processes all along the way. While more could be said on these matters, it is time to turn from the story scholars tell about the Pentateuch to the story the Torah itself tells.

THE STORY THE TORAH TELLS

The first five books of the Old Testament are always found in the order we now have them: Genesis through Deuteronomy. The ordering of books in the other divisions of the Hebrew Bible does not enjoy the same kind of stability (see Chapters 3–4).

GENESIS (*BERESHITH*)

The English title for the first book in the Old Testament corresponds to the name of the book in the Greek Septuagint: *Genesis*. The word *geneseos*, which means "beginning" or "origin," is used in the Septuagint's translation of Gen 2:4 and 5:1. The Greek title made its way into Latin (*Liber Genesis*) in the translation known as the Vulgate, and then, eventually, into English versions. In the Hebrew Bible, the first book is called by the very first word of the very first verse: *Bereshith*, a word (and accompanying verse) that can be translated in more than one way (see above)!

Both the Greek and Hebrew titles convey that Genesis is a book about beginnings. Chapter 1 speaks of the beginning of the world, after all (as does chaps. 2–3), but other beginnings are also mentioned in the book: the beginning of culture, for instance (4:17–22), the beginning of the people of Israel (Gen 12:1–4), and so on.

One of the ways the beginnings in Genesis are identified is by what is called the *toledoth* formula. The Hebrew word *toledoth* is typically translated into English as something like, "these are the generations of ..." or "these are the descendants of ...." The term occurs 13 times in Genesis (each *toledoth* is italicized):

2:4	These are the *generations* of the heavens and the earth ...
5:1	This is the list of the *descendants* of Adam ...
6:9	These are the *descendants* of Noah ...
10:1	These are the *descendants* of Shem, Ham, and Japheth, Noah's sons ...
10:32	These are the families of Noah's children, according to their *generations*, in their nations ...
11:10	These are the *descendants* of Shem ...
11:27	And these are the *descendants* of Terah ....
25:12	These are the *descendants* of Abraham's son, Ishmael...
25:13	These are the names of Ishmael's children, by name, according to their *generations* ...
25:19	These are the *descendants* of Abraham's son, Isaac ...
36:1	These are the *descendants* of Esau ...
36:9	These are the *descendants* of Esau, the ancestor of the Edomites...
37:2	These are the *descendants* of Jacob ...

Repetition of key terms is common in ancient literature and often used as a structuring device to divide compositions into various subparts. In the case of Genesis, the subparts are connected to significant characters who go on to become the ancestors of various people groups. Human history in Genesis is thus not a simple matter of population growth; it is, instead, the growth of a particular family tree. The first instance of *toledoth* in Gen 2:4 is especially noteworthy in this regard because it indicates that even the heavens and the earth have a heritage! The created world is also viewed as kin, related to the family. Perhaps this makes the world a bit more manageable or understandable because it is now viewed on a human scale: creation, too, is just one more branch on the family tree.

The repeated use of the *toledoth* formula helps to explain the presence of the several extended genealogies in Genesis (5:1–32; 10:1–32; 11:10–32; 36:1–43): that is, after all, what a *toledoth* is. Modern readers find these genealogies tiresome if not downright boring, but they perform an important function beyond simply dividing the book into smaller chunks. Genealogical lists offer both a history of and an orientation to the world—they are a kind of cultural map. Ancient readers of these genealogies could quickly see how, on the one hand, they were related to famous persons of old, and, on the other hand, how they were also related to every other human family—even to the heavens and the earth (2:4). Indeed, according to the genealogies, everyone on earth, ultimately, is extended family.

The genealogies in Genesis are often ascribed to the Priestly source which, according to some scholars, is a product of the exilic period, when the people of Israel were under the thumb of the Babylonian Empire (see Chart 2.1). That social-historical location makes good sense: a smaller immigrant group amidst a colonial superpower might draw great comfort from knowing they descended from great heroes of old. Having a noble lineage that traced back to the very origins of the world would be encouraging and empowering to those who had been thoroughly humiliated by the Babylonians. The significance of heritage is not restricted to difficult circumstances, however, and so the genealogies could provide similar encouragement and empowerment in other social-historical contexts as well.

Regardless of the *toledoth* formula, the structure of Genesis can be understood in more than one way, with the content of the book falling nicely into three parts: chapters 1–11, which deal with the creation and early history of the world; chapters 12–36, which contain stories about the ancestors of Israel, especially Abraham, Isaac, and Jacob, their wives, and children; and chapters 37–50, which contain the dramatic story of Joseph, the youngest son of Jacob, and his life in Egypt.

Genesis 1–11 is often called *the primeval history* since it deals with primordial time prior to Abraham, the first great ancestor of Israel. The opening chapters of Genesis have already been touched on above. What was not mentioned earlier, however, is the story of disobedience found in Genesis 3. Often called "the Fall" or the first instance of "sin" in Scripture—though neither term is found in Genesis 3—this story introduces several key themes that reappear in the rest of the primeval history. One of these themes is that problems occur when the distinction between human and divine realms is inappropriately crossed or blurred in some fashion. Adam and Eve try to be "like God" (3:5) and they are expelled from the garden because of it (3:24). In the very next chapter, the first sibling rivalry ends in murder. When God confronts Cain about Abel's missing person status, Cain is dodgy and asks in reply "Am I my brother's keeper?" (4:9). Cain's question isn't entirely disingenuous because nowhere else in the Bible are people instructed to "keep" other people. Instead, it is God who is sometimes described as the one who keeps Israel (Ps 121:4–5, 7–8). So, no, Cain is not Abel's keeper—not like God is. But despite that fact Cain has, for all intents and purposes, acted in that role: wielding the power of life and death that properly belongs only to the Divine Keeper. In this story, too, the divine/human distinction has been blurred, and with disastrous outcomes. Another instance of this theme, with the problem this time originating from the divine side of things, is the very odd and enigmatic story of the divine beings who wish to have sexual relations with human women (6:1–4). The story indicates that the offspring of these unions were the Nephilim, heroic giants of old, whose descendants will cause problems later in the Torah (e.g., Num 13:33). It is also significant that this strange account leads directly into the flood narrative (Gen 6:5–8:18). Finally, the Tower of Babel story (11:1–9) may be yet another instance of the theme because the builders are said to desire a tower "with its top in the heavens" (11:4). They are unsuccessful, since God must "come down" to even see the tower (11:5). Why, then, does God decide to confuse their language and disperse them across the earth? Apparently because the people are inclined to hunker down and stay put—actions that are directly opposite to what God had commanded (see 1:28; 9:1, 7). God's action is thus less a judgment on human hubris and a haughty building project than a divine enablement of humanity to fulfill the creational commands of God.

The last remark highlights a second important theme in the opening chapters of Genesis: the recurrence of human disobedience and the response of God. If the world God creates is not just "good" but "very good" (1:31), it is nevertheless clear that it is also complicated if not despoiled by human disobedience. That begins already in the

Garden of Eden (Genesis 3) but gets worse quickly, especially in terms of violence (see 4:8, 23–24; 6:5, 11–12). In each case, God responds to the problems caused by humankind—sometimes with judgment, as in the flood, but oftentimes with a gracious act of some sort, even if that accompanies the divine judgment. Examples include God's provision of clothes for the first couple (3:21); God's ensuring that Cain is not killed, despite his murderous act (4:15); God's saving the human species by warning Noah about the flood, then remembering him and the animals on the ark and promising to never flood the earth again (6:13–21; 8:1, 21–22); God's scattering of the people to inhabit the entire world, per God's wishes in creation, despite humankind's desire to stay put (11:8–9). If the very good world has gone awry due to human disobedience, then the opening chapters of Genesis show a God who is working hard to set things aright.

This divine responsiveness is also at work in the next block of text, chapters 12–36, which are often called *the ancestral narratives*. Already at the end of chapter 11, the Book of Genesis begins to narrow in on one family, the family of Terah, and specifically on Terah's son Abram whose wife, Sarai, is said to be barren, incapable of having children (11:30). Suddenly, out of the blue, God speaks to Abram, calling him to leave his family and homeland and journey to a new land (12:1–3). God promises to prosper Abram and make him into a great nation with the result that "all the families of the earth" will be blessed because of him. The specific mention of "families of the earth," shows that the concerns of Genesis 1–11 are still operative in this second block of text: God still intends to bless all human peoples, all genealogical units, wherever they are found. That is not new. What is new in Genesis 12 is that we have reached a new stage in divine responsiveness. Prior attempts to set things straight have yielded mixed results: expulsion from the garden, flood, dispersal from the tower. God now seems to adopt a new approach, focusing on one particular family in order to ultimately bless all. This makes good sense, of course, since everyone is ultimately related per the *toledoth* formula.

This central section of Genesis is primarily concerned with Abram and Sarai, whose names are formally changed to Abraham and Sarah in Gen 17:5, 15. This section also has much to say about their grandson Jacob and his 12 sons. In the case of Abraham and Sarah, the plot is driven by the initial question posed by considering God's call in 12:1–3 after the crucial detail of 11:30: How can

Abraham become the father of a great nation if he and his wife cannot have children? The question is not lost on Abraham and Sarah, who engage in various activities that endanger Sarah's motherhood of Abraham's child (e.g., the deceptions with Pharaoh and Abimelech; see above) or that attempt to produce a viable heir via another process—most notably by Hagar who bears Abraham a son, Ishmael (16:1–16; see also 15:2–3). The book's ultimate answer to this question is Isaac, the child of promise who is born to Abraham and Sarah at an advanced age (21:1–7).

It is apparently Abraham's mixture of faithful and less-than-faithful responses to God's calling and promise that gives rise to the famous (or infamous) text found in Genesis 22. This chapter is called the near sacrifice of Isaac, or, in Hebrew, the *Akedah* (the "binding" of Isaac, given the use of the verb "to bind" in 22:9). This chapter is troubling in content and poignant in presentation. The narrator is clear from the start that the entire thing is a "test" (22:1)—one that, in the end, yields conclusive evidence of Abraham's allegiance (22:12). But the rest of the story indicates that this test takes its toll: Isaac and Abraham are never portrayed as speaking to each other after this point in Genesis. Interpreters throughout the centuries have struggled with why God would design such a brutal test.

Genesis 22 is a turning point, regardless. Prior to this chapter, it seems as if God is unsure if the latest step in the divine strategy—using one family to bless all families—would work, especially in light of Abraham's history of faith*less*ness alongside his more faithful moments. Perhaps God will have to go another route. But not after Genesis 22. "Now I know that you revere God," says the angel who stays Abraham's hand (22:12), and from that point forward the question is not *if* the divine promise will go through Abraham's offspring but *how*, exactly, it will do so, especially once the family gets large.

Isaac is the long-awaited child of promise, but Genesis does not devote much time to him. After his crucial role in chapter 22, the critical issue is finding Isaac a spouse so the family line can continue. Once she is located, Isaac's wife, Rebekah, is every bit as if not more important than Isaac is, especially when she learns she is pregnant with twins. God tells her that the older one, Esau, will end up serving the younger one, Jacob (25:21–24). Rebekah is instrumental in making sure that Jacob obtains (by deception) the blessing that should have gone to Esau as firstborn (27:1–29). Not surprisingly, significant strife between the brothers ensues, and Jacob is forced to flee for his life (27:30–45). During his time away, Jacob ends up reunited with some distant kin and marries two sisters, Leah and Rachel (29:16–30). Between these two sisters and their two maid-servants, Bilhah and Zilpah, 12 sons are born to Jacob (29:31–30:24; 35:16–18). Because Jacob's name is changed to Israel (twice: 32:29 and 35:10, usually ascribed to E and P, respectively), these children become known as the "twelve tribes of Israel."

Genesis 37–50 focuses on the 12 sons, especially on the second-to-last born, Joseph. Here we find more instances of sibling rivalry and the favoring of the youngest over the oldest—a motif established as early as the story of Cain and Abel and repeated several times since. In this case, problems arise because Joseph is Jacob's favorite (37:3). His brothers despise him for it (37:4) and sell him into slavery because of it (37:18–28). Joseph ends up in Egypt where, the text reports, God was with him (39:2). Through a series of fortunate, unfortunate, and then fortunate events—replete with accusations of sexual assault (39:11–18) and insightful interpretations of dreams (40:1–41:32)—Joseph eventually finds himself as second in command to Pharaoh himself (41:37–45).

The plot thickens when Joseph's brothers, back in Canaan, find themselves in a famine and must journey to Egypt to seek food (42:1–5). Joseph recognizes them when they arrive (42:7) but puts them through a series of trying circumstances. These read as no small amount of payback, but they are also a way for Joseph to force his older brothers to bring the youngest sibling, Benjamin, to Egypt (42:9–44:17).

The Joseph story is widely considered to be among the best, in terms of narrative art, in the Bible. The account culminates in Joseph revealing his true identity to his brothers, forgiving them, and being reunited with his father Jacob (45:1–28; 46:28–34; 50:15–21). As Genesis draws to a close, we have come a long way: from a story of fratricide (Cain and Abel) to a story of fraternal forgiveness (Joseph and his brothers). Abraham's family is once again reunited and reconciled … in Egypt. This latter detail poses an immediate problem for those who remember God's initial promises to Abraham about the land of Canaan (Gen 12:1, 7). Egypt is not the promised land—far from it, in fact, as the opening chapters of Exodus make painfully clear.

EXODUS (*SHEMOTH*)

Like Genesis, the English title for the second book of the Torah stems from the Septuagint: *Exodos Aigyptou*, "the departure from Egypt," shortened to just *Exodos*. The Hebrew name for the book comes from the second Hebrew word in the first verse: "And these are the *names of* [*shemoth*] the children of Israel who went down to Egypt with Jacob" (Exod 1:1). The fact that the Book of Exodus begins with the conjunction "and" demonstrates that it does not exist in a vacuum but is closely connected with what has come before.

This connection is evident from the story itself, but it is also true of Pentateuchal sources, assuming for the moment that such sources did in fact (once) exist. In source-critical theory, the various sources are the building blocks that produced the Torah as we now have it and extend across the five books of the Pentateuch (see Figure 2.3). In terms of the unfolding narrative, Exod 1:1–6 harkens back to Gen 46:8–27. In terms of Pentateuchal sources, the specific language used in Exod 1:7 to describe the fertility and proliferation of the Israelite people in Egypt uses words that are also found in Genesis 1 (esp. vv. 20, 28) and 9 (esp. vv. 1, 7), suggesting that this verse in Exodus belongs to the same source as those texts—in this case, P.

Exodus does not only look back, however; it also looks forward. The end of Exodus, with its details about the divine cloud filling the tabernacle (Exod 40:36–38), anticipates the information about the cloud that comes later in Num 9:15–23. Other details serve to connect Exodus to the Book to Leviticus. The instructions about the ordination of Aaron and his sons as priests are given in Exodus 29, for example, but aren't enacted until Leviticus 8–9. Another example would be how the instructions for the tabernacle (Exodus 25–30) and its subsequent construction (Exodus 35–40) are an essential prelude for the cultic activity described in Leviticus.

Exodus, in brief, is not alone.

Despite its connections to other books, Exodus stands apart from them as arguably the most important book in the Torah, if not the whole Old Testament, because it contains the fundamental saving act in the Hebrew Bible: the delivery of the Israelites from Egypt. This important event has proven very difficult for historians to fix in time, however, in part because one of the central characters in the story—the pharaoh himself—goes unnamed. Given this difficulty, some scholars argue that the exodus is best understood in terms of cultural or collective memory. That would mean, among other things, that the memory of the exodus grew and changed over time. That is to be expected when the memory in question is preserved in literature like the Pentateuch, which has a complex internal development and a long history of transmission. Whatever the case, the book of Exodus and the exodus that it recounts—along with related topics like the Passover, the covenant, the Ten Commandments, and so forth—function paradigmatically for other texts and traditions in the Old Testament. Indeed, insofar as the New Testament Passion accounts take place during the Passover celebration, a case could be made that the primary saving act in the New Testament is also dependent on the exodus, making the exodus the act of salvation par excellence in Scripture, with the Book of Exodus the most important in the Christian Bible.

Exodus can be divided into two, roughly equal parts: chapters 1–18 relate the events in Egypt and the journey from there to the arrival at Mount Sinai; chapters 19–40 then cover the covenant at Sinai, including the famous story of the golden calf. The content and ordering of these two parts are important. First, Exodus recounts what God has done for Israel; only after that does the book outline what Israel must do for God in grateful response.

The opening verses of Exodus 1 tell of the proliferation of the Israelite people, which is proof of God's blessing given at creation and reiterated to Abraham and his offspring in Genesis. The problem is that the divine promises are coming to fruition, not in the land that God promised Abraham but down in Egypt. The problem is exacerbated by an Egyptian king who didn't know all that Joseph had done for Egypt (1:8). The current pharaoh cares only about possible military outcomes (1:9–10). Initially he decides to control the foreign element within his country by enslaving them (1:11–14). He quickly escalates matters by trying to eliminate the Israelites altogether by deviously murdering the Hebrew boys at birth (1:15–16). This atrocious plan is only narrowly avoided thanks to the civil disobedience of two midwives, Shiphrah and Puah. These two are brave enough to disobey Pharaoh and to lie directly to his despotic face (1:18–19). Their action is motivated by godly reverence (1:17), and so it is not surprising that God rewards them for their deeds

(1:20–21). Maniacs like Pharaoh don't give up, however. He moves from covert murder-by-midwife to public decree to kill every baby boy born to the Hebrews (1:22). The baby girls can live, but they will effectively be assimilated by intermarriage. Pharaoh intends nothing less than the end of Israel.

Exodus next recounts the birth of Moses, of the tribe of Levi; his mother hides him as long as possible, and then, when it isn't, sends him down the Nile in a basket (2:1–4). Miraculously, baby Moses survives this perilous journey and is rescued by Pharaoh's daughter (2:5–9). She gives him the name "Moses"—a common name in Egyptian—though the biblical text offers a Hebrew, non-Egyptian etymology for why she picked it (2:10).

In the very next verse, Moses is now an adult (2:11) and gets in trouble when he sees an Egyptian beating a Hebrew. For whatever reason, Moses intervenes. He kills the Egyptian and then buries the body (2:11–12). The next day, when Moses attempts to break up a fight between two Hebrews, it becomes clear that everyone knows what he has done (2:13–14). Moses is now wanted for homicide (2:15) and escapes to Midian, where he marries and becomes a father (2:16–22).

Meanwhile, things are getting worse in Egypt, but there is a twist: God is now alert to Israel's plight (2:23–25). God remembers the covenant with the ancestors and in the next chapter calls Moses to deliver the Israelites from Egypt. The extended dialogue between Moses and God in Exodus 3–4 contains a number of well-known details such as the giving of the divine name, "I Am Who I Am" (3:14; see Box 2.1), the staff that can turn into a snake (4:2–4; cf. 7:12), and Moses' difficulties in speaking (4:10).

God talks Moses into the job. He returns to Egypt with his brother Aaron. In their first audience with Pharaoh, the Egyptian king makes clear that he has never heard of a deity named *Yhwh* and he will not give into this God's demands to let the Israelites go (5:2). Nothing short of a cosmic battle ensues, in which God inflicts ten plagues on Pharaoh and his land (7:8–10:29). In Hebrew, these are typically called "signs" not "plagues" because they function as public displays that demonstrate to Pharaoh, Egypt, and the whole world who this God is. Pharaoh didn't know *Yhwh* before, but now he does—up close and in personal and painful detail. The tenth and final sign, the death of the firstborn, is given an extended introduction and is to be memorialized in the future through the Passover meal (11:1–12:28). When the tenth plague takes place, it is told tersely (12:29–30)—perhaps due to its gravity. This final sign leads to Israel's immediate release (12:31–32). But Pharaoh subsequently reconsiders and pursues the Israelites, cornering them with their backs against "the reed sea" (Hebrew *yam suf*).

The miracle at the sea of reeds is found in Exodus 14 in what appears to be a complicated mixture of J, E, and P traditions. Some stories, evidently, were so important that the main traditions each had some version of it. Or perhaps the final editor(s) felt that the most important stories should include as many traditions as possible, even if the final product is somewhat convoluted as a result. In Exodus 14, there is confusion with regard to how the sea was parted: God drove it back with a wind in J; in P, the sea split into two walls of water as Moses stretched out his hand. The next chapter of Exodus contains a poem celebrating God's victory at the sea which offers yet another, third perspective on the event (cf. 15:1, 4, 6–8, 10, 12). Some scholars think this poem is one of the earliest texts preserved in the Hebrew Bible and may predate the earliest Pentateuchal source by a century or more.

In Exodus 19, exactly three months after leaving Egypt, the Israelites arrive at Mt. Sinai. According to the biblical chronology, Israel remains at Sinai more than 11 months. They are not said to depart until Num 10:11. Sinai is where God enters into a covenant (*berit*) with Israel—a kind of formalized relationship similar to political treaties of that day. The essence of the Sinai covenant is that the Lord will be Israel's God and Israel will be the Lord's people. Right at the start of the covenant, Israel is described as a kingdom of priests and a holy nation (Exod 19:6). This connects Israel's covenantal duties to God's purposes to set the world aright as laid out in the primeval history of Genesis 1–11 and in the selection of Abraham and Sarah and their descendants in the ancestral narratives of Genesis 12–50.

The specifics of the covenant relationship are many and detailed. They begin with the Ten Commandments, also called the Decalogue ("ten words," which is what they are called in Hebrew; see Exod 34:28; Deut 4:13; 10:4). The Ten Commandments are given in Exod 20:1–17 and repeated again in Deut 5:6–21. The Decalogue is just the beginning of the covenantal legislation, but the people have heard enough after only hearing that much! They are frightened by the pyrotechnics on the mountain and they ask Moses to serve as their intermediary from that point forward (Exod 20:18–19).

What follows is often called the Book of the Covenant or the Covenant Code (20:22–23:19). It is one of several legal collections in the Pentateuch and is probably the earliest. The Ten Commandments are instances of *absolute law*. "You must not murder!" is unqualified, but its enforcement and the punishment for its violation are left unspecified. Most of what is found in the Book of the Covenant and the other law collections in the Torah is *case law*. "If (or when) *x* happens, then *y* must happen." In the Old Testament, case law frequently clarifies absolute law which is often broader in reach and ramification but far briefer in formulation. Israel's covenant with God at Sinai is ratified in 24:9–18.

Next come two large blocks of text that are concerned with the construction of the tabernacle. The tabernacle is effectively a mobile temple for Israel's worship of God while they journey from Egypt to Canaan. Chapters 25–31 provide all of the instructions for this elaborate structure: its furnishings, its personnel, their cultic duties, and so forth. But intervening between this block and the second, chapters 35–40, where the instructions are carried out, is the famous golden calf story. The profundity of the disobedience that takes place in this event is sometimes likened to committing adultery on one's wedding night. At the very moment when the Israelites are receiving the covenant, they break it by violating the first and second commandments about worshiping other gods, especially in the form of an idol (32:1–6).

All seems to be lost. God is ready to shut down the current phase in the divine set-the-world-aright strategy because Abraham's offspring have ruined everything (32:7–8). God proposes to start all over from scratch, with Moses as a new and improved Abraham, promising to make Moses into a great nation (32:9–10; cf. Gen 12:1–3). Only Moses' rhetorically savvy intervention talks God down (Exod 32:11–14).

But the disobedience leaves its mark on all parties. God is reluctant to continue on the journey with the Israelites. Once again Moses must intervene (33:1–3; 33:12–34:9). In this second intervention, God reveals further insight into the divine name and the divine character with a snippet of poetry that is repeated enough times elsewhere in the Bible (see, e.g., Num 14:18–19; Deut 7:9–10;

Neh 9:16–19; Ps 25:4–11; 86:15; 103:8; Jonah 4:2; Joel 2:23; Nah 1:2–3) that some scholars have deemed it the closest ancient Israel got to a creedal statement of belief:

> The LORD! The LORD!
> a God who is compassionate and merciful,
> > very patient,
> > full of great loyalty and faithfulness
> > showing great loyalty to a thousand generations,
> > forgiving every kind of sin and rebellion,
> > yet by no means clearing the guilty,
> > punishing for their parents' sins
> > their children and their grandchildren,
> > as well as the third and fourth generation. (Exod 34:6b–7, CEB).

There is also a new set of stone tablets (34:1) with a new set of commandments. The new set is often called "the cultic Decalogue" because it includes a number of commandments about worship—the golden calf was a profound failure on exactly that point (34:10–28).

The interlude about the golden calf explains the extensive and elaborate repetition that comes in the second block of text devoted to the tabernacle (Exodus 35–40). Modern readers can find this repetition mind-numbing, but it plays a crucial role in the Book of Exodus because it shows that Israel, after the golden calf, is now willing and able to be completely obedient to the divine will. The repeated notice that everything was done "exactly" as God commanded is no small matter but proof that Israel can keep the promise it made at the very start of the covenant-making process: "We will do everything that the LORD has said" (19:8).

It is no wonder, therefore, but a truly wondrous thing, that Exodus ends with the glory of God filling the tabernacle (40:34–35).

LEVITICUS (*VAYYIQRA*)

Like Genesis, the Hebrew name for Leviticus comes from the first word of Lev 1:1 (*wayyiqra*, "and he [God] called out"), and, like Exodus, Leviticus is closely connected with has preceded it. What has preceded it is Genesis–Exodus, but most immediately Exodus, which ended with the glory of God filling the tabernacle. Leviticus provides detailed instruction for what is to take place in that tabernacle. A rabbinic designation for the book captures this cultic focus quite nicely: *torat kohanim*, "priestly law." Source-critical analyses concur, determining that the majority of the book belongs to the Priestly stratum of the Pentateuch. The English title, "Leviticus," comes from the Septuagint's *Leuitikon* via the Vulgate (*Liber Levitici*), though the book is about far more than just the Levites.

It is precisely because the book is about more than just the priests that some scholars have argued that Leviticus, too, is composite—just like the other books of the Pentateuch. Though there is little debate that the majority of Leviticus belongs to the P source, many have noted differences between chapters 1–16 and chapters 17–27. The earlier chapters speak primarily of the holiness (the "set apart-ness") of the priests and their work, but the latter chapters speak of the holiness of "the entire congregation of the people of Israel" (19:2). The last part of Leviticus, therefore, has sometimes been called the Holiness Code or Holiness Collection, abbreviated H, which now joins the other, more familiar abbreviations J, E, D, and P. And, just like those other sources, H may be less a singular "document" from a single author but something more akin to a "Holiness Tradition" from a "Holiness School" (HS). While there is much debate about all these matters, scholars who ascribe to an H "source" or "tradition" are generally agreed that it postdates P. There may even be traces of H in the P portions of Leviticus (chaps. 1–16), which might indicate that H had the final editorial say in Leviticus or at least that there are editorial additions from H (or HS) in the earlier P materials.

According to the internal biblical chronology, Israel is at Sinai for just shy of a year, but a third of the Torah is devoted to this period, with the entirety of Leviticus taking place within a period of one month (see Exod 40:17 and Num 1:1). If Sinai is the dominant centerpiece of the Pentateuch, then Leviticus is the very center of that centerpiece. This is an important fact about the book—one that underscores its significance. The framework to Leviticus provided by Exodus and Numbers, most immediately, and Genesis and Deuteronomy, more distantly, is also crucial since it provides the justification, motivation, and explanation for the many instructions found in the Torah's center attraction: Leviticus.

Leviticus is noteworthy for a number of reasons. Many practices and institutions in contemporary Judaism are to be found here—Yom Kippur, for instance (Leviticus 16), or laws about diet (Leviticus 11)—with Jewish children traditionally beginning their study of the Bible with Leviticus given the importance of its commandments. Most Christians do not observe Jewish festivals or food practices, but they, too, know of Lev 19:18, "love your neighbor as yourself," since it is quoted, along with Deut 6:5, by Jesus in the New Testament as the "Great Commandment" (see Matt 22:34–40; Mark 12:28–34; Luke 10:25–28). Much later Christian writers such as Saint Augustine in North Africa (fourth to fifth century CE) and John Wesley in England (eighteenth century CE) took Deuteronomy's love of God and Leviticus' love of neighbor as the quintessential description of the Christian life. Not to be missed in this regard is Lev 19:34, which commends the same kind of love and care for immigrants—a point that is also found elsewhere in the Torah (Exod 22:21; 23:9) and in the New Testament (e.g., Matt 25:34, 38, 40, 43–45; Luke 10:25–37).

Leviticus begins with what might be called an instruction manual on sacrifice (chaps. 1–7). These chapters outline various kinds of offerings: their distinct types, purpose, and so forth. Coming hard on the heels of the tragic, near-fatal disobedience with the golden calf (Exodus 32), this instruction manual is crucial for Israel's continuing life with its holy God. While this makes sense of the narrative flow from Exodus into Leviticus, it remains somewhat curious that Leviticus should reveal so much of what is, properly speaking, the special purview of the priests. On the one hand, this indicates that much of Leviticus may have been originally "for priests' eyes only." On the other hand, in its current form and placement, Leviticus 1–7, no less than the H material in Leviticus 17–26, functions to democratize priestly holiness by making it widely available—if not in terms of family lineage (only some Israelites were Levites by birth), then at least in terms of literary access.

It can be difficult for modern readers to move from the mostly narrative materials in Genesis and the first half of Exodus to the more legal and cultic texts in the second part of Exodus and the opening seven chapters of Leviticus. Leviticus 8–9 returns to narrative, however, and covers the matter of the ordination and initiation of the priests that was first mentioned in Exodus 29. This section is followed immediately by the unusual story of Nadab and Abihu, two of Aaron's sons, who are struck down after offering "unauthorized fire" (CEB) before God (Lev 10:1–7). What, exactly, these two individuals did wrong is not entirely clear; what is abundantly clear, however, is that the story underscores the dangerous nature of cultic practice and priestly leadership. These are serious matters with life-and-death consequences.

Leviticus 11–15 returns to cultic matters, detailing a great deal of instructions about purity. Topics covered in these chapters include food, childbirth, and the mysterious skin disease called *tzara'at* in Hebrew. This disease in English translations is often referred to as "leprosy," though it is certainly not the same malady as modern-day leprosy (Hansen's disease) since *tzara'at* can show up on clothing and in the walls of houses, not just on people's skin (Lev 13:47–58; 14:33–53). This section of Leviticus culminates in chapter 16 which concerns the Day of Atonement (Yom Kippur), a yearly ritual in which everyone's sins are cleansed and removed (Lev 16:16, 21–22). This remarkable ritual stands at the very center of Leviticus, which stands at the very center of the Torah. It is hard to imagine a better way to signal the Torah's (and its God's) interest in reconciliation.

Leviticus 17–26 shifts the focus from the priests and their sanctuary service to their work outside the sanctuary and to the congregation of Israel as a whole (see 17:1–3; 18:1; 19:1; etc.). One frequently encounters in these chapters an odd mixture of inspirational commands like the injunctions to love one's neighbor and the immigrant (19:18, 34), to show respect for the elderly (19:32), or to exercise care for the disabled (19:14) with laws that make very little sense now, like the rule forbidding clothing of mixed fabrics (19:19) or other laws that are unclear as to precise motivation or specific referent (19:27–28). What *is* clear about this holy hodge-podge, however, is that its ultimate grounding is in the identity of God (note the recurring refrain "I am the LORD") and God's holy nature, both of which serve as motivation for Israel's own holiness and obedience (see 19:2). In some way, that is, God and God's holiness are thought to be made manifest in this often curious collection of laws and their enactment in Israel's life in the world. Readers of Leviticus must thus wrestle with the entire complex—no easy task—and not be too cavalier in dismissing this or that verse, especially when compared to others. To put the situation differently, with categories frequently found in later Christian writing about Old Testament law, the legal material in Leviticus (and elsewhere in the Torah) is not easily divided into civil, ceremonial, and moral laws, with some or most of the former two categories quickly jettisoned. The Pentateuchal laws will not come apart so neatly, and that means that the civil, ceremonial, and moral categories are ill-suited to the Pentateuch. Many, if not most of the Torah's many commandments function in more than one of these ways—even simultaneously. That means that each one deserves careful consideration and thorough study.

NUMBERS (*BEMIDBAR*)

The Book of Numbers is called *Bemidbar,* "In the wilderness," in Hebrew since that is the first distinctive word found in Num 1:1. The English title, "Numbers," comes from the Greek (*Arithmoi*) and Latin (*Liber Numeri*) translations. Both the Hebrew and other titles are instructive and capture something of the book's content. In the case of Hebrew *Bemidbar,* the book can be organized into three sections, around three primary geographical locations, each of which, in its own way, is "in the wilderness":

- At Mt. Sinai—Num 1:1–10:10;
- On the trek through the desert on the way to Transjordan—Num 10:11–21:35; and
- In the plains of Moab—Num 22:1–36:13.

In terms of the larger Pentateuchal "plot," the main twist in Numbers is the story about the spies found in chapters 13–14. Second only to the golden calf incident, this incident is another major setback for Israel on its way to the promised land of Canaan. Israel's unfaithfulness in the spy account leads to their wandering in the desert for 40 years—a temporal span that is schematic, designating the changeover of a generation. Numbers covers two generations, therefore: the one that initially came out of Egypt and proved unfaithful after the spy report and a second, new generation that is allowed entry into Canaan. These generations are counted in two censuses (chaps. 1 and 26), which, along with their numerical totals, have given rise to the title "Numbers." Though the book is not primarily interested in the mathematical sums themselves, Numbers is very much concerned with the generations that are counted, with their respective characters (faithful or not), and with the transition from the first to the second. The censuses thus offer another way to divide the book up into two, unequal parts:

- First generation—Numbers 1–25;
- Second generation—Numbers 26–36.

Like Leviticus, the Book of Numbers is sometimes neglected by modern readers, which is ironic, since it contains some of the best known stories in the Old Testament, including the priestly or Aaronic benediction (6:22–27), the spy story with the heroics of Caleb and Joshua (chaps. 13–14), Moses' and Aaron's disobedience when bringing water from the rock (20:1–13), and Balaam's talking donkey (22:22–35), among others.

Numbers, which like Exodus and Leviticus also begins with the conjunction "and," picks up in the second month of the second year since the exodus from Egypt (1:1). The first census of the people is ordered for the sake of military preparations and is described in chapter 1. This is followed by instructions about the layout of the camp and additional laws of various sorts, from purity in the camp to the dedication of the tabernacle to details about the Passover celebration—all of which suggests that the majority of this material comes from the Priestly source (chaps. 2–9). Numbers as a whole, however, is easily the most complicated in the Torah when it comes to source-critical analysis and its complex mixture of various genres.

After almost a year at Sinai and some 59 Pentateuchal chapters, Israel is finally commanded to leave the mountain and set out for Canaan (10:11). At this point, we encounter stories that are reminiscent of the early days after the escape from Egypt, especially when the people complain about food (11:4–35; cf. Exod 15:22–17:7). In Numbers, as earlier in Exodus, the people's needs are provided for with the miraculous provision of manna and quail, though the discerning reader will note that God is far less patient in Numbers than was the case in Exodus. This seems strange. Shouldn't God be even more favorably disposed toward the people after the covenant-making at Sinai? The narrative suggests the exact opposite, however. The problem, it seems, is not on the divine side of the equation but the human one: After Sinai, Israel is God's covenant people and should know better about the Lord who is gracious and merciful (Exod 34:6–7). With the covenant now in place, a new stage in the God-Israel relationship has been reached. The covenant at Sinai can be seen as kind of *bar mitzvah*, with Israel now a "son of the commandment." More can be and is expected of the people after the covenant than before the covenant was formalized.

A similar logic may underlie Numbers 13–14, the story of the spies who are sent to scout out the land and bring a report back to the people. The report begins positively: the land is every bit as good as Israel hoped, proverbially "flowing with milk and honey" (13:27). Proof of the land's fertility is provided by a massive cluster of grapes so large it has to be carried by two of the spies (13:23, 26). After this good word and indisputable evidence, the report turns sour. The spies report that there are people living in the land in fortified settlements (13:28–29). One of the scouts, Caleb, reassures the people that they are capable of the job ahead of them (13:30), but his testimony is not enough (Joshua chimes in similarly in 14:5). The other spies insist that the job is impossible. They renege on their prior report of the land's goodness, and say, instead, that the land eats up its inhabitants—though not, evidently, the ones living there presently! They go on to specify that the present inhabitants are not only stronger than the Israelites (13:31), they are also physically bigger because some of them, like the Anakim, are the direct descendants of the Nephilim (13:33)—the mythic figures that were the offspring of divine and human intercourse way back when in Genesis 6.

Things quickly go from bad to worse with the entire congregation turning against Moses and Aaron and threatening to kill them (Num 14:1–10). What follows is highly similar to what transpired in the golden calf debacle: once again, God is finished with the people and offers to start over from scratch with Moses as a new Abraham/ Israel upgrade (14:11–12), but once again Moses intercedes with a rhetorically savvy prayer (14:13–19). After that prayer, God once again stands down, but not without indicating some long-term consequences for this second, near-fatal instance of unfaithfulness (14:20–35). The consequences this time are even more dire than they were in Exodus 32–34. In Numbers, the divine decree is that the entire generation that came out of Egypt, 20 years and older, is condemned to die in the wilderness and not enter the promised land. The only exceptions to this rule are the two faithful spies, Caleb and Joshua. (The notable absence of Moses and Aaron from this list of exceptions is a foreshadowing of what comes later in Numbers 20.) This is presented as poetic justice of a sort: the unbelieving generation will, in fact, experience defeat—but not at the hand of the Anakim or other Canaanite peoples; and they will, in fact, die in the desert—just as they wished (14:2). The punishment is also heavily ironic: the people worried about their children being taken by the enemy (14:3), but God promises that it will be those very children who will be the ones to enter and inherit the land. Here, then, is another instance of divine judgment like those found in the early chapters of Genesis. It is two-edged—punitive, on the one hand, and gracious, on the other. The similarities bear witness to the consistency and ultimate purposes of God in the Torah.

The rest of the Book of Numbers covers the events that transpire until the death of the first generation is complete. Here is where the story about Moses and Aaron bringing water from the rock is found (Numbers 20). This is another installment in the Bible's collection of highly enigmatic stories. *Something* clearly goes wrong here. God is not pleased with how Moses and Aaron execute the miraculous provision, but the exact reasons for God's displeasure go unspecified. Should Moses have struck the rock only once, not twice? Or is it that Moses is not allowed to show displeasure or impatience with the people? The text does not say, but the divine decision is quite unambiguous: neither Moses nor Aaron will enter the promised land (20:12). Aaron dies shortly thereafter (20:23–29). Moses' death will be delayed until the very end of the Pentateuch.

With the slow and steady demise of the first, exodus generation, the action focuses increasingly on the next generation of Israelites and their movement into the region of Moab, across the Jordan river from Canaan (Num 22:1–36:13). The second census of the new generation is taken in chapter 26, which is followed by laws pertaining to inheritance (27:1–11; 36:1–12) and by details about the distribution of the land of Canaan by Israelite tribe (32:1–42; 33:50–35:34). Both are important. In the case of *inheritance*, Numbers 27 tells the story of the daughters of Zelophehad, who died without a male heir. This raised the question of who should inherit Zelophehad's estate. When Moses brings this matter for divine consultation, God sides with the daughters: they deserve to inherit their father's estate rather than their uncles. Only if the deceased is without any children whatsoever should the estate go to siblings or next of kin. Numbers 36 adds an additional requirement to this legislation: when daughters inherit, they must marry within the tribe to ensure that the wealth does not go outside the clan.

As for *land distribution*, the most crucial point is that the tribes of Reuben and Gad and half of the tribe of Manasseh prefer to settle down in land east of the Jordan River. Their request is granted but these tribes are not released from the military service they owe their fellow Israelites across the Jordan in Canaan (chap. 32).

The last verse of Numbers states: "These are the commandments and regulations that the LORD enjoined upon the Israelites, through Moses, on the steppes of Moab, at the Jordan near Jericho" (36:13; NJPSV). This serves as an apt summary of the book, but the language that is used here is also very similar to what is found in the next book of the Torah, so the verse also serves as an excellent transition to Deuteronomy.

DEUTERONOMY (*DEVARIM*)

The English title for the final book of the Pentateuch once again comes from the Greek translation of the Bible, *Deuteronomion*, via the Latin (*Liber Deuteronomium*). The Greek title is taken from the Septuagint's translation of Deut 17:18, which, in Hebrew, speaks of a "copy of this law" (*mishneh torah*). The Septuagint understood this phrase to mean "second law," as did the Vulgate. *Mishneh torah* is sometimes used of Deuteronomy in rabbinic literature, which also calls the book *sepher tokachot*, "book of exhortations (or admonitions)." The most common Hebrew title, however, is simply *Devarim*, "words," since that term appears prominently in the first verse of the book.

As with other books in the Pentateuch, each of Deuteronomy's different names affords helpful insight on the book as a whole. The Greek and Latin titles capture the fact that Deuteronomy does indeed seem like a *second law*. It seems to revise much of what has preceded it in the Torah. Deuteronomy also supplements earlier material (see 29:1). And yet, despite revision and supplementation, Deuteronomy is still very much in line with what has come before—it repeats a good bit of that narrative and law and so the book can be seen as (just) another *copy of the law*. Deuteronomy's literary style is idiosyncratic. What scholars call D is easily distinguished from P and other non-P and non-D texts. One aspect of this Deuteronomic style is its "preachy" tone. The book abounds in *moral exhortation* and so the rabbinic designation is spot on. Finally, Deuteronomy is definitely a book of *words* since there is more reported speech in Deuteronomy than in any other book in the Torah. The Hebrew title, *Devarim*, captures this fact nicely.

The best word to describe Deuteronomy, however, is *torah* because that is how the book identifies itself. This begins already in Deut 1:5: "Moses began to explain this *torah* as follows." Deuteronomy's self-designation as *torah* shows up elsewhere—even outside of Deuteronomy in places that likely have Deuteronomy in mind. One example is Josh 1:8, which speaks of Joshua's need to attend to "the book of the law" given through Moses. This is a rather obvious cross-reference to Deuteronomy, especially coming so quickly on its heels. Another example is 2 Kgs 22:8, the famous mention of the discovery of "the book of the law" in the temple which has led scholars since de Wette to peg Deuteronomy, or some part(s) of it—the D source—to the reforms of King Josiah ca. 622 BCE (see above and Chart 2.1).

What part(s) of Deuteronomy, exactly, should be connected to King Josiah's period is a matter of considerable debate. Many scholars think that the central law collection of Deuteronomy (chaps. 12–26) is the most likely section since much of what Josiah does in terms of religious reforms conforms to this material in Deuteronomy, especially chapter 12 which stresses the importance of one and only one center for worship. Whether D was recovered or actually composed at the time of Josiah is yet another matter of scholarly discussion. Whatever the case, the connection between Deuteronomy and Josiah is underscored in the fact that he is portrayed as incarnating the famous text of Deut 6:4–10 (called the Shema):

> Hear, O Israel: The LORD is our God, the LORD alone. You shall love the LORD your God with all your heart, and with all your soul, and with all your might. Keep these words that I am commanding you today in your heart. Recite them to your children and talk about them when you are at home and when you are away, when you lie

down and when you rise. Bind them as a sign on your hand, fix them as an emblem on your forehead, and write them on the doorposts of your house and on your gates. (NRSV)

The Book of Kings applies this to Josiah (the key terms are italicized):

He established the words of the law that were written in the book that the priest Hilkiah had found in the house of the LORD. Before him there was no king like him, who turned to the LORD *with all his heart, with all his soul, and with all his might,* according to all the law of Moses; nor did any like him arise after him. (2 Kgs 23:24b–25; NRSV)

The citation of Deut 6:4–10 is unmistakable with Josiah's example unsurpassed. No other person in the Bible instantiates the Shema as he does.

For reasons like these, some scholars have wondered if Deuteronomy best belongs not with the story of the Torah but the story of the Prophets. This perspective will be discussed more fully in the next chapter. An important consideration when judging Deuteronomy's role in the Pentateuch and/or in the Prophets deserves to be mentioned here, however, and that is how Deuteronomy interrupts the Torah's narrative flow. At the end of Numbers, Israel is poised in Moab across the Jordan from Jericho. Readers know from Numbers 20 that Moses will not enter Canaan, even if the exact reasons for that remain murky. Israel's entry into Canaan does not take place until the Book of Joshua. All that is needed to move directly from Numbers to Joshua—in terms of the development of the Torah's story—is for Moses to die. Coming between Numbers and Joshua, however, is the very large book of Deuteronomy. Only at the very end of Deuteronomy do we finally hear of Moses' death (chap. 34).

Deuteronomy thus arrests the Torah's story for 33 chapters. Before dying, Moses delivers a series of valedictory addresses that urge Israel to obedience in Canaan and that provide old, new, and revised legislation for Israel's life therein. Each of these speeches is preceded by a third-person introduction that sets the stage:

Introduction to the First Speech—1:1–5
The First Speech—1:6–4:43

The length of the second speech is noteworthy. The second speech includes the central Deuteronomic law collection (chaps. 12–26), preceded with a summarizing and revising recapitulation (chaps. 4–11) of some of the narratives in Exodus and Numbers. Even the Ten Commandments are repeated and revised in Deuteronomy (5:6–21)! The most famous revisions occur in the motivation for the Sabbath commandment (in Deuteronomy, it is because the Israelites weren't given any breaks in Egypt; in Exodus, it is because God rested in creation) and in the coveting commandment (in Deuteronomy, coveting another's wife is placed in a separate category from coveting property; in Exodus, these are treated together). Changes like this show how Deuteronomy's take on *torah* is dynamic, capable of being updated due to different times and changed circumstances. The book also shows that humanitarian and egalitarian considerations play crucial roles in legal amendment.

The legal revisions in Deuteronomy demonstrate that this book, like the others in the Pentateuch, had a long compositional history. Different layers of tradition seem to be identifiable. Scholars often point to Deut 4:25–31; 28:45–57; and 30:1–6 as texts that betray knowledge of the Babylonian exile. "Multi-layering" like this proves the importance of Deuteronomy: its words were deemed relevant not only for the literary audience (Israel in Moab) but also to later generations of Israelites, from Joshua through Josiah, even into the exile and beyond. In fact, Deuteronomy is one of the most frequently cited Old Testament books in the New Testament (e.g., Deut 6:4–5 in Matt 22:37; Mark 12:29–30; Luke 10:27; see above). This should come as no surprise since Deuteronomy is explicitly concerned not only with past history or past generations but also, and far more importantly, with the present and future generations (Deut 5:3; 29:14–15). What Moses bequeaths to Israel in Deuteronomy, therefore, is a surrogate. He will not accompany Israel into the land, but this dynamic polity or "constitution" will. This is why God can say, at the end of the book, that when all seems lost, the song that is Deuteronomy's *torah* will make sure it isn't (31:19–22).

To sum up: Deuteronomy is both a climax to the Pentateuch and a fulcrum on which the Hebrew Bible pivots from the Torah to the Prophets. Deuteronomy looks backward as a kind of definitive summary of the Torah, capped by the death of the Pentateuch's most important human character. Deuteronomy also looks forward, exerting its influence upon and serving as interpretive key for all that follows in the Prophets—as we will see in the next chapter.

WHAT THE TORAH IS ALL ABOUT: TWO THINGS

Given its length (187 chapters across five books), the Torah is about a large number of things. Its scope is vast, running *from creation to Canaan*. To reduce such a dense and wide-ranging collection to only two items is difficult to say the least. Even so, in an attempt to provide some initial help toward comprehending the entirety of the Pentateuch, especially for those new to this material, the following two things may be highlighted as particularly important in any discussion of "what the Torah is all about."

DIVINE CREATION(S)

First, the Torah is about *divine creation(s)*. The Torah begins with the famous story—or, rather, stories (plural)—about the creation of the world, but the importance of creation is not limited to the opening chapters of Genesis. Instead, those opening chapters initiate what becomes a wide-ranging and robust discussion of creation throughout the Old Testament. The creative activity of God that is first attested in the divine command "Let there be light" (Gen 1:3) is actually just the beginning when it comes to creation in the Hebrew Bible. God starts anew with different strategies of restoration in the primeval history (Genesis 1–11) and, again, with the calling of Abraham (Genesis 12). In the case of the latter, God creates a people out of a situation that, from a human perspective, was impossible, "formless and void" (Gen 1:2)—namely, Sarah's barrenness and the two ancestors' advanced age (Gen 11:30; 15:3; 18:12; see Rom 4:19–21; cf. Luke 1:36–37). But a new nation is created with the birth of a baby boy named Isaac and the same is true for the people who come from Abraham's older son, Ishmael (Gen 21:13, 18, 20).

Skipping ahead to Exodus, there is the opposite of creation—the *de*creation of nature—that is manifest in the plagues on Egypt. In the plagues, Pharaoh comes to know who God is (cf. Exod 5:2), but so do the Israelites who are slowly but surely *re*created, no longer as slaves, but as God's treasured possession (19:5–6). Indeed, the poem that celebrates the crossing of the reed sea contains these key lines:

> Terror and fear fell on them [the Egyptians].
>> Because of your mighty arm, they became as still as stones!
> Until your people, O LORD, crossed over,
>> until the people *that you created* crossed over. (Exod 15:16)

But, as the old saying goes, you can get the people out of Egypt, but it is hard to get Egypt out of the people. This is shown in the murmuring narratives in Exodus and Numbers where the people complain about food and water. Upon further reflection, such complaints are thoroughly understandable. The biblical chronology has Israel in slavery in Egypt for more than 400 years (see Gen 15:13; Exod 12:40–41; cf. Acts 7:6; Gal 3:17). It is easy to imagine how such an experience created a culture of profound despair and mistrust, with Israel good only for someone else's labor. In the 40 years of Sinai and wandering before they reach Canaan, the Israelites learn a new identity, however. They are no longer Pharaoh's slaves, they are servants of God. This is just another instance of the many divine creations that mark the Torah. This last mentioned creation, like the others, is created (!) in no small measure, by the second key element of what the Torah is all about.

DIVINE COMMAND(S)

The second thing the Torah is all about is *divine command(s)*. From the start, God creates by divine command, uttering the imperatives to be fruitful and multiply (Gen 1:22, 28), and issuing the first laws in the Garden of Eden regarding what should and should not be eaten (Gen 2:16–17). Command is built into the very tissue of creation.

Divine command, like divine creation(s), is actually plural because the commands of God are found throughout the Torah. God's establishment of a new people through Abraham, Sarah, and their offspring begins with the command to leave one land and go to another one (Gen 12:1). Later, in the Sinai covenant, Israel receives a vast number of divine commands—both detailed and specific. These order life and also create a new society, one that is at odds with the rapacious economics that marked the politics of Pharaoh (Deut 5:12–15; 15:15; 16:12; 24:18, 22). These commands also remind Israel of who the true Creator and Landholder is (Exod 19:5b–6; Lev 25:23). In this way, the commands create the community of Israel—a community that must also, by direct divine command, care about other communities (Exod 23:9; Lev 19:18, 34).

The tangible relationship between divine command(s) and divine creation(s) helps to explain why the notion of land, which is so important early on in the Pentateuch, is relegated by the end of the Torah. Abraham is promised a land early in Genesis but dies with only a burial plot to his name (Gen 23:1–20; 25:9–10). The Torah concludes with Moses, the great hero of the Pentateuch, dying outside Canaan. Fulfillment of the long-delayed promise of land must wait until Joshua. And yet, in a very real way, no physical turf is necessary for the Torah to accomplish its work because, as the Torah itself makes clear, God can create anew and create again in various ways and by diverse means, including via divine command(s), and because God's commands are both pliable and portable.

Two aspects of divine creation(s) and divine command(s) should be underscored. The first, again, is that each is a pluriform phenomenon. There is not one creation in the Old Testament, but *many*; not one command, but *many*—at least 613 according to the rabbis. The second is how creation and commandment are profoundly interconnected. God does not create and then call it quits. Neither does God create Israel as a people by getting them out of Egypt and then letting them go. No, in each case, God's activity is *ongoing*. Creation is set on its course, and, even when it goes awry—even before then—God is on the scene giving commands: to the natural world and the human community (Genesis 1), to the first human couple (Genesis 2–3), and to the first ancestors of Israel (Genesis 12). Later, God commands a people descended from those couples, showing them that there are new ways to be in the world, especially the world outside of Egypt (Exodus 20–Deuteronomy 34). Commands help to create, and creation involves command. These two go together. They are not easily, if ever, extricable in the Torah. Neither are they easily, if ever, extricable in the Torah's description of God. God's ways in the world—in terms derived from later Christian theology but perfectly applicable to the Old Testament—involve creating, redeeming, and sustaining. These are not, in the end, separable steps or "progressive" moments in the divine revelation. They are of one inseparable piece. *Creation(s)* and *command(s)*: those two things, which may, in the end, be finally just one, are a large part of what the Torah is all about.

SUGGESTIONS FOR FURTHER READING

Good overviews of the Pentateuch may be found in Jean-Louis Ska, *Introduction to Reading the Pentateuch* (Winona Lake: Eisenbrauns, 2006); Thomas B. Dozeman, *The Pentateuch: Introducing the Torah* (Minneapolis: Fortress, 2017); and Johanna W. H. Van Wijk-Bos, *Making Wise the Simple: The Torah in Christian Faith and Practice* (Grand Rapids: Eerdmans, 2005).

The classic study by Julius Wellhausen is his *Prolegomena to the History of Israel*, first published in German in 1878 and translated into English in 1885 (reprint ed.; Atlanta: Scholars, 1994). The dates given above for the four sources reflect the work of Martin Noth, *A History of Pentateuchal Traditions* (Chico: Scholars, 1981). A popular presentation of the Documentary Hypothesis is found in Richard Elliott Friedman, *Who Wrote the Bible?* (San Francisco: HarperSanFrancisco, 1997). Friedman calls Welllhausen's late dating of P "a brilliant mistake." For a translation of the Torah with the sources in different colors, see Friedman's *The Bible with Sources Revealed: A New View into the Five Books of Moses* (San Francisco: HarperSanFrancisco, 2003)—though of course the "new view" in question is actually now several hundred years old! A different presentation, without colors, is found in Anthony F. Campbell and Mark A. O'Brien, *Sources of the Pentateuch: Texts, Introductions, Annotations* (Minneapolis: Fortress, 1993).

The most significant challenge to the Documentary Hypothesis in neo-fragmentarian form is Rolf Rendtorff, *The Problem of the Process of the Transmission of the Pentateuch* (Sheffield: JSOT, 1990). A neo-supplementarian approach, with later dating of the sources and a revised order, is John Van Seters, *Prologue to History: The Yahwist as Historian in Genesis* (Louisville: Westminster John Knox, 1992). For a recent return to the idea of four, originally independent documents (but with differences from Wellhausen) and just one compiler, see Joel S. Baden, *The Composition of the Pentateuch: Renewing the Documentary Hypothesis* (New

Haven: Yale University Press, 2012). A very different approach that reckons with the role of memory among scribes and the evidence from the extant manuscripts is represented by David M. Carr, *The Formation of the Hebrew Bible: A New Reconstruction* (New York: Oxford University Press, 2011). The theology of the sources is probed in Walter Brueggemann and Hans Walter Wolff, *The Vitality of Old Testament Traditions* (2nd ed.; Atlanta: John Knox, 1982).

For the literary approach, see Robert Alter, *The Art of Biblical Narrative* (rev. ed.; New York: Basic, 2011)—my definition of type scene follows his (59–60). The canonical approach is the distinctive achievement of Brevard S. Childs, *Introduction to the Old Testament as Scripture* (Philadelphia: Fortress, 1979). Another type of integrated approach is Israel Knohl, *The Divine Symphony: The Bible's Many Voices* (Philadelphia: Jewish Publication Society, 2003).

Rosenzweig's remark about R first appeared in a German newspaper in October 1928. It is published in English in Martin Buber and Franz Rosenzweig, *Scripture and Translation* (Bloomington: Indiana University Press, 1994), 22–26. I borrow the phrases "the human from the fertile *humus*" and "a human 'soul' from the soil" from William P. Brown, *Sacred Sense: Discovering the Wonder of God's Word and World* (Grand Rapids: Eerdmans, 2015), 33. The notion of the genealogies as "cultural maps" is from Theodore Hiebert, "Genesis," in *The CEB Study Bible* (Nashville: Common English Bible, 2013), 2. For Sinai as a kind of *bar mitzvah*, see Jay A. Wilcoxen, "Some Anthropocentric Aspects of Israel's Sacred History," *Journal of Religion* 48 (1968): 333–350. Christoph Uehlinger, *Weltreich und "eine Rede": Eine neue Deutung der sogenannten Turmbauerzählung (Gen 11, 1–9)* (Freiburg, Schweiz: Universitätsverlag, 1990), is the scholar who identified four distinct stages in the Tower of Babel story.

For the Garden of Eden story, see Phyllis Trible, *God and the Rhetoric of Sexuality* (Philadelphia: Fortress, 1978); and Mark S. Smith, *The Genesis of Good and Evil: The Fall(out) and Original Sin in the Bible* (Louisville: Westminster John Knox, 2018). For the movement from Genesis 4 to Genesis 50, see Matthew Schlimm, *From Fratricide to Forgiveness: The Language and Ethics of Anger in Genesis* (Winona Lake: Eisenbrauns, 2011). For the plagues as an instance of divine *de*creation, see Terence E. Fretheim, "The Plagues as Ecological Signs of Historical Disaster," *Journal of Biblical Literature* 110 (1991): 385–396. Fretheim has written about the dynamic nature of biblical law in "Law in the Service of Life: A Dynamic Understanding of Law in Deuteronomy," in *A God So Near: Essays in Old Testament Theology in Honor of Patrick D. Miller* (eds. Brent A. Strawn and Nancy R. Bowen; Winona Lake: Eisenbrauns, 2003), 183–200. For the role of revision in biblical law, see Bernard M. Levinson, *Deuteronomy* and the Hermeneutics of Legal Innovation (New York: Oxford University Press, 1997). See S. Dean McBride, Jr., "Polity of the Covenant People: The Book of Deuteronomy," *Interpretation* 41 (1987): 229–244, for Deuteronomy as a kind of constitution.

A convenient listing of the 613 commandments of the Torah may be found in Rabbi Joseph Teluskin, *Biblical Literacy: The Most Important People, Events, and Ideas of the Hebrew Bible* (New York: William Morrow, 1997), 513–592. Of these 613, Genesis has 3 commands, Exodus has 111, Leviticus has 247, Numbers has 52, and Deuteronomy has 200.

THE PROPHETS (*NEVI'IM*)

The second division of the Hebrew Bible is called the Prophets (*Nevi'im*). At some point in the Middle Ages, the Prophets were divided in two: the Former Prophets (*Nevi'im Rishonim*), which includes Joshua, Judges, 1-2 Samuel, and 1-2 Kings; and the Latter Prophets (*Nevi'im Acharonim*), which includes Isaiah, Jeremiah, Ezekiel, and the Book of the Twelve Minor Prophets (Hosea–Malachi). Ruth and Daniel, which are found mixed into these other books in most English Bibles, aren't included here because, in the Hebrew Bible, they are found in the third division known as the Writings (*Ketuvim*), discussed in Chapter 4.

The designation *former* vs. *latter* when it comes to the prophetic books refers mostly to which come first and which second in their present ordering within the Hebrew Bible. It shouldn't be understood as a definitive chronological indicator at any rate since some of the books in the Latter Prophets (or at least some parts of them) were likely written *before* some of the books in the Former Prophets (or at least some parts of them). It is nevertheless true that the time period covered by the Former Prophets begins long before the time period of the Latter Prophets. Moreover, while most of the Latter Prophets fit within the timeframe suggested by the Former Prophets, a few do not. These date from periods later than the events described at the end of 2 Kings.

1-2 Samuel, 1-2 Kings, and the Book of the Twelve Minor Prophets count as one book each (see further below). Altogether, then, the Prophets is a nicely balanced collection: eight compositions subdivided into two major categories of four books each:

Former Prophets: Joshua, Judges, (1-2) Samuel, (1-2) Kings
Latter Prophets: Isaiah, Jeremiah, Ezekiel, Book of the Twelve.

The overall rubric for this second division of the Hebrew Bible suggests that these very different compositions may nevertheless share something in common—something "prophetic." The two subdivisions suggest that each is nevertheless different somehow from the other group. For example, the Former Prophets are primarily prose, while the Latter Prophets are primarily poetic in form. The stories found in the Former Prophets are told by a narrator; the poetry of the Latter Prophets abounds in first person discourse that is frequently uttered in God's name. The Former Prophets continue the story begun in the Pentateuch; the Latter Prophets do no such thing, though they add some informative details along the way.

What does it mean to call these various books the Prophets? The designation seems straightforward in the case of the Latter Prophets since these are largely collections of speeches or sermons by various named and unnamed individuals known as "prophets." Perhaps the Books of Joshua through Kings are considered "Prophets" due to the prominence of prophetic figures in those books—though the first prophet of any great significance, Samuel, doesn't come along until the third book into this section (but note the brief mention of an anonymous prophet in Judg 6:8). After Samuel, however, there are quite literally hundreds of other prophets mentioned in the narratives of the Books of Samuel and Kings (see, e.g., 1 Kgs 18:4, 13, 19; 22:6). Some of these individuals are named and famous in the Old Testament: Elijah, Elisha, and Nathan, for example.

Another reason to consider Joshua–Kings prophetic has to do with their literary function. Like the Latter Prophets, the Former Prophets announce God's message to the people. Even if the Latter Prophets do this in a slightly different manner, these books, too, deserve to be considered "prophetic." In fact, in some ways, the Former Prophets may be even more effective than the Latter Prophets because they make their prophetic point by means of a large narrative arc that many modern readers will find easier to grasp than the often dense poetry of the Latter Prophets.

The present form of the Hebrew Bible with Torah first and Prophets second may suggest that the Former and Latter Prophets are to be viewed as authoritative interpretations of the Torah. (Note that Jewish liturgy pairs selections from the prophetic texts—called *haftorot*—with weekly Torah readings.) The prominence of the Pentateuch is underscored in this perspective since it sets the agenda for all that follows. But the significance of the Prophets is equally featured because they are privileged interpreters. This understanding of the relationship between the Pentateuch and Prophets was challenged by Julius Wellhausen, who argued that, regardless of the literary ordering, historically speaking, the prophets *preceded* the Torah, or at least some of it—especially the P source (see Chapter 2).

If the Torah tells the story *from creation to Canaan*, the Prophets tell the story from the *taking of the land to the loss of that land* (in Joshua–Kings, especially) along with the *reasons for that land loss* and the *future with God that lies beyond it* (in Isaiah–Malachi, particularly). It is worth recalling, though, that the order of the Hebrew Bible differs from most English Bibles, and not just on the matter of where Ruth and Daniel fit. This is an appropriate place to begin the scholarly story of the Former Prophets.

THE SCHOLARLY STORY OF THE FORMER PROPHETS

English Bibles, depending in part on the Greek Septuagint, reflect a four-part division of the Old Testament as opposed to the three-part scheme of the Hebrew Bible (see Charts 1.1 and 1.2). Apparently due to comparable genre as well as overlapping content, the four-part arrangement associates Ruth, Chronicles, Ezra-Nehemiah, and Esther with Joshua through Kings to create what is often called the "Historical Books." This designation is somewhat misleading, however, because biblical scholars debate how far these books reflect ancient reality as that can be known through historical reconstruction and the careful sifting of sources, literary and archaeological, that are available to us now. One difficulty is found in the fact that a good bit of material is repeated in some of the biblical compositions and these repetitions sometimes disagree with each other on various details. Such disagreement complicates any simple and straightforward access to history "as it really was" in the so-called Historical Books. Still further, these biblical compositions frequently indicate that they are not interested in the kind of historiography that is common in the modern world. The Book of Kings, for instance, provides very little information about Omri, devoting only six verses to this Israelite king who reigned ca. 879–869 BCE (1 Kgs 16:23–28). The extrabiblical evidence, however, demonstrates that Omri must have been a significant leader (see further below). Kings cares only if Omri was faithful to God. He wasn't and so Kings moves on. A very similar situation is found in the case of the Judean king Manasseh, who reigned ca. 698–644 BCE (see 2 Kgs 21:1–18). Perhaps the "Historical Books" are better called the "Theological Books"!

The creation of a "Historical Books" category affects how other biblical books are viewed as well—a point taken up further below (see also Chart 1.2 and Chapter 4). For now, it is enough to observe how the addition of Ruth, Chronicles, Ezra-Nehemiah, and Esther to the Former Prophets continues their narrative arc, but not very far. According to the biblical chronology (see Chart 2.1), the stories recounted in Ezra-Nehemiah and Esther take place only a century or two after the latest events recounted in Kings. The chronological payoff of "continuing the story" by adding these books to the Former Prophets isn't very significant, and the downside, by way of contrast, is considerable. The downside is felt mostly in the fact that one simply can't read the sequence Kings → Chronicles without encountering some vertigo, especially due to the repetition of material found in Chronicles. There is a major break after Kings, whether what comes next is the Latter Prophets or the Historical Books.

If there is a major break between the Former Prophets and what comes afterwards, the opposite seems to be the case for how the Former Prophets relate to what precedes them in the Torah. One obvious point of connection is how Deuteronomy flows directly into the first chapter of Joshua (see esp. vv. 1–2, 5, 7–8)—but the same is true for more chapters than the first, and more books than just Joshua. The story the Torah tells is closely related to the story told in the Former Prophets. As a result, the scholarly story about these two parts of the Hebrew Bible is also closely intertwined.

We might begin with the (relative) importance of land in the Torah. Already in Genesis 12, land is a part of God's call to Abraham and Sarah. That promise is reiterated later, with the acquisition of the land of Canaan a major driver in the plot of the Pentateuch, especially when the Israelites find themselves enslaved in another land, Egypt. The significance of the promise of land led earlier scholars to believe that it was too important for its culmination—the settlement of Canaan—to have been absent from the early versions of Israel's traditions. These scholars argued that the sources that made up the Torah according to the Documentary Hypothesis must have once extended into Joshua, at least, and maybe even further into the Former Prophets. If they went into Joshua, one would need to speak of a Hexateuch (six books) rather than a five-part Pentateuch. In no small measure, this theory was driven by the supposition that if the land was promised early on in a (theoretical) source, then that source would surely also have recounted the actual taking of the land.

This inference makes good enough sense. Unfortunately, there is no way to prove it, and so other scholars began to tell different stories about the way(s) the Torah and Former Prophets were related. A very influential theory came on the scene in the middle of the twentieth century that focused on the importance of one of the Pentateuchal sources: D, the Book of Deuteronomy, or some portion of it, that was known in the late seventh century (see Chapter 2 and Chart 2.1). The idea was not that D extended into Joshua per se, but rather that D exerted a great deal of influence—theological pressure, as it were—on the books that come after it.

This theory is known as the Deuteronomistic History Hypothesis. In its initial formulation by the German biblical scholar Martin Noth, the theory held that one individual—the Deuteronomist (abbreviated Dtr)—was responsible for the entirety of the complex that stretches from Deuteronomy through Kings (excepting Ruth). Noth dubbed this complex the Deuteronomistic History (abbreviated DtrH or DH). Contrary to earlier scholars who posited that the J source continued into Joshua, Noth's theory sliced the Pentateuchal pie differently, effectively reducing the Torah to a Tetrateuch (four books) since Deuteronomy, in his account, belongs more with what follows it than what precedes it.

For present purposes, the most important points in Noth's theory are that Dtr was an author who wrote in the exilic period under the profound influence of Deuteronomy. Dtr used a form of D as the preface or first part of a grand history of Israel and Judah (DtrH). According to Noth, DtrH was for all intents and purposes a history of disastrous failure. Joshua through Kings repeatedly show Israel falling short of God's commands, especially—and here is a key observation—as those commands are now found in Deuteronomy. For example, following the division of the kingdom, the northern realm of Israel is constantly portrayed as unfaithful because it did not worship in Jerusalem (the capital city of the southern kingdom of Judah). The ancestors in Genesis worshipped wherever they wished, but Deuteronomy 12 makes clear that for Israel's life in the land, there is only one rightful place to worship God. Cult centralization is imperative, therefore, and the rulers of Israel and Judah are consistently, and in some cases solely, judged on whether or not they keep this injunction.

The Deuteronomistic History Hypothesis has a great deal of explanatory power, and the theory remains popular to this day. Even so, just as in the case of the Documentary Hypothesis for the Pentateuch, subsequent scholarship has identified problems with Noth's theory and has refined and improved it or offered alternatives in its place. So, in contrast to the Noth's view of DtrH as a depressing history of failure, some scholars observed that some positive notes are occasionally sounded along the way, some of which are too important to ignore and, taken together, suggest that the tone of DtrH is not nearly as dour as Noth would have it. There are, for example, numerous instances in the Book of Judges where Israel repents of wrongdoing which leads directly to divine deliverance. A clear high point in DtrH is the promise to David that his dynastic house will endure forever (2 Samuel 7). There is also the brief notice, at the very end of DtrH, that King Jehoiachin, held captive in Babylon, was released from prison (2 Kgs 25:27–30). Perhaps this is a harbinger of a new day that includes a return to self-sovereignty back in the homeland. If there is something like a Deuteronomistic History, it seems clear that the history in question is not univocal and cannot be easily reduced to just one point, whether glum (with Noth) or otherwise.

Other refinements of Noth's theory have less to do with DtrH's message than with the process by which it came to be. Even at this point, the matter of tone plays a role, with the main result of the debates over compositional history similar to scholarly revisions of DtrH's central message(s)—namely, that this material is more complex than Noth's theory allowed. Some scholars, noting the extremely positive assessment of Josiah in the Book of Kings, posited two major editions of DtrH. They dated the first version, called Dtr$_1$, to the preexilic period. It would have run up through Josiah's reign and may have been promulgated by him as part of his reform program (see 2 Kings 23). The second version, Dtr$_2$, belongs to the exilic period. It updated the history of Judah after the death of Josiah and continued through the fall of Jerusalem and the release of Jehoiachin.

After the compositional debates around the Torah that were discussed in Chapter 2, it comes as no surprise to learn that still more and more complex understandings of DtrH have been offered. Numerous redactional layers have been postulated in DtrH and are distinguished not just by numbers but by letters that specify their special emphases. For example: DtrN ("N" for *nomos*, "law"), a strand of DtrH with legal interests; or DtrP, with the "P" in this case indicating, not the Priestly source of the Torah but a prophetic focus within DtrH. Each of these strands, and many others, could be—and has been!—further subdivided. The result is a highly technical morass that only the most committed source critics can endure for long. Others will find their patience tried by such complexity and their credulity strained by the amount of speculation involved.

It is clear, regardless, that the story scholars tell about the Former Prophets, no less than the story they tell about the Pentateuch, is a complicated one. In fact, most scholars would agree that, even if there really is (or was) something like a DtrH in ancient Israel, each of the books in the Former Prophets has its own literary history, quite apart from how they now fit into the DtrH. Still further, these books' literary history was likely lengthy and complex—just like what was seen with the Torah. As an example, it is evident that Joshua 1–12 and Judges 1 seem to be at odds with one another regarding the taking of the land of Canaan. Joshua 1–12 suggests a largely successful endeavor during Joshua's lifetime; Judges 1 indicates there is still much to do after Joshua's death. Despite differences like these, there is also a good bit of coherence in the Former Prophets, especially in Samuel and Kings. Such coherence demonstrates that there is still value in the idea of a Deuteronomistic History, even if Noth's version isn't the final word (and it isn't).

The Torah and Former Prophets also cohere, and not just with respect to the influence of Deuteronomy on DtrH. For example, Gen 50:25 states that Joseph's bones should be buried in Canaan; next, Exod 13:19 mentions that the bones were taken by the Israelites when they left Egypt; finally, Josh 24:32 recounts the reburial of Joseph's remains. Details like these have suggested to some scholars that ultimately what we have on our hands is an Enneateuch—a nine-book complex stretching from Genesis through Kings. (As noted in Chapter 1, some scholars call this the Primary History, as compared to the Secondary History of Chronicles and Ezra-Nehemiah; see further Chapter 4). If that is correct, some kind of process is needed to explain it: a final editor, perhaps, of the entire complex—one who introduced certain links or forged certain connections between various books, texts, or traditions.

Imagining a single literary genius lying behind the Enneateuch, or even just the Former Prophets, recalls an alternative academic perspective that was also encountered in the case of the Pentateuch. Scholars holding to this other viewpoint think that investigating compositional processes that lie behind the biblical texts proper are mostly exercises in missing the literary point. A far better approach, in their opinion, is to engage these books' literary art directly, especially as there is wide agreement that the Former Prophets contain some of the best narratives in the Old Testament. This is where we read of the walls of Jericho "tumbling down" (Joshua 6); of the mighty Samson, defeated by a haircut (Judges 16); of the madness of King Saul who threw spears at his son and his rival (1 Sam 18:10–11; 19:9–10; 20:33); and of the rise and fall of King David: adulterer, murderer, bereaved parent, faithful friend (1 Samuel 16-1 Kings 1). As in the case of the Torah, the literature of the Former Prophets is *there*, manifest in a way that hypothetical compositional processes are not. It is appropriate, then, to turn from the story scholars tell about the Former Prophets, to the story the Former Prophets themselves tell.

THE STORY THE FORMER PROPHETS TELL

JOSHUA (*YEHOSHUA*)

The Book of Joshua picks up immediately where Deuteronomy left off. Moses has died and Joshua has been commissioned. Joshua succeeds Moses but, as a leader, always lives in Moses' shadow, subject to the law "Moses commanded you" (Josh 1:6)—which is another way to refer to Deuteronomy. Joshua's first five chapters discuss preparations for the battles that will take place in Canaan. The conquest of the land is then recounted in chapters 6–12. The invasion revolves around three geographical locations: the central country (chaps. 6–8), the southern region (chap. 10), and the north (chap. 11). Following the last battle at Hazor, the conquest is summarized (11:16–12:24) before the land is apportioned to the tribes by lot (chaps. 13–21). After this, and not unlike the ending of Deuteronomy, though on a much smaller scale, Joshua calls the people to renew their commitment to God (chaps. 23 and 24). Joshua makes explicit reference to "the book of the law of Moses" (23:6) and records the words of the covenant renewal "in the book of the law of God" (24:26). He then dies at 110 years of age (24:29–30), a decade shy of Moses' 120 years (Deut 34:7). One of the last verses in the book occasions worry: "Israel served the LORD all the days of Joshua, and all the days of the elders who outlived Joshua and had known all the work that the LORD did for Israel" (Josh 24:31; NRSV). Readers will wonder what will happen next, after the elders themselves die. Will Israel continue to serve the Lord? That is a question that the rest of the Former Prophets will address in considerable detail.

The conquest of Canaan is the primary subject matter of Joshua. It is also a primary stumbling block for contemporary readers who frequently find themselves repulsed by this kind of violence, aimed at a specific people group in a particular location, within the pages of what is supposed to be sacred literature. The conquest is an important and complex topic—one that cannot be engaged here in the depth it deserves. Even so, two points should be made that might prove helpful in thinking about this difficult issue.

1. The first involves a single text, Josh 5:13–15. According to this text, Joshua encounters a man with a drawn sword in the vicinity of Jericho. Joshua reasonably asks if the man is friend or foe. The individual responds: "Neither! I'm the commander of the LORD's army. I have now come!" (v. 14). He then instructs Joshua to take his shoes off since he is on holy ground (v. 15; cf. Exod 3:5). The exact connection between this story and the next one, where Jericho is captured, remains indirect. One thing seems clear, however: when Joshua asks this angelic general if he is for or against the Israelites, the response is "neither." Standing, as it does, at the start of a series of battle accounts, Josh 5:13–15 serves as a sharp and unexpected rebuke to anyone—ancient or modern—who would claim "God is on our side," especially when the side in question is a military side. Whatever role God may play in the conflicts to come, in Joshua or elsewhere, this little unit suggests that the Lord of Israel is *above* the fray. That includes being above Israel, too (cf. Amos 9:7; John 10:16). So, among many other things that might be said, it should be stressed that the warfare recounted in the Book of Joshua should not be described as "holy war." The Bible never once speaks of "holy war," neither does it ever describe warfare as "holy."

2. The second point is more wide-ranging. It is that the conquest itself is *not* wide-ranging. What appears in some parts of Joshua as an all-out, aggressive blitzkrieg is, upon closer inspection, nothing of the sort. Despite claims that the conquest of "all" the land was thorough-going (11:16, 23), the book includes a decent number of notifications that the situation on the ground was far more complicated than that (Josh 13:1–7; 15:63; 16:10; 17:12–13; 23:5–13). Other texts, like Judges 1, confirm that much of the land was not, in fact, taken at the time of Joshua, which means that the Canaanites continued living in the land—even into much later periods (even New Testament times according to Matt 15:21–28!). What some parts of Joshua portray, therefore, is an idealized representation of the conquest; other parts of the book are far less sanguine about all that. Joshua also includes notable exceptions to the otherwise harsh treatment of the Canaanites, whether by confession of faith, as seems to be the case with Rahab (Josh 2:9–13), or by shrewd, even deceptive negotiation, as in the case of the Gibeonites (9:1–27). Both of these stories, along with others that might be mentioned, demonstrate that much of what is recounted in the Book of Joshua is ultimately religious in orientation and far less aggressive than typically thought. The name "Joshua" (*Yehoshua*) means "the LORD saves," after all, and so much of the conflict is presented in theological, even liturgical terms. The very first battle at Jericho begins with a ritual procession around the city with the Ark of the Covenant (see Exod 25:10–22; 37:1–9) part of the parade. Several of the other battles in the book are presented as defensive. In these, Israel responds to Canaanite aggression that is produced, in part, by the Canaanites' refusal to heed the news about God (see Josh 9:1–2; 10:1–5; 11:1–5; cf. 2:10–11; 5:1). Only Jericho and Ai are directly attacked. All of this suggests a far more nuanced picture of the conquest in Joshua. To this could be added the additional fact that archaeologists have failed to corroborate destruction layers in many of the cities said to have been captured in Joshua. This, too, suggests a more nuanced understanding: perhaps the literary presentation in the book is overstated, hyperbolic, idealistic in some fashion; or perhaps "taking" some of these locations did not involve their destruction. Most important of all, however, is the observation that the conquest motif has a very limited shelf life in the Old Testament. That can be contrasted with how lively the exodus motif is throughout the Hebrew Bible. The contrast highlights that the Bible itself seems to

be worried about the violence of the conquest. It also demonstrates one way that violence can be contained: by restricting it to a specific time and place—one in the far distant past—and to a process that was, at best, only partially successful, and that is not to be replicated, not even as a metaphor for the life of faith.

JUDGES (SHOFETIM)

The Book of Judges takes its name from the 12 leaders who are said to rule Israel during the time after Joshua and before the establishment of the monarchy in the Book of Samuel. These figures are called "judges" (*shofetim*) but a translation like "chieftains" (NJPSV) or "leaders" (CEB) better captures their function. The book condenses a large chronological expanse—over 400 years according to the internal biblical chronology. The book also combines and synthesizes material that was probably originally disparate in origin though perhaps concurrent in time. It is possible, therefore, that the leaders in the Book of Judges overlapped one another rather than followed each other sequentially. It is also possible that their influence was far more local than the "all-Israel" perspective that the book presently conveys.

Judges picks up immediately after Joshua's death (Josh 24:29; Judg 1:1; 2:8–9) though not without a surprise or two, especially the information in Judges 1 that much of the land was still in need of settling (see above). If Joshua lived in the shadow of Moses, never quite attaining to his stature (cf. Exod 33:11; Deut 34:10), then it is safe to say that the judges never quite live up to Joshua. The 12 leaders who are mentioned—Othniel, Ehud, Shamgar, Deborah, Gideon, Tola, Jair, Jephtah, Ibzan, Elon, Abdon, and Samson—have their fair share of ups and downs. Of these 12, Othniel, Ehud, Deborah, Gideon, Jephthah, and Samson are called "major" judges because they have more than a few verses devoted to them. The rest are deemed "minor" judges given their briefer treatment. The first few chieftains are presented in a fairly positive light, but things begin to go downhill with Gideon, especially during the short rule of his son Abimelech (Judges 9). Despite the downward slide, the stories about the major judges frequently showcase the theme of God working in unexpected ways through unlikely agents. Ehud, for instance, is from the tribe of Benjamin, a name that means "son of the right hand," but is explicitly identified as left-handed (3:15). Deborah, one of the most successful of the judges—the only one, apparently, who actually heard legal cases (4:5)—is female, a unique situation in the patriarchal culture of the time. Gideon is said to be from an insignificant clan and he claims to be the least important member of his family (6:15). Jephthah, though a mighty warrior, is said to be the son of a prostitute (11:1). Samson delivers Israel from the Philistines, but only after he has been imprisoned and blinded, and even then only by killing himself in the process (16:23–31).

Why Israel needs these all-too-human leaders in the first place, and why they should need 12 of them (a symbolic number) requires comment. As noted earlier, the end of the Book of Joshua seemed to hint that things wouldn't go as well as they had been going after Joshua dies (Josh 24:31). Joshua's death is recounted again in Judg 2:6–10 and what was just a hint before becomes blatant fact:

> The people worshipped the LORD all the days of Joshua, and all the days of the elders who outlived Joshua, who had seen all the great work that the LORD had done for Israel ... that whole generation was gathered to their ancestors, and another generation grew up after them, who did not know the LORD or the work that he had done for Israel. (Judg 2:7, 10; NRSV)

The phrase "not knowing the Lord" recalls Pharaoh's ignorance of God way back in Exod 5:2. According to Judges, the results of Israel's not knowing are no less deadly than they were in Egypt according to Exodus. Judges 2:11–22 proceeds to outline the repetitive cycle that marks Israel's life according to the book:

- Stage 1: Israel disobeys, especially by worshiping other gods. Because of this, God hands them over to enemies who oppress them.
- Stage 2: God is moved to pity because of their oppression (2:18; cf. Exod 2:23–25) and so raises leaders up who deliver the people from their enemies. After that, Israel lives in peace.
- Stage 3: After the death of the chieftain, the people return to Stage 1 and the cycle repeats itself.

This cycle establishes a kind of rhythm to the Book of Judges, though it must be said that mixed in along the way are plenty of blues—not only from the repeated periods of oppression from various enemies (especially the Philistines) but also from the missteps made by several of these leaders, especially the further one reads into the book. Slowly but surely, Israel enters into an inescapable downward spiral. The judges are part of this spiral, evidence that it is taking place. Jephthah, for instance, utters a rash vow and, as a result, ends up sacrificing his own daughter (Judg 11:29–40). Samson, the last of the 12 chieftains, seems more interested in satisfying his lust for women and battle than in delivering Israel. As noted earlier, only at the very end of his life, as a blind prisoner of war, does he finally address the Philistine threat. And yet, even at this point, his prayer is only for revenge, to "pay back the Philistines for my two eyes" (16:28).

The Judges cycle comes to an end with Samson's death, but the Book of Judges is not yet complete. Devoid of leaders raised by God, the final chapters of the book show Israel left to its own devices … and vices. Chapters 17–18 tell an inauspicious story about the tribe of Dan. The Danites acquire different territory than their original allotment (cf. Judg 1:34) and set up of an unlawful worship site, facilitated by an idol that was made by a man who employed a priest-for-hire to maintain it. All of that is far from the demands of the Torah, or even just Deuteronomy. Judges 19 then tells the gruesome story of a rape and murder, followed by the dismemberment of the victim that summons the tribes to enact terrible justice against the tribe of Benjamin, where these horrific events took place. The Benjaminites are nearly wiped out (chap. 20). They only survive by kidnapping women from Shiloh to marry (chap. 21).

These final chapters rarely mention God—Judges 20:18, 23, 28, 35; 21:15 are the exceptions, and they are all with reference to the punishment that is due the Benjaminites. Framing these God-forsaken chapters is an important refrain that indicates something else is missing, too:

> In those days there was no king in Israel; all the people did what was right in their own eyes. (17:6; 21:25; NRSV)

This refrain also occurs in abbreviated form in chapters 18 and 19:

> In those days there was no king in Israel. (18:1; NRSV)
> In those days, when there was no king in Israel … (19:1; NRSV)

These four notices do at least two things. First, the longer forms in 17:6 and 21:25 make clear that what transpires in these final chapters of Judges is nothing short of chaos and bedlam: everyone doing whatever seems right to them and them alone. But what *seems right* to them is, by means of the refrain and the downward spiral of Judges 17–21, shown to be *exactly wrong*—it is precisely what is *not* to be done because it is damaging, even lethal to Israel's worship, women, and tribes. Second, all four notices suggest in no uncertain terms that things may very well be different—that they could be different, should be different, and will be different—if only there were a king to establish order and just rule.

Enter the Book of Samuel.

SAMUEL (*SHEMUEL*)

English Bibles, following the tradition of the Septuagint, divide Samuel into two parts. The name of the book is taken from the primary character of the first half of the composition. Samuel is the last of the judges (see 1 Sam 7:6, 15–16; cf. 4:18; 8:1) as well as the first of the major prophetic figures in the *Nevi'im* (1 Sam 3:21–4:1). Although he dies in 1 Sam 25:1, Samuel is so significant that he makes a comeback from the grave just a few chapters later (1 Samuel 28).

The Book of Samuel begins not with Samuel himself, however, but with his family, especially his mother, Hannah, who prays that she might conceive a child. When she does, she gives him the name "Samuel" (*Shemuel*), saying, "I have asked him of the LORD" (1 Sam 1:20; NRSV). Hannah's comment seems to treat the name *Shemuel* as if were related to the Hebrew verb "to ask" (*sha'al*). It isn't, but the meaning of *Shemuel* itself is debated. It may mean something like "His name is *El*" (the "his" would refer to God; *El* is a common Hebrew word for "God").

The first main section of Samuel provides the background—not only for Samuel but for all that follows (1 Sam 1:1–7:17). At this point in the larger narrative of the Former Prophets, Israel is still very much in the time of the judges. Eli, the priest at Shiloh, is said to have "judged" Israel (4:18), just like those earlier leaders from the Book of Judges. The wickedness of Eli's sons (2:11–17) leads God to choose Samuel, not them, as Eli's successor (3:1–4:1a). One "intra-Israelite" problem is thus taken care of, but a major "extra-Israelite" problem continues: the Philistines. In 1 Sam 4:1b–7:1, the Ark of the Covenant is captured by the Philistines. It is eventually returned after a series of miraculous events, ending up housed in a town called Kiriath-jearim. Scholars sometimes deem this section, along with its sequel in 2 Samuel 6, as "the Ark Narrative," thinking that it may have been one of the sources drawn upon by the author(s) of the Book of Samuel (or the larger DtrH) when it was composed.

The next section deals with the inauguration of the monarchy in Israel (1 Samuel 8–15). Here one finds a number of interleaved perspectives that are, in one moment, in favor of the establishment of kingship, and, in the next, quite opposed to it. The people's request to have a king "like the other nations" (e.g., 8:5, 20; etc.) has an ominous ring to it, especially after stories about less-than-stellar foreign monarchs earlier in the Bible. In fact, the people's request is said to be a rejection of God own rule over the people (8:7). When the specific habits of royalty are detailed for Israel's consideration, the accent is on acquisition: kings *take* and *tax*, which means, in the end, that Israel will end up crying out under its own king, just as it had previously done under Pharaoh and the various enemies discussed in the Book Judges. Only this time, Samuel says, God will *not* listen (8:11–18).

But the people are decided. Saul, Kish's son, is selected and anointed as the first king (1 Samuel 9–10). Saul is a Benjaminite (9:1) from the town of Gibeah (10:26; cf. 11:4). This is the same tribe and the specific location that figured so prominently in the horrific ending of the Book of Judges. Some interpreters have seen these details as a not-so-subtle critique of Saul and his kingship. But another way to view them is to see the movement from Judges 17–21 into Saul's kingship in Samuel as a *redemptive* one: even a tribe guilty of the greatest of atrocities can provide Israel's ruler. The tribe of King David, Judah, is no less a mixed bag (see Genesis 38; 49:8–13; Josh 7:1; 15:63).

Saul is said to be both handsome and tall (1 Sam 9:2). He experiences God's spirit and goes into a type of prophetic frenzy (10:9–16; cf. 19:23–24). He is acclaimed king by the tribes of Israel and has military success against the Ammonites (10:17–11:15). So far, so good. But things quickly take a turn for the worse, presaged by Samuel's farewell address in chapter 12. Though Samuel is handing the reins (and reign!) over to Saul, the rest of the narrative—indeed from this point forward through the very end of the Book of Kings—will show that the prophetic voice is far from obsolete, even after the coming of the king. In fact, once the monarchs are in place, the prophetic "word of the Lord" is needed more than ever. And so, when Saul operates on his own, he makes a series of blunders: an unlawful sacrifice in chapter 13 (cf. Leviticus 10); a rash oath that would have required killing his own son had the people not intervened (1 Sam 14:24–46; cf. Judges 11); and a violation of the complete ban on the Amalekites (1 Sam 15:1–9). Unfortunately for Saul, Samuel always shows up just when he has made his worst mistakes (1 Sam 13:10; 15:12). After the last one, there is no going back: God regrets making Saul king (15:10) and then rejects his kingship (15:26). Chapter 13 foreshadowed as much: Saul's first major mistake there gives God reason to cancel any chance for a Saulide dynasty. Instead of Saul's descendants, "the LORD will search for a man following the LORD's own heart" (v. 14; CEB). After chapter 13, and especially after chapter 15, the questions that drive the narrative are: who is the one who follows God's heart and how long will it take Saul to exit the stage?

We don't have to wait too long for an answer to the first question. After Saul's divine rejection, the very next chapter introduces David, who is quickly anointed king (1 Sam 16:1–13). Israel has, in effect, two kings from this point forward—but of course there can only be one. So, again, how long will it take Saul to be deposed?

The next major section is the story of David's rise to power (1 Sam 15:35–2 Sam 5:10). It recounts the many dramatic twists and turns by which Saul slowly fades from the scene, ultimately dying an ignominious death (1 Samuel 31), while David grows ever more popular, eventually becoming king of all Israel with his capital city in Jerusalem (2 Samuel 5). The vividness of many of the stories in this section led some earlier scholars to posit that it was written by someone close to the action, perhaps even by a member of David's (or Solomon's) court. This view is no longer widely held, if only because genres like modern fiction and fantasy prove that well-written literature can be composed by people who have made the whole thing up. Whatever the case, it is clear that this section of Samuel is complex and probably composite. For example, David is first introduced to Saul in 1 Sam 16:14–23 and plays the lyre for the king to help him feel better. But in the very next chapter, David is introduced to Saul for a second time, as if they'd never met before (1 Sam 17:55–58)! This seems like a doublet—just like the ones in the Pentateuch (see Chapter 2)—preserving two, originally distinct traditions about when David met Saul. If not, the juxtaposition of the two stories has to be seen as a rather awkward way to demonstrate that Saul's powers are failing. The fact that he lets a shepherd boy do his dirty work with Goliath is further evidence of the same.

Once David's reign is consolidated, details of his rule are provided (2 Sam 5:11–12:31), followed by the account of his son Absalom's revolt against him and its aftermath, including a second revolt under Sheba (2 Sam 13:1–20:25). The Book of Samuel then concludes with what some scholars think is a kind of appendix of miscellaneous stories about David (2 Samuel 21–24).

Much of what comes in 1 Samuel demonstrates the many sides of David's character: his loyalty to Jonathan, for instance, or his shrewdness when living as an outlaw and mercenary (1 Samuel 20; 21:10–15). But the material in 2 Samuel is even more revealing. Here is where we read of the divine promise to build David an eternal dynasty (2 Samuel 7). This is quickly followed by the narrative recounting of David's profound abuse of power in the affair with Bathsheba and the murder of her husband Uriah (2 Samuel 11). That leads into the famous showdown between David and the prophet Nathan where David is confronted with his wrongdoings, confesses his guilt, and is forgiven, though he must still face dire consequences—many of which are played out in the poignant story of Absalom's seizing the throne from him (2 Samuel 15).

In the end, then, what the Book of Samuel presents is a profoundly human, profoundly flawed, and profoundly faithful David. "A man after God's own heart" (1 Sam 13:14) probably goes too far, especially since that statement is made *before* David even steps on the scene, and so is not explicitly said of him. It is, furthermore, uttered long before his egregious failures in 2 Samuel 11. But many readers have nevertheless found this description somehow fitting for the very human, very flawed, and very faithful David. Whatever the case, it is clear that the figure of David looms large in the very next book, Kings, and almost entirely in a positive way (see 1 Kgs 3:3, 14; 9:4; 11:4, 6, 12–13, 32–34; 15:3, 11; 2 Kgs 8:19; 14:3; 16:2; 18:3; 19:34; 22:2). That judgment is even truer for the Book of Chronicles (see Chapter 4).

KINGS (*MELAKHIM*)

The Book of Kings (also divided into two, more manageable halves) continues the narrative of the Book of Samuel without skipping a beat—except, perhaps, for the beats found in 2 Samuel 21–24 (see above). The Septuagint, recognizing the close relationship between Samuel and Kings, lumped them together as 1–4 Reigns or 1–4 Kingdoms. In fact, some scholars believe that a "succession narrative" (2 Samuel 9–20 + 1 Kings 1–2) once circulated independently and was used by the author(s) of Samuel and Kings (or DtrH) as a source. Whatever the case, the fact that the story of David's succession extends from Samuel into Kings underscores the close relationship between the two books.

Despite elements of continuity, differences are also evident. Samuel focused on several key figures—primarily Samuel, Saul, and David. Kings, on the other hand, has a much larger cast of characters. In fact, once the kingdom is consolidated under Solomon, the Book of Kings moves on to tell a complex parallel account of various kings ruling two independent but interrelated kingdoms, Israel and Judah (see Chart 3.1). Once again both the Hebrew (*Melakhim*, "Kings") and Greek (Reigns, Kingdoms) names for the book capture something essential about its content. It is a book about specific monarchs, their reigns, and two kingdoms.

Before all those many kings in the northern and southern kingdoms, however, is the one king over all Israel: David, and, after him, Solomon, who rules in his stead. David's last days, in Kings, are as ambivalent as his earlier ones, in Samuel. His final words to Solomon include encouragement to walk in God's ways—language that is familiar from Deuteronomy. In fact, just in case someone missed the allusion, David specifies that what Solomon must do "is written in the law of Moses" (1 Kgs 2:3). But David's final words also commend vicious payback for Shimei. Earlier, during Absalom's rebellion, Shimei had cursed David, but David acknowledged that his cursing was at God's direction (2 Sam 16:5–14). But that was then. Here and now, in Kings, things are different. Though David had previously sworn to spare Shimei's life, he now says the matter is up to Solomon. In case Solomon missed the allusion, David once again clarifies: "Give him a violent death" (1 Kgs 2:9; CEB). With that, the life of David, Jesse's son—flawed and heroic, faithful and vengeful king of Israel—comes to an end.

The next nine chapters of Kings focus on Solomon's reign (chaps. 3–11). Born to the purple, Solomon is a different kind of ruler than his father. He expands the boundaries of the kingdom, not by war but by strategic treaties, symbolized by his many marriages, since political agreements were often ratified in the ancient world by the intermarriage of the parties. Solomon is said to have had 700 wives in addition to 300 concubines (1 Kgs 11:3). That number is shocking; also shocking is that one of his many wives was Pharaoh's daughter (3:1). Solomon, it seems, is a shrewd and opportunistic politician not overly concerned with or constrained by Israel's terrible past with Egypt.

Solomon is also interested in public works: he builds the temple that David was denied. The design and construction of the temple takes up several chapters and is full of technical detail, a good bit of which is now lost on us (5:1–7:51). Upon its completion, Solomon dedicates the temple, culminating the ceremony with a lengthy prayer that sounds a lot like themes familiar from Deuteronomy (1 Kgs 8:22–53).

Bracketing the stories about the temple construction and its dedication are two encounters between Solomon and God. In the first, Solomon prays for wisdom (3:4–15). God is pleased with this request and grants it. Solomon then displays his wisdom on both local and international stages (3:16–20; 4:21–34; 10:1–13). In the second encounter (9:1–10), God repeats to Solomon the divine promises originally made to David, though in the latest installment they are far more contingent. In 2 Samuel 7, God seems to expect disobedience and promises punishment in return: "*Whenever* he does wrong, I will discipline him …" (v. 14). But the dynasty was secure regardless: "But I will *never take my faithful love away* from him like I took it away from Saul" (v. 15). Things are different in 1 Kings 9. The key term now is *if*, which is followed by a disastrous *then*. If there is obedience, *then* the dynasty is secure (1 Kgs 9:4–5); *if* there is disobedience, *then* all bets are off (vv. 6–9). The obedience is described in Deuteronomic terms, as one would expect from a passage now found in DtrH. The disobedience, too, is described in Deuteronomy's terms, as is the punishment, which is thoroughgoing and devastating (cf. 1 Kgs 9:8–9 with Deut 29:24–28).

God's stern warning proves necessary because mixed in among Solomon's high points are numerous indicators that things aren't so

great. Construction of the temple took immense manpower and re-
sources. Solomon got both by resorting to forced labor and taxation
(1 Kgs 5:13–18; cf. 9:15)—proof of Samuel's warning about monarchs (1 Sam 8:10–18) and a surefire way to breed dissention among
the populace. Also revealing is the detail that Solomon's palace took
almost twice as long to finish as the temple, with the palace twice as
big (1 Kgs 6:38; 7:1–2; 9:10). Solomon is also fabulously wealthy, and
the list of his various acquisitions and wives (1 Kgs 10:14–29; 11:1–3)
seems as if it was carefully crafted to demonstrate how he is in egregious violation of Deuteronomy's law of the king (Deut 17:14–20).
The *coup de grâce* is found in 1 Kgs 11:1–10, which mentions Solomon's many foreign wives but also, and more importantly, their many
foreign gods. "Solomon clung to these in love," 1 Kgs 11:2 reports. In
contrast to what some English translations imply, the meaning of this
verse in Hebrew seems to be that what Solomon clung to in love was
not his wives, but their gods! The narrator connects the dots in 1 Kgs
11:4–10, remarking that Solomon's "heart was not true to the Lord
his God, as was the heart of his father David" (v. 4). Then Solomon
encounters God once more (vv. 11–13). The divine decree this time
is that Solomon's rule is over; but, because of David, not all is lost.
The kingdom will be divided into two, with most of the tribes going
to a rival, but Solomon's heir will remain on the throne of Judah—
because of David. The rest of 1 Kings 11 tells us about Solomon's
opponents (vv. 14–40), then he dies (vv. 41–43).

Things go south quickly. Solomon's son, Rehoboam, attempts to
hold things together but with no success. The complaints from the
northern tribes that Rehoboam refuses to take seriously confirm
that Solomon's "golden age" was gilded by the sweat of people
whose lives suffered so as to make his shine. With Solomon, Israel
finally got a king "like the nations," especially like the nation to their
south, Egypt. The language used for the "forced labor" or "work
gangs" that Solomon conscripted is also found in Exod 1:11, where
Pharoah places taskmasters over Israelite "work gangs." Solomon
followed suit, appointing Adoniram the chief taskmaster (1 Kgs 4:6;
5:14). In 1 Kings 12, Solomon's son wants to continue the family
business, with business as usual—but actually much worse (vv. 6–14).
No wonder the northern tribes secede, disavowing any heritage in
"David" (v. 16), or, evidently, David's sons. When Rehoboam sends
Adoniram north to do his dirty work, "all Israel stoned him to

death" (v. 18). All out civil war is only narrowly avoided (vv. 21–24), though Kings later says that it raged throughout the reigns of Rehoboam and Jeroboam (14:30).

From this point forward (ca. 922 BCE), there are two kingdoms, Israel in the north and Judah in the south (see Chart 2.1), though readers of the Old Testament should be cognizant of the fact that the term "Israel" is often used to encompass both kingdoms after 922 and even after 722 when the northern kingdom came to its geopolitical end. Retelling the story of Kings after the kingdom divides is difficult given the number of monarchs the book touches on: 19 in the north, 20 in the south (Chart 3.1). Kings covers a great deal of ground, then, from David's deathbed (ca. 965) to the release of Jehoiachin from prison in Babylon (ca. 560). Only the Books of Genesis and Judges cover longer periods of time. As a result, the Book of Kings is highly selective in what it includes.

This selectivity was already noted with reference to Kings' highly abbreviated treatment of Omri. Texts from ancient Near Eastern cultures referred to the northern kingdom of Israel as "the House of Omri" long after Omri died, indicating that he must have been a very important figure on the international scene. But what ultimately matters for the Book of Kings, part of the *Deuteronomistic* History, is not political impact but theological commitment. That commitment is primarily measured in Deuteronomic terms: the First Commandment—allegiance to God (see Deut 5:7; 6:5; cf. Exod 20:3)—and its correlate: worship in the one sanctuary of the one God (Deut 12:2–28). Even the great but ultimately flawed kings of the united monarchy, David and Solomon, are judged by these standards … and found wanting. Even so, the Book of Kings is part of the Deuteronomistic *History* and so is still very much a history of sorts. It refers to other sources of information, for example—especially the Annals of the Kings of Israel (1 Kgs 14:19; 15:31; 16:5, 14, 20, 27; 22:39; 2 Kgs 1:18; 10:34; 13:8, 12; 14:15, 28; 15:11, 15, 21, 26, 31) and the Annals of the Kings of Judah (1 Kgs 14:29; 15:7, 23; 22:45; 2 Kgs 8:23; 12:19; 14:18; 15:6, 36; 16:19; 20:20; 21:17, 25; 23:28; 24:5). A number of the monarchs discussed in Kings are also mentioned in non-biblical texts from the ancient Near East. These texts not only prove these monarchs lived but also support the specific sequence of rulers that is preserved in Kings. The author(s) of Kings, therefore, wasn't making things up whole cloth. The author(s) was just interested in more than

United Monarchy

Saul (1025-1005)
David (1005-965)
Solomon (968-928)

Divided Monarchy

Judah (South)	Israel (North)
Rehoboam (928-910)	Jeroboam I (928-906)
Abijam/Abijah (909-907)	
Asa (906-878)	Nadab (905-904)
	Baasha (903-882)
	Elah (881-880)
	Zimri (seven days)
	Omri (879-869)
Jehoshaphat (877-853)	
	Ahab (868-854)
	Ahaziah (853-852)
Jehoram (852-841)	
	Jehoram (851-840)
Ahaziah (840)	
Athaliah (839-833)	Jehu (839-822)
Joash/Jehoash (832-803)	
	Jehoahaz (821-805)
	Joash (804-789)
Amaziah (802-786)	
	Jeroboam II (788-748)
Uzziah/Azariah (785-760)	
Jotham (759-744)	
	Zechariah (six months)
	Shallum (one month)
	Menachem (746-737)
Jehoahaz I/Ahaz (743-728)	
	Pekahiah (736-735)
	Pekah (734-731)
	Hoshea (730-722)
Hezekiah (727-699)	
	Fall of Samaria (722)
Manasseh (698-644)	
Amon (643-642)	
Josiah (641-610)	
Jehoahaz II (three months)	
Jehoiakim (608-598)	
Jehoiachin (three months)	
Zedekiah (596-586)	

Fall of Jerusalem (586)

Here, as also in Chart 2.1, all dates are approximate, with the earliest the most sharply contested and different dates often offered by historians. Note that the internal biblical chronology doesn't always correspond with what is provided here; further, Versions like the Septuagint sometimes preserve different dates from those preserved in the Masoretic Text. The presentation here follows, with slight modification, J. Maxwell Miller and John H. Hayes, *A History of Ancient Israel and Judah* (2nd ed.; Louisville: Westminster John Knox, 2006), 222.

Chart 3.1 Rulers of Israel and Judah

"raw" facts or "mere" history. Most people are, even today. The difference between now and then would be that modern historiographers consider things like politics, society, and economics as primary causes or drivers of historical change. The author(s) of Kings, however, considers a theological cause, God, to be operative throughout the history of Israel and Judah. "If you are interested in mundane matters of state, go look them up in the official annals," is what Kings effectively says. "Read me," it would continue, "if you want to know the real, *religious* reasons for why things happened the way they did."

The religious commitments of Kings (and DtrH)—especially the importance of the temple and its location in the south, in Jerusalem—mean that the northern kingdom and its monarchs are at an immediate and profound disadvantage in the book's perspective. This is no doubt partly due to the fact that Kings (and DtrH) comes from an author(s) who lived in the south (or once did, before being exiled to Babylon, if Noth is right). History is written by the winners, as the old saying goes, though in this specific case it would be better to say that history is written by the losers. The south lost to Babylon—badly—even if that came a bit later than the north's loss to Assyria (see Chart 2.1).

The first king of the north, Jeroboam I, does his best to counter Jerusalem's monopoly on the temple (the gold standard in Deuteronomy and DtrH) by setting up rival worship centers in Bethel and Dan (1 Kgs 12:25–33), replete with calf statues that harken back to the golden calf debacle at Sinai (Exodus 32). This was a shrewd move on Jeroboam's part—perhaps well-intentioned to boot—but for the Book of Kings it is nothing less than apostasy. Jeroboam's rival worship sites become the paradigmatic failure, not just for him but for all who follow him, and for the entire history of the northern kingdom. These are the "sins of Jeroboam" or his "way"—phrases that are used repeatedly throughout Kings (1 Kgs 14:16; 15:30; 16:2, 19, 26, 31; 2 Kgs 10:29, 31; 13:2, 6, 11; 14:24; 15:9, 18, 24, 28) as shorthand for the north's errors. These errors culminate in the destruction of Israel and its capital city, Samaria, in 722 BCE (2 Kgs 17:5–23). The final reference to Jeroboam's sins, committed at the start of the northern kingdom, is found at its very end:

> **And the Israelites continued walking in all the sins that Jeroboam did. They didn't deviate from them, and the LORD finally removed Israel from his presence. That was exactly what he had warned**

> through all his servants the prophets. So Israel was exiled from its
> land to Assyria. And that's still how it is today. (2 Kgs 17:22–23; CEB)

Despite the north's negative press in Kings, it is nevertheless constantly connected with the south through a system that synchronizes the reigns of the different northern and southern rulers. For example: "In the eighteenth year of King Jeroboam son of Nebat"—that is Jeroboam I, king of the north—"Abijam became king over Judah" in the south (1 Kgs 15:1). Unfortunately, these synchronisms cause chronological problems because the numbers don't add up. Scholars have written books on "the mysterious numbers of the Hebrew kings," trying to make the numbers crunch. The significance of the synchronisms isn't chronological or mathematical, however, but literary and religious: they provide a structure for the book and also demonstrate how the north, even if divided from the south, still plays a role in God's people. Part of that role is surely to provide a cautionary example for the south (and for readers of Kings/DtrH)—disobedience will end in punishment and exile like 722 BCE. But the role isn't only a grim one because DtrH is not exclusively dour (see above). And so, even after 722, kings like Josiah appeal to those still living in the north to participate in worship at Jerusalem (see 2 Kgs 23:15–23), and prophets active in the exile and thereafter envision a reunited Israel and Judah (see Ezek 37:15–28; Zech 8:13).

The fall of the northern kingdom is recounted tersely in 2 Kgs 17:1–6. This is followed by a sermonette on why it happened (vv. 7–23). The reasons given are Deuteronomic to the core: proliferation of rival worship sites where other gods and idols were venerated, refusal to listen to God's warnings and heed God's commandments, and so on and so forth. The Book of Deuteronomy, especially chaps. 28 and 29, is the playbook 2 Kings 17 follows.

While the north is negatively marked by "the sins of Jeroboam," the south is positively marked by God's promises "for the sake of my servant David" (e.g., 2 Kgs 19:34). And yet, despite David's legacy, only three southern kings receive positive commendations: Asa (1 Kgs 15:11–15), Hezekiah (2 Kgs 18:5–6), and Josiah (2 Kgs 23:24–25). As noted in Chapter 2, many biblical scholars associate Josiah's reform with Deuteronomy or some form of it, given the similarities. Another point of connection is how Josiah turns to God "with all his heart, all his soul, and all his strength in agreement with everything in the Law (*torah*) of Moses" (2 Kgs 23:25), a clear echo of Deut 6:5 and Deuteronomy as a whole. Links like these have led some scholars to posit a Josiaic edition of DtrH (Dtr$_1$; see above).

The southern kingdom was more stable than the north: it lasted 136 years longer with only one more king, all from one dynasty. This may have been due in part to geography. The north was larger in area, more exposed, and, as a result, more cosmopolitan—not to mention more strategic as a buffer zone when it came to international politics, conflict, and war. But despite outlasting the north for more than a century, the end of the south is told quickly in eight short chapters (2 Kings 18–25). The brevity of this account may be evidence that a second edition of DtrH (Dtr$_2$) was only lightly retouched with a supplement on Judah's fall. But the brevity might also downplay the importance of the south, or, at least suggest that the story of the north, its rise and demise, is every bit as if not more instructive than the south's—even if only as a cautionary tale. If so, the south doesn't learn the lesson very well. Despite a few high points along the way, the south is portrayed as every bit as culpable as the north. Already in the reign of its very first king, Judah is reported to have done "evil in the LORD's eyes" building rival worship sites "on top of every high hill and under every green tree" (1 Kgs 14:22–23; CEB). The similarities to Jeroboam's sins in the north are obvious.

In sum: From the beginning and throughout, the story told in the Book of Kings (and in DtrH generally) is a theologically motivated one—or perhaps better, a *prophetic* one: what matters is religious commitment. The fact that both kingdoms ended in exile means, in such a perspective, that their stories are largely ones of profound religious *failure*. That failure, in part, was due to a failure to hear God's words, especially as delivered through the prophets (e.g., Judg 6:7–10; 2 Kgs 17:13–14, 23; 24:2). It is time to turn to the words of some of those figures as preserved in the second half of the *Nevi'im*.

THE SCHOLARLY STORY OF THE LATTER PROPHETS

Readers will find themselves in new territory when they move from the Former Prophets to the Latter Prophets. As noted above, the Latter Prophets traffic heavily, sometimes exclusively, in poetry and poetry requires more from its readers. As Wendell Berry has said, good poetry "cannot be written or read in distraction." The Latter Prophets contain some of the greatest poetry in the Bible and will thus require careful attention to be fully appreciated. A further difficulty is that the Latter Prophets—as a whole and individually—are more like *an anthology of poetry*, much of which is not in any discernible order, and certainly not in a straightforwardly chronological order.

The Latter Prophets is comprised of Isaiah, Jeremiah, Ezekiel, and the Book of the Twelve Minor Prophets—typically in this order. The Twelve are called "minor" because they are short in comparison to the "major" prophets. Together, these 12 can fit on one scroll whereas the three larger prophets demand an entire scroll each. The 66 chapters of Isaiah, which encompasses material from the eighth century BCE through the postexilic periods (see below), set the tone and an expansive time range for the Latter Prophets. Next come Jeremiah and Ezekiel, who are active in a far more compressed period since both prophesy right around (both before and after) the fall of Jerusalem and the Babylonian exile. The Latter Prophets are then concluded by the Twelve, which come in at 67 chapters, and, like Isaiah, cover material from a wide chronological range. This order isn't invariable, however. The Babylonian Talmud puts Jeremiah first before Ezekiel and Isaiah, while two of the great Septuagint manuscripts put the Twelve in initial position, perhaps for chronological reasons since the biblical dates for Hosea and Amos precede that of Isaiah.

As noted earlier, the Historical Books category can be somewhat misleading if one confuses the prophetic history of Joshua–Kings with modern historiography. But even if contemporary readers miss the prophetic edge of the Former Prophets, it is impossible to miss the prophecy of the Latter Prophets. These are *the prophetic books* par excellence in the Old Testament with their authors known as *the writing prophets*. Each of the italicized words in the preceding sentence requires further discussion in light of the story scholars tell about the Latter Prophets.

1. We may begin with the definition of the term *prophet*. The Hebrew Bible uses several different terms to designate individuals who have some sort of special relationship with the divine. Some

of these terms, like *ro'eh*, "seer," and *ḥozeh*, "visionary," are derived from verbs having to do with sight. The use of these words suggests that the prophets had experiences in which they saw God, God's throne room and heavenly council, or things to come (see, e.g., Isa 1:1; 6:1–13; Jer 1:11–19; Ezek 1:1–3:15; 37:1–14; Amos 1:1; 7:1–9; 8:1–13; 9:1–4; Obad 1; Hab 1:1; Zech 1:7–6:8; cf. 1 Kings 22). Another word for prophet is *navi'* (plural *nevi'im*). This word means "one who is called" or "one who calls." The former, passive understanding captures the notion that the prophets were *individuals called by God* to a special mission or task. Some prophetic books contain records of such calls (see Isa 6:1–13; Jer 1:4–10; Ezek 1:1–3:15; Amos 7:10–17; cf. 1 Kings 22). The active understanding of *navi'* signals that the prophets were *those who called out to others*, proclaiming God's message to all who would hear. Either way, the prophets are intermediaries between the divine realm and the human one. They were not, generally speaking, forecasters of the future—at least not the far distant future. Instead, the prophets were keenly aware of the current political scene and brought a divine message to bear on that.

Most of the prophetic books begin with a superscription that locates them in time and space, especially with reference to the sitting monarch (see Isa 1:1; Jer 1:1–3; Ezek 1:1–3; Hos 1:1; Amos 1:1; Mic 1:1; Zeph 1:1), which in two instances is a foreign king (Hag 1:1; Zech 1:1). Situating the prophetic word during the reigns of particular kings is not coincidental. The rise of prophecy in Israel is closely connected to the rise of kingship. Similarly, with the demise of kingship, prophecy also decreases in significance or at least goes through something of a transformation. Samuel portrayed Israel's initial desire for a king as a rejection of God's kingship (1 Sam 8:7). In such a perspective, God's leadership has been usurped, and so the prophet becomes a necessary representative of the divine to rulers and those ruled. The prophets can be seen as political preachers, therefore, deeply interested in persuading the people and their leaders to turn to God and God's ways. In this light, it is not surprising to find the prophets using various and artful genres and literary forms to accomplish these means, poetry and imagistic language above all else. Some prophets also preached with their bodies, performing various acts—some quite bizarre—that symbolized their message (see, e.g., Jer 13:1–11; 16:1–13; 32:1–25; Ezekiel 4; 12; etc.). Isaiah, for example, walks around Jerusalem naked for three years because the Judeans would be taken into exile naked (Isa 20:1–6). A final, very important point is that women, not just men, served as prophets in ancient Israel (see, e.g., Exod 15:20; Judg 4:4–10; 5:1; 2 Kgs 22:14; Isa 8:3; Neh 6:14).

2. An earlier generation of scholars was fascinated with the personalities or psychologies of the prophets. According to one such scholar: "the average prophet was tall, spare, and nervous"! More recent interpreters have been more cautious. The presentations of the prophets found in the Bible are literary portraits, after all. These may or may not correspond to real, historical individuals from the past. This brings us to the *specifically written* aspect of the writing prophets and *the prophetic books*. Initially, scholars thought that prophets uttered their messages in short, poetic form—often introduced and/ or concluded by formulas like "Thus says the LORD," "the word of the LORD," or "the oracle of the LORD" (see, e.g., Jer 1:1; Ezek 1:2; Nah 1:1; Hab 1:1). Subsequent scholarship did not deny the existence of oral forms or the use of various formulas but frequently expressed doubt that all of a prophetic book necessarily went back to its namesake. This is a shift from *prophetic person* to *prophetic speech* and especially to *prophetic literature in written form*. What we now have access to is not Isaiah, Amoz's son (Isa 1:1), in this perspective, but only the literary work that bears his name. Even very important, even personal things—like the story of a prophet's calling—can be told in remarkably formulaic ways, which seems to *de*personalize those things to some degree (cf. Isa 6:1–13 with Jer 1:4–10 and Ezek 1:1–3:15; see also Exod 3:1–12; Judg 6:11–17). While much of what is presented as prophetic speech may go back to originally oral forms, all we have now is the written form. And so, the more they dug into things, the more scholars became convinced that some— perhaps much—of that written form didn't go back to the prophet who lent their name to the book. Instead, scholars deemed it likely that a prophet like Amos delivered some prophetic messages but that the Book of Amos was more than just that. The Book of Amos is the result of a long set of processes that preserved Amos' original words—or some of them, at any rate—while also adding to them over the years, updating and expanding them in various ways. This means that the books of the Latter Prophets, no less than those found in the Pentateuch and Former Prophets, also have complex compositional histories.

The most recent scholarly development is to focus squarely on *the prophetic book*. Some later prophetic texts, like Ezekiel, may have been written compositions from the start. Ezekiel makes extensive use of prose, as does Haggai. Nahum 1:1 is interesting in this regard, too, since it titles the composition that follows "the *book* of the vision of Nahum of Elkosh." Recent scholarship is far less interested in prophetic personalities than in the growth of the prophetic books—both separately as individual texts and together as a "prophetic corpus." While much of this compositional-critical work remains speculative, as it does in the case of the Torah and Former Prophets, it nevertheless indicates that the term *writing prophets* should be generously defined. It includes a prophet like Amos, since there is a book bearing his name. But it also includes all those who preserved and edited Amos' prophecies, which may have been exclusively oral until his disciples put them down in a scroll. These disciples and editors are also "among the prophets" (cf. 1 Sam 10:11–12; 19:24). The compositional-critical approach has demonstrated how these later editorial additions updated the prophets. Such updating is proof of the ongoing relevance of the prophetic word to different time periods. Updating also facilitated that ongoing relevance.

To summarize and simplify: the story scholars tell about the Latter Prophets has moved from one centered on prophetic individuals to one focused on prophetic books, from oral forms to written texts—texts that seem to have been updated in various ways and by varying means. Unfortunately, the Latter Prophets frequently lack the distinctive marks that *require* composition-critical theorizing such as the doublets and triplets encountered in the Pentateuch (see Chapter 2; but note Isa 2:2–4 and Micah 4:1–4; Obad 1–7 and Jer 49:7a, 14–16, 9–10; Joel 3:16a and Amos 1:2a). The absence of such markers makes a compositional approach to the Latter Prophets even more speculative than in the case of the Torah and Former Prophets. Be that as it may, it seems that the Latter Prophets have been intentionally edited to move from an emphasis on *God's judgment* to *hope beyond judgment*. To repeat an earlier formulation: if the Former Prophets tell the story of the *taking of the land to the loss of that land*, the Latter Prophets offer *reasons for land loss* and also the possibility of a *future life with God* beyond judgment. That, in the broadest sweep, is the story that the Latter Prophets tell, though more about this story deserves to be told.

THE "STORY" THE LATTER PROPHETS TELL

Given their extensive use of poetry and nonlinear presentation, not to mention the fact that the books of the Latter Prophets may have been gone through several editorial editions, it is much harder to tell their story, beyond the general remarks just made. Indeed, *story* may not be the right word for these books at all. The following summaries are thus brief and also insufficient to capture what are often long, complex, and fascinating *non*-narrative compositions. Each of the prophetic books also has its own set of interpretive issues and so a bit of the stories scholars tell about these books has also been mixed in with the "stories" each of these books tells.

ISAIAH (*YESHAYAHU*)

The Book of Isaiah has been called the Shakespeare of the Old Testament and the Fifth Gospel of Christianity. It is among the most beloved of prophetic books and is also among the most difficult since, according to current scholarly perspectives, it contains material that spans hundreds of years, from the time of the eighth-century prophet, Isaiah the son of Amoz, of Jerusalem, all the way through the Babylonian exile and well into the postexilic period. It has long been a scholarly standard to divide Isaiah into three unequal parts that reflect this range:

- Isaiah 1–39, called *Proto-* or *First Isaiah*;
- Isaiah 40–55, called *Deutero-* or *Second Isaiah*;
- Isaiah 56–66, called *Trito-* or *Third Isaiah*.

This division associates each of the major parts with a different time period and author(s):

- First Isaiah with the *eighth-century* prophet, *Isaiah of Jerusalem*, who was active from 738 until at least 701, maybe even as late as 688 BCE;
- Second Isaiah with an *anonymous prophet* active during *the later years of the Babylonian exile* (ca. 545–539 BCE); and
- Third Isaiah with an *anonymous prophet (or prophets)* who lived *after the edict of Cyrus* in 538 BCE that allowed the Judean exiles to return home (see Chart 2.1).

Not surprisingly, many scholars have found this division too neat and tidy. According to many, not all of Isaiah 1–39 can be confidently traced back to the eighth century because this lengthy block of material is itself obviously composite. Isaiah 36–39 is a mostly prose narrative borrowed from the account in 2 Kgs 18:13–20:19 (see also 2 Chr 32:1–24). These chapters of Isaiah seem to function as a bridge from Isaiah 35 to Isaiah 40, where Second Isaiah begins. Scholars have also noted that the themes that are so pronounced in Second Isaiah—themes of comfort and hope—are also found in Isaiah 34–35, which presently stands in First Isaiah. Perhaps this is a sign that the author responsible for Second Isaiah edited First Isaiah.

As for Third Isaiah, most scholars think Isaiah 56–66 is not nearly as coherent as Second Isaiah. Does this mean that more than one anonymous prophet was responsible for Third Isaiah with the result being that the number of "Isaiahs" should be increased beyond three? Some interpreters believe that the core of Third Isaiah, chapters 60–62, bear notable similarity to Second Isaiah. Perhaps that is a sign that the "Third" (or higher number) Isaiah is responsible for the final editing of this lengthy book. Or does it mean that there are really only two "Isaiahs," First and Second, with the latter extending from chapter 40 through chapter 66? Another vexed interpretive question is if these units—however many are identified—were originally discrete, existing independently of one another, or if Second Isaiah was from its inception conjoined with First Isaiah, or Third Isaiah with Second (and First) Isaiah.

Here, as in all instances of composition- and redaction-critical analysis, much remains uncertain and, finally, unknowable. What is clear, regardless, is that the Book of Isaiah, no less than other books in the Hebrew Bible—and in truth perhaps far more than most of them—is the end result of a long set of processes. It is also clear that the tone of the book shifts rather markedly in chapter 40. First Isaiah, or at least those parts of chapters 1–39 that scholars attribute to the eighth-century prophet, is marked by oracles that announce judgment on Jerusalem and Judah for wrongdoing, especially concerning matters of social injustice. First Isaiah also warns of the coming of Assyria, which God will use as a punitive tool against Judah (see, e.g., Isa 7:20; 10:5–15). In some ways, this thematic comes to its conclusion in chapter 39 where Isaiah promises

King Hezekiah that destruction and exile are imminent (vv. 5–7). But then, unexpectedly, Isaiah 40 rings out:

> Comfort, O comfort my people! says your God.
> Speak tenderly to Jerusalem, and cry to her
> that she has served her term, that her penalty is paid,
> that she has received from the LORD's hand double for all her sins.
> (40:1–2; NRSV)

Most interpreters are agreed, not only on the basis of this verse, but of all else that follows in chapters 40–55, that the "penalty" that has been paid here refers to the destruction of Jerusalem, the fall of Judah, and the exile to Babylon. Second Isaiah is thus something of an extended poetic argument convincing the exiles that, despite judgment and punishment, God now intends to do a "new thing" (43:19). That new thing involves a return from exile that is comparable to a new exodus (see, e.g., 43:16–21; 51:9–11).

This shift is quite unexpected after the first 39 chapters. Equally unexpected is that one of the ways God will do this new thing is by using the Persian king, Cyrus, who is mentioned in 44:28 and 45:1, with the latter verse going so far as to call Cyrus the "anointed one" or Messiah of God! The specific mention of Cyrus by name is one of several reasons that scholars date Second Isaiah to the time of the Babylonian exile. Prophets, after all, were not primarily concerned with predicting far distant events (see above). Though the prophetic books frequently do discuss eschatological elements—texts that speak about the end (*eschaton* in Greek) of the world or of an epoch/era—they typically do not detail specific names of rulers hundreds of years before they are born. As one noted scholar put it, if chapters 40–55 were spoken by the eighth-century prophet Isaiah, seeking to address the needs of exiles who lived a century and a half after he lived, "it would be a situation without parallel in the rest of the Old Testament."

Whatever the case, there is wide agreement that Second Isaiah contains some of the most beautiful poetry in the Hebrew Bible. Many scholars also believe that Second Isaiah comes closest to what we would today call abstract or theoretical monotheism: that there are no other gods besides the Lord (see, e.g., Isa 44:8; 45:5–6, 14, 18, 21–22; cf. 40:18–20; 44:9–20).

As already noted, Third Isaiah doesn't have the same feel as Second Isaiah. In fact, there are hints here and there that this material comes from a later period than Second Isaiah—after the return home from exile and the rebuilding of the temple (see 66:1)—and that things haven't turned out as well as Second Isaiah envisioned. In Third Isaiah, Judah seems highly fractious, and a general note of disappointment about the time period is sounded—something that is echoed in other postexilic prophets like Haggai and Zechariah (see below).

In the current form of the Book of Isaiah, all three "Isaiahs" are connected and attributed to Isaiah of Jerusalem (Isa 1:1). This shows, on the one hand, that the words of the prophets were thought to be lively and highly relevant for future times. It also shows, on the other hand, that for this very reason the (original) words of the prophets were regularly expanded upon and updated to demonstrate their significance for later generations. This could be seen as a kind of "accretion model"—not entirely unlike supplementary hypotheses for the Pentateuch (see Chapter 2)—but it shouldn't be understood as indicating that the various accreted parts of Isaiah have little or nothing to do with one another. On the contrary, the Book of Isaiah, as it now stands, contains *all* of this material: it is a book-length testimony to the interrelationship between these various, sometimes distinct parts—even if that relationship isn't always clear now.

In some cases, however, the relationship of the parts seems quite clear. Scholars have identified a number of unifying themes that appear across all parts of Isaiah. These include the emphasis on God, who is frequently referred to as "the Holy One of Israel" (e.g., Isa 1:4; 29:19; 40:25; 60:9), and special interest in Jerusalem (Zion), which God has chosen and is thus treasured and special. Writing much later, in the second century BCE, the author of Sirach (see Chart 1.1) captured some of the range and themes of the Book of Isaiah as we now have it in a brief, but memorable, way, attributing all of it to Isaiah, Amoz's son, from Jerusalem:

> In Isaiah's time, the sun moved backward,
>   and he extended the king's life.
> By his great spirit, he saw what was to come,

> and he comforted those who mourned in Zion.
> He revealed forever what would be
> and hidden things even before they happened. (Sir 48:23–25; CEB)

JEREMIAH (*YIRMEYAHU*)

The second of the three major prophets, Jeremiah, is another lengthy and complex book. It too, no less than Isaiah, bears evidence of being composite in nature. Scholars often identify three different kinds of material in the book: (1) early poetic oracles in chapters 1–25 that go back to the prophet himself, who was likely active from ca. 627 to 581 BCE; (2) prose material in chapters 36–45 that is written about Jeremiah and sometimes ascribed to his scribe, Baruch; and, finally, (3) material peppered throughout the book that seems closely connected to Deuteronomy (e.g., Jer 25:1–14), which leads some scholars to wonder if the book went through some process of Deuteronomistic editing (perhaps Jeremiah is meant to be the "prophet like Moses" promised in Deut 18:15–22). The combination of different kinds of material from different hands, if not also different time periods, means that the Book of Jeremiah often contains more than one perspective on the difficult topics it treats: trauma, hope, God.

An interesting fact about the book is that the Hebrew version is different, in both order and length, than the version preserved in the Septuagint. Many scholars believe the shorter Greek version is probably the earlier and more original. Some of the copies of Jeremiah found among the Dead Sea Scrolls demonstrate that the shorter form does go back to a Hebrew original. English translations of Jeremiah, however, are almost always taken from the longer Hebrew form.

To borrow words from Isaiah, the prophet Jeremiah could be appropriately described as "a man of sorrows, and acquainted with grief" (Isa 53:3; KJV). The book that bears his name takes Judah and Jerusalem into the great tragedies of defeat, destruction, and exile and then brings them out again on the other side. A verse that occurs in Jeremiah's call narrative in the very first chapter functions like a motto for the book as a whole (God is speaking to the prophet):

> This very day I appoint you over nations and empires
> to dig up and pull down,
> to destroy and demolish,
> to build and plant. (Jer 1:10; CEB; cf. 18:9; 24:6; 31:28; 42:10)

Six important commissioning verbs are used here. Four are negative and have to do with judgment and destruction; two are positive and connect with themes of hope and the future. The emphasis is clearly on the four, negative verbs, which outnumber the positive verbs two to one. And yet, like the other prophetic books, Jeremiah contains both judgment and promise—in that order. In fact, those two rubrics roughly correspond to the two halves of the book, with chapters 1–25 dominated by judgment and chapters 26–52 offering glimpses of hope. An especially important section about restoration is called the "Book of Consolation" (chaps. 30–33). Here is where the famous text about "a new covenant" occurs:

> The time is coming, declares the LORD, when I will make a new covenant with the people of Israel and Judah. It won't be like the covenant I made with their ancestors when I took them by the hand to lead them out of the land of Egypt. They broke that covenant with me even though I was their husband, declares the LORD. No, this is the covenant that I will make with the people of Israel after that time, declares the LORD. I will put my Instruction within them and engrave it on their hearts. I will be their God, and they will be my people. They will no longer need to teach each other to say, "Know the LORD!" because they will all know me, from the least of them to the greatest, declares the LORD; for I will forgive their wrongdoing and never again remember their sins. (Jer 31:31–34; CEB, altered)

The "new covenant" language recurs, later in the language of "new testament" (Luke 22:20; 1 Cor 11:25; cf. Heb 8:8; 9:15), making Jeremiah 31, a text about God's covenant with Israel, the ultimate origin of the title later used for the canonical collection of early Christian writings!

A series of judgment oracles against other nations, including Babylon, is found in the latter part of Jeremiah (chaps. 46–51). Judgment on an enemy is good news, and so these oracles against the nations are included in the second, hopeful half of the book—a situation found in other prophetic books as well. The last chapter of Jeremiah is a kind of historical appendix that contains material borrowed from 2 Kgs 24:18–25:30.

More than other prophetic books, the figure of the prophet himself is a significant feature of the Book of Jeremiah. This appears to afford us increased access to the prophet's personality. He is often called "the weeping prophet" because of passages like Jer 9:1; 13:17; 14:17–18 (cf. also 2 Chr 35:25). But in some of these weeping passages, the speaker is God, not the prophet. Perhaps it would be better to call Jeremiah not the weeping prophet but the prophet of the weeping God! Whatever the case, the sorrow contained in the book led to the tradition that Jeremiah was responsible for writing the Book of Lamentations (see Chapter 4).

Other parts of the book seem to cast light on Jeremiah's persona, especially the passages that are called his "confessions" (Jer 11:18–23; 12:1–6; 15:10–21; 17:14–18; 18:18–23; 20:7–18). These are not confessions of sin or wrongdoing but powerful complaints Jeremiah utters against God—largely because of the hardships facing the prophet. In one of these "confessions," Jeremiah says he gladly ate God's words, but God disappointed him: "You have become for me as unreliable as a spring gone dry!" (15:18). In another, Jeremiah accurses God of enticing him (20:7). In these texts, one gets a sense of the intense and personal strain that accompanied the prophetic task. And Jeremiah seems to have a point: the book contains several passages that indicate that the prophet was frequently at odds with the king and other political powerbrokers (e.g., 11:18–23; 26–28; 37:11–38:6). It was often only because of the protection of an important family, the clan of Shaphan, that he was able to escape punishment or worse (see 26:24; 29:3; 39:14; 40:5; 43:6).

Two texts cast light, not only on Jeremiah the prophet but also on Jeremiah the book—perhaps even prophecy more generally (both oral and written). In the first, Jeremiah finds himself in a head-to-head conflict with another prophet named Hananiah (chap. 28). Hananiah is convinced that the exiles who had been removed to Babylon would return soon, and he proclaims this message, in God's name, to King Zedekiah. Jeremiah is unconvinced and claims the exact opposite. True prophets, Jeremiah asserts, are the ones who prophesy "war, disaster, and disease"; any "prophet who prophesies peace is recognized as one ... sent by the LORD only when that prophet's message is fulfilled" (28:8–9). This chapter is fascinating because both prophets speak in the name of God, use prophetic speech formulas, and engage in symbolic actions that support their messages. It would have been very hard, on the ground, to know which was the true prophet and which the false, especially since both men are called "prophet" (navi', vv. 1, 5) in Hebrew! The

Septuagint solved this conundrum for its Greek readers: in the very first verse, it calls Hananiah a "false prophet" *(pseudoprophetes)*. In the midst of the showdown, however, things would have been harder to sort out. As a result, the rulers who depended on prophetic advice were often at a loss. When the issues were urgent or the situation volatile, monarchs didn't have the luxury to wait around and see which prophecy came to pass (28:9; cf. Deut 18:15–22; 1 Kings 22).

The second text shows that kings often didn't like prophets—especially the ones who critiqued them or caused problems by hindering their plans, if only by condemning their deeds as unjust (see 1 Kings 21). In Jeremiah 36, the prophet sends Baruch to read a scroll of his prophecies in the temple. The scroll is eventually taken to King Jehoiakim and read to him:

> And whenever Jehudi read three or four columns of the scroll, the king would cut them off with a scribe's knife and throw them into the firepot until the whole scroll was burned up. Neither the king nor any of his attendants who heard all these words were alarmed or tore their clothes. (Jer 36:23–24; CEB)

But Jehoiakim's bonfire cannot stop the prophet—or the prophetic word! Right after the first scroll is burned, God tells Jeremiah to write a second scroll that repeats all the words of the first one (v. 28). The last verse of the chapter reports that that is exactly what Jeremiah does, and then adds pointedly, "many similar words were added to them" (v. 32). This chapter seems to afford a rare glimpse, not only on the conflict between kings and prophets but also on how prophetic scrolls might have been rewritten and expanded. Whatever the case, Jeremiah 36 shows that the prophetic word—perhaps especially in revised and expanded form—cannot be stopped. It triumphs over any and all instances of human rule, foreign or domestic (cf. 51:59–64).

EZEKIEL *(YECHEZKEL)*

According to Ezek 1:1–3, the prophet Ezekiel was a priest who was among the first wave of exiles deported to Babylon in 597 BCE. There, along the banks of the Chebar River, quite unexpectedly—especially for a priest obsessed with the temple and its purity—Ezekiel had a vision of God's throne-chariot coming into exile too. As a priest, Ezekiel is especially circumspect about describing this vision, saying, in the end, that he saw something several times removed from saying he actually saw God: it was only "the *appearance* of the *likeness* of God's *glory*" (1:28). This vision leads immediately into Ezekiel's call to be a prophet (2:1–3:27).

This is just one of three visions Ezekiel has about God's glory (*kavod*). The next one, in chapters 8–11, is similar to a flashback that provides the reason why God's glory shows up in Babylon in the first place: because the glory abandoned the temple in Jerusalem. The third and final vision in chapters 40–48 concerns a future after the exile, with the land reorganized, a new temple constructed, and a new capital city with a new name. In this last vision, the glory of God comes full circle. Ezekiel watches it return from the East—from Babylon—to reenter the temple (43:1–5). After this reentry, the eastern gate is permanently shut, since God will never need to use it again (44:1–2). In other words, God won't be abandoning the temple or the city ever again!

These three visions provide one way of structuring Ezekiel. Another way to do that is by means of the 13 chronological notifications in the book that specify when the prophet delivered specific oracles or performed particular actions (1:2; 8:1; 20:1; 24:1; 26:1; 29:1, 17; 30:20; 31:1; 32:1, 17; 33:21; 40:1). These dates range from 593 to 571 BCE. Some scholars believe these notices prove that the book was, from the start, a piece of written literature without going back to any oral precursors.

While that point might be debated, it is clear that Ezekiel didn't shy away from non-verbal communication. Early in the book, God is said to shut up his mouth (3:26–27; reversed only much later: see 24:27; 33:21–22). Perhaps for this reason, Ezekiel is a master of what might be called prophetic street theater. Isaiah and Jeremiah also engaged in prophetic actions that were symbolic in some way, but Ezekiel takes this performative art to a new level. No less than 12 distinct sign acts are recounted in the book; some are odd, others downright troubling (e.g., 4:1–3). Included in the troubling category is how Ezekiel is forbidden from mourning his wife's death. His stoicism was to symbolize how no one would mourn the destruction of Jerusalem when it took place (24:15–27). "So I spoke to the people in the morning, and at evening my wife died. And on the next morning I did what I was commanded," Ezekiel reports laconically (24:18; NRSV). Ezekiel's audience of fellow exiles was accustomed to his unusual, prophetic sign acts, however, as is clear from the question they immediately ask him: "Won't you tell us what these things mean *for us*, that you are acting like this?" (24:19). And so he does; the performance art worked.

The symbolic actions, along with various other details in the book, led earlier scholars to wonder about Ezekiel, with some going so far as to psychoanalyze him. More recently, given his status as an exile forcibly deported after military defeat, some interpreters have suggested that Ezekiel may have suffered from posttraumatic stress disorder (PTSD). While most scholars no longer think that the prophetic books grant direct access to the prophets' psyches (see above), many still think that the Book of Ezekiel is an instance of trauma literature. If so, the book reflects trauma and may also be an attempt to work through trauma: the trauma of exile and the trauma of Jerusalem's ultimate defeat.

One way the book "works through" these traumas is by the shift that takes place halfway through. When the worst case scenario finally happens—the death of Ezekiel's wife, which parallels Jerusalem's fall—the book turns from material focused on judgment (chaps. 1–24) to texts devoted to hope, restoration, and the future (chaps. 25–48). This same movement was also observed in Isaiah and Jeremiah. The ending of Ezekiel goes further than any biblical prophet, however, in offering a lengthy and detailed vision of life in the land after exile. As noted briefly above, in Ezekiel's final vision (chaps. 40–48), the tribes are reorganized with some of the northern tribes shifting to the south. This means that the northern tribes will no longer be able to claim, as they did when they seceded way back in 922 BCE: "What share have we in David?" (1 Kgs 12:16). In fact, according to Ezekiel, the future is altogether devoid of a king. There is mention only of a "prince" or a "leader" (*nasi*). The capital city is given a new, altogether religious name—one that symbolizes God's presence: "The LORD is There" (48:35). The restored temple is said to fructify the entire land, making even the Dead Sea flow with fresh water once again (47:1–12).

Ezekiel's vision was never realized in the postexilic period. Perhaps that failure is what led to the disappointment that can be discerned in parts of Third Isaiah, Haggai, and Zechariah. Ezekiel's visions of God's glory were formative in other ways, however: for certain types of Jewish mysticism and for eschatological hope in both Judaism and Christianity.

THE BOOK OF THE TWELVE MINOR PROPHETS

The Twelve Minor Prophets are Hosea, Joel, Amos, Obadiah, Jonah, Micah, Nahum, Habakkuk, Zephaniah, Haggai, Zechariah, and Malachi. That is the order found in modern Bibles, but it has varied at points in time. Some Septuagint manuscripts, for example, have a different order for the first six books: Hosea, Amos, Micah, Joel, Obadiah, Jonah. This is apparently due to chronological considerations, which is what led some manuscripts to put the Twelve before the Major Prophets (see above).

As already noted, the Twelve are called "minor" prophets only because of their brevity. The longest books are Hosea and Zechariah, each with 14 chapters; the shortest is Obadiah, which contains only 21 verses (just 291 words in Hebrew). Although most of these compositions were once independent, it became convenient, given their concision, to combine them into one "book," since they could all comfortably fit on a scroll that was comparable in size to Isaiah, Jeremiah, or Ezekiel. This produces a four-book Latter Prophets that corresponds to the four-book Former Prophets.

The Twelve may perhaps also be considered "minor" insofar as they don't add drastically to what the three "major" prophets already convey. But this would be to underestimate the distinctive content of each of the Twelve. Furthermore, since Hosea predates Isaiah and some of the other Twelve date from the postexilic period, the Minor Prophets can be seen as encompassing the entire time span of the Major Prophets, further extending the chronological range of the prophetic word in Israel as recorded in the Hebrew Bible.

The precise dating of the various Minor Prophets is a vexed question, however. Like the other books of the Old Testament, these small prophetic books have been subjected to extensive compositional analyses which have argued that only some of the material in, say, Amos, goes back to the prophet from Tekoa (see Amos 1:1; cf. 7:14–15). Other parts of Amos would come from the prophet's first circle of disciples or followers. That material, in turn, would have been further expanded through centuries of editing and transmission. So, to stay with Amos as an example, the end of that book, which speaks of restoring David's fallen dynasty (9:11–15), strikes a very different chord than the earlier chapters which are chock full of harsh judgment. Accordingly, many scholars see this ending as secondary, probably added long after Amos prophesied in the eighth century BCE (and in the north!) since at that time David's dynasty hadn't yet fallen (in the south!). This kind of editorial addition, moreover, is in line with the other prophetic books that seem to be organized in a judgment → promise sequence. This sequence and the compositional development of a book like Amos are familiar from the other prophets discussed in this chapter and from the story scholars tell about them.

Also familiar from the preceding discussion, and operative in the Minor Prophets as well, is the more recent trend that cares less about recovering the "original Amos" than it does to paying attention to the literary artistry of the Book of Amos and, indeed, of the Book of the Twelve as a collection. Many scholars now think that some of the Minor Prophets were developed in tandem (Hosea and Amos, for example). It is possible, that is, that a few of these compositions never existed independently, and so do not go back exclusively to oral sermons by a named prophet. Instead some may have been entirely *literary* compositions from the start (cf. above on Ezekiel).

It is intriguing, in this regard, to note how similar Malachi is to Zechariah. In Hebrew, "Malachi" means "my messenger." Perhaps "Malachi" is a proper name in Mal 1:1, therefore, but it could just as easily be a generic title, which is how the Septuagint understood and translated it. That is also what the word *malachi* seems to mean in 3:1 where it is usually translated as "my messenger." Also intriguing is how Mal 1:1 identifies what follows as "a burden" (*massa*). Nahum and Habakkuk also use this term, but it is found twice in the latter part of the Book of Zechariah (9:1; 12:1), which immediately precedes the Book of Malachi. Zechariah 9–14 is sometimes identified as "Second Zechariah" and differentiated from "First Zechariah" (chaps. 1–8). Given similarities in content between Second Zechariah and Malachi, some interpreters have often wondered if the "burden" of "my messenger" that begins in Mal 1:1 is simply the third in a sequence of additions to Zechariah 1–8 that begin at Zech 9:1 and continue in Zech 12:1 and Mal 1:1. If so, what is now the Book of Malachi may have once been just a part of Zechariah which was only later separated out as an independent composition, perhaps in part to produce a 12-part Minor Prophet collection, since that numerical total can hardly be coincidental. Other scholars think Malachi was its own composition from the get go, whatever possible relationships it might (and does) have with Zechariah and the rest of the Twelve.

There are other signs of intentional editing of the Twelve as a collection. These include their rough chronological sequencing with Hosea, Amos, and Micah clustering around the eighth century; Nahum, Habakkuk, and Zephaniah around the late seventh century; and Haggai, Zechariah, and Malachi around the late sixth century. Of course if the Minor Prophets are composites, then even an early prophetic book may contain material from much later times. Beyond chronology, the Twelve seem to be arranged in now familiar judgment → promise sequence. The earlier books in the collection are dominated by judgmental prophecies, while the latter sound a more positive note. Of course, as already noted, each prophetic book usually has elements of both judgment and salvation, typically in that order, though they are sometimes interleaved in interesting ways (e.g., Micah has judgment in chaps. 1–3 and 6, salvation in chaps. 4, 5, and 7).

The Twelve might be categorized in various ways, especially in terms of theme. So, for example, Hosea, Amos, and Micah—like Isaiah of Jerusalem—are all eighth-century prophets that demonstrate a special interest in *social justice*. Jonah, Obadiah, and Nahum all manifest a particular concern with *foreign nations*. Joel and Zechariah emphasize *eschatological themes*. And, though chronology is always a topic of debate among scholars, most interpreters agree that Joel, Jonah, Haggai, Zechariah, and Malachi probably come very late in Israel's history. Four of these five evidence a different kind of literary style than the other prophets:

- Jonah is a satirical short story that seems out of place in the Twelve. It is generically far more similar to something like the stories of Ruth and Esther in the *Ketuvim* (see Chapter 4) than it is to Amos or Micah in the *Nevi'im*. Or, since it is a story about an individual prophet, perhaps it could fit in Kings alongside accounts of Elijah, Elisha, and others. Indeed, the only other place we hear of someone named "Jonah the son of Amittai" outside of the Book of Jonah is 2 Kgs 14:25.

- Like Jonah, Haggai is apparently a prose, not a poetic composition, as is also Malachi and parts of Zechariah. Both Haggai and (especially) Malachi make extensive use of rhetorical questions, in a dialogue or disputation form (see, e.g., Hag 1:4; 2:3; Mal 1:2–5, 6–8, 9–13; 2:10–15, 17; 3:2–6, 7–12, 13–15). Considerations like these may be further proof of what was said before: that after the demise of the monarchy, prophecy also declines, or, probably more accurately, transforms into something new.

- Zechariah, which combines prose and poetry, includes eight visions that are highly imagistic and symbolic (chaps. 1–6). Other prophetic books contain visions (e.g., Isa 6:1–13; Ezekiel 1–3; Amos 7:1–9; 8:1–3; 9:1–4; etc.) but here again is a sign of something new since Zechariah's visions anticipate a literary genre—apocalyptic—that doesn't come to full fruition until a bit later (see below and Chapter 4).

One final item might be mentioned that unifies the Twelve Minor Prophets and that is that nearly all of them make mention of the "Day of the LORD" (see, e.g., Hos 9:5; Joel 1:15; 2:1, 11, 31; Amos 5:18–20; Obad 15; Mic 2:4; Nah 1:7; Hab 3:16; Zeph 1:7, 9–10, 14–16, 18; 2:2–3; 3:11; Hag 2:23; Zech 14:1; Mal 3:1–3; 4:1, 3, 5). This motif is found in the Major Prophets as well (e.g., Isa 13:6, 9), but it is especially pronounced in the Twelve, which can be seen as an extended reflection on what this "Day" is and entails. On the one hand, there are perspectives like that of Amos, for whom the day is one of doom (5:18–20). For Zephaniah, too, it is a "day of wrath, a day of distress and anguish, a day of ruin and devastation, a day of darkness and gloom, a day of clouds and thick darkness" (1:15; NRSV). The devastation in question can be of Israel (see Mic 2:4; Hab 3:16; Zeph 1:9; Mal 4:1) or of other nations (Obad 15). It can even be a time of cosmic disorder (Joel 2:31). On the other hand, the "Day of the LORD" can be a time of worship (Hos 9:5; Zeph 1:7) and hope—when new political leaders can be expected (Hag 2:23) or when the exiles will be gathered up with God as "king over all the earth" (Zech 14:9). Even Jonah, the one book in the Twelve that doesn't explicitly mention the "Day of the LORD" can be considered to contribute to the theme because of the rest of the Twelve. In this light, Jonah's contribution would be to show that God's day might include divine forgiveness for the worst of enemies—a point that is implicit in some of the other prophets as well (e.g., Isa 19:19–25; Zeph 3:9–12). Finally, the present sequence of the Twelve moves the interpretation of the Day of the Lord from an imminent one, full of judgment for God's people, to a more distant, futuristic and eschatological day that is marked by the deliverance and salvation of God's people (Joel 2:28–3:21; Zech 14:6–7; Mal 4:5). Eschatological themes are also found in the Major Prophets (see Isaiah 24–27; Ezekiel 38–39; 40–48) but are found in most pronounced form in the apocalyptic books of Daniel, in the Old Testament (see Chapter 4), and Revelation, in the New.

Given these futuristic, salvation-rich themes, it is not surprising that—in contrast to the ordering of the Hebrew Bible—Christian versions of the Old Testament end with the Twelve and, ultimately, with Malachi 4, which refers to the coming Day of the Lord:

> Look, the day is coming, burning like an oven. All the arrogant ones and all those doing evil will become straw. The coming day will burn them, says the LORD ... But the sun of righteousness will rise on those revering my name; healing will be in its wings so that you will go forth and jump about like calves in the stall.
>
> Remember the Instruction (*torah*) from Moses, my servant, to whom I gave Instruction (*torah*) and rules for all Israel at Horeb. Look, I am sending Elijah the prophet to you, before the great and terrifying day of the LORD arrives. Turn the hearts of the parents to the children and the hearts of the children to their parents. Otherwise, I will come and strike the land with a curse. (Mal 4:1–2, 4–6; CEB)

This ending appears intended to unite the Twelve, and probably the entire prophetic corpus, with the Pentateuch since it mentions Moses and the Torah. The mention of Elijah, from the Former Prophets, and his imminent return is also a pregnant image, one that was used by the New Testament authors who compared him to John the Baptist (see Matt 11:14; 17:12; Mark 9:13; Luke 1:17) and who reported his appearance in Jesus' transfiguration (Matt 17:3; Mark 9:4; Luke 9:30). In Protestant Bibles, in particular, it is a very short hop, skip, and a jump from Malachi to Matthew. A very different effect is created by the order of the Hebrew Bible which ends, not with Malachi and Elijah but with Chronicles and King Cyrus of Persia (see Chart 1.2)—but that is a topic for the next chapter.

WHAT THE PROPHETS ARE ALL ABOUT: TWO THINGS

If it was hard to boil the Torah down to two things in Chapter 2, it is even harder to do so in the case of the Prophets in the present chapter. The *Nevi'im* contain eight books to the Torah's five and 380 chapters to the Torah's 187. This second section of the Hebrew Bible is not only longer than the first, it is far more disparate as a collection, offering new types of literature not contained in the Pentateuch, including, most of all, *prophecy*. Summarizing "what the Prophets are all about," therefore, is even trickier than saying "what the Torah is all about." Even so, epitomizing a vast amount of data remains a worthy endeavor, especially for new readers trying to get a grasp on the whole. To that end, here are two things that begin to capture what the Prophets "are all about."

GOD'S MIRROR

The Prophets are, first, about God's mirror. These books hold up a mirror to society to show what it has become. Occasionally, that picture is good, but most of the time it is not. In the case of the Former Prophets, the grand sweep of the narrative from Joshua–Kings is one of serious decline: *from the taking of the land to the losing of the land*. The Latter Prophets would chime in *with reasons* for that land loss, though the Former Prophets have some of that already specified (e.g., Joshua 23–24; 2 Kgs 17:5–23).

God's mirror is sometimes held up to society with very little or no commentary. The downward spiral of decline at the end of Judges, for instance, is virtually devoid of moralizing remarks. But none are needed. Readers who have made it from Genesis to this point in Judges, or from Deuteronomy to Judges, or from Joshua to Judges—of even who have read just Judges alone—know that the events that take place in chapters 17–21 of that book can in no way be thought of as God's plan or desire for Israel. To put it bluntly: not everything in the Bible is *prescriptive literature* to be emulated and repeated. Far from it! A good bit of the Bible is a cold hard reckoning with the ugly facts of life, even life among God's people. It is *descriptive literature*: the brutal truth of looking in the mirror and not liking what you see. The editorial comment in Judg 17:6; 18:1; 19:1; 21:25, that at that time there was no king around, is thus hardly necessary. The sobering look in the God's mirror, the prophets, is enough. The Former Prophets, by telling a somewhat unified story from Joshua through Kings, do not simply warn of the dreadful consequences of terrible choices, they recount that ultimate end: destruction, defeat, exile.

The Latter Prophets, too, hold up God's mirror to society. Though the Latter Prophets frequently lack "the rest of the story" since they do not always narrate the fall of Israel or Judah, these prophets nevertheless show, with spine-tingling rhetoric, how serious God is about the wrongdoing perpetrated in society. To borrow words from Franz Kafka, a text like Amos is a book of "ill-fortune" that distresses us deeply, "like the death of one we love better than ourselves, like suicide." Those kinds of book are necessary, Kafka says, because we need "an ice-axe to break the sea frozen inside us." There can be no doubt that a good bit of prophetic rhetoric shocks and disturbs contemporary readers—the marriage metaphor of God and God's people may be the paramount example, especially when it is mingled, as it sometimes is, with language of sexual violence (e.g., Ezekiel 16, 23; Hosea 2; Nah 3:5–7). It seems likely that such language was equally shocking in ancient Israel, a culture that was far less desensitized to graphic violence and sexuality on a day-to-day basis than our own. Whatever the case, the Prophets are quite literally dead set to do whatever they can to shock God's people back to their senses: back to doing justice, to loving mercy, and to walking humbly with God (Mic 6:8). They hold up a cold, hard mirror as a way to do so and force Israel, and us, to look.

GOD'S *MISHPAT-AND-TZEDAQAH*

The Prophets are also all about *mishpat* and *tzedaqah*. *Mishpat* means "justice." *Tzedaqah* means "righteousness." The two can be closely conjoined, as if they were one (*mishpat*-and-*tzedaqah*), because they often occur together, sometimes appearing as corresponding terms in lines of Hebrew poetry. An excellent example is Amos 5:24, made famous in more recent days by Martin Luther King, Jr. in his "I Have a Dream" speech:

> But let justice (*mishpat*) roll down like waters,
> and righteousness (*tzedaqah*) like an ever-flowing stream. (NRSV)

Mishpat and *tzedaqah* are not, strictly-speaking, synonyms, however. They are different words, each with their own range of meaning, even if they are often combined as they are in Amos 5 (see, e.g., 1 Kgs 10:9; Isa 1:21, 27; 5:16; 9:7; Jer 4:2; 22:3; Ezek 45:9; etc.). Taken together, *mishpat*-and-*tzedaqah* evoke the range of prophetic concern: *justice* in the society writ large and *righteousness* that includes the most personal of matters. These two things—or, rather, this one thing—is what God seeks and what God often finds lacking, as nicely captured in the NJPSV's rendition of the word-play in Isaiah 5:

> For the vineyard of the LORD of hosts
> Is the House of Israel,
> And the seedlings he lovingly tended
> Are the men of Judah.
> And He hoped for justice (*mishpat*),
> But behold, injustice (*mishpach*);
> For equity (*tzedaqah*),
> But behold, iniquity (*tze'aqah*)! (Isa 5:7)

The close relationship of *mishpat* and *tzedaqah* explains why God's mirror frequently highlights instances of gross social injustice (e.g., 2 Sam 11:14–27; 1 Kgs 5:13–17; Amos 2:6–7a) and what goes on, as it were, behind closed doors (e.g., 2 Sam 11:1–15; 1 Kings 21; Amos 2:7b). Such texts, and the Prophets writ large, show how deeply God desires *mishpat* and *tzedaqah*. The absence of these things brings God's judgment; their presence facilitates God's blessing.

This point affords a crucial insight into the nature of divine wrath in the Bible. To borrow from the great twentieth-century rabbi, Abraham Joshua Heschel, the God of Scripture is not a God of wrath (*Deus irae*)—angry all the time or mad inexplicably. Instead, God *has* wrath (*ira Dei*) about *specific things*: injustice and unrighteousness, the lack of *mishpat* and *tzedaqah*. But when *mishpat* and *tzedaqah* are restored, God's wrath dissipates and disappears (see, e.g., Jer 3:12–14; 18:5–11; Ezek 18:21–32; 33:10–20; Jonah 3:10). God's mirror shows how dire and desperate, mean and malicious human life is when it is absent *mishpat* and *tzedaqah*. God's mirror also occasionally reveals, in the future if not also here and there, now and then, how beautiful the human community can be when it is marked by those selfsame qualities (see, e.g., Isa 2:1–4; 11:1–9; Zeph 3:11–20).

In the end, then, not only are *mishpat* and *tzedaqah* intertwined as *mishpat*-and-*tzedaqah*, so, too, is *mishpat*-and-*tzedaqah* inextricably related to God's mirror. Their intimate association is not unlike the close relationship between God's creation(s) and God's command(s) in the Torah.

SUGGESTIONS FOR FURTHER READING

The classic articulation of the Deuteronomistic History Hypothesis is Martin Noth, *The Deuteronomistic History* (2nd ed.; Sheffield: JSOT, 1991). For a more recent reassessment, see Thomas Römer, *The So-Called Deuteronomistic History: A Sociological, Historical and Literary Introduction* (New York: T & T Clark, 2005). A useful presentation, that includes Deuteronomy, is found in Anthony F. Campbell and Mark A. O'Brien, *Unfolding the Deuteronomistic History: Origins, Upgrades, Present Text* (Minneapolis: Fortress, 2000).

For the interpretive issues surrounding the conquest accounts, see especially: Stephen B. Chapman, "Martial Memory, Peaceable Vision: Divine War in the Old Testament," in *Holy War in the Bible: Christian Morality and an Old Testament Problem* (eds. H. A. Thomas, J. Evans, and P. Copan; Downers Grove: Intervarsity, 2013), 47–67; Lawson G. Stone, "Ethical and Apologetic Tendencies in the Redaction of the Book of Joshua," *Catholic Biblical Quarterly* 52 (1991): 25–36; Douglas S. Earl, *Reading Joshua as Christian Scripture* (Winona Lake: Eisenbrauns, 2010); and Christian Hofreiter, *Making Sense of Old Testament Genocide: Christian Interpretations of* Herem *Passages* (Oxford: Oxford University Press, 2018).

The problems of royal chronology are treated in Edwin R. Thiele, *The Mysterious Numbers of the Hebrew Kings* (rev. ed.; Grand Rapids: Zondervan, 1983); and John H. Hayes and Paul K. Hooker, *A New Chronology for the Kings of Israel and Judah and Its Implications for Biblical History and Literature* (Atlanta: John Knox, 1988). For the history of Israel and Judah more generally, see J. Maxwell Miller and John H. Hayes, *A History of Ancient Israel and Judah* (2nd ed.; Louisville: Westminster John Knox, 2006); Megan Bishop Moore and Brad E. Kelle, *Biblical History and Israel's Past: The Changing Study of the Bible and History* (Grand Rapids: Eerdmans, 2011); and Victor H. Matthews, *A Brief History of Ancient Israel* (Louisville: Westminster John Knox, 2002).

There are many excellent books on the prophets but two stand out above all others: Abraham Joshua Heschel, *The Prophets* (New York: Perennial, 2001); and Walter Brueggemann, *The Prophetic Imagination: 40th Anniversary Edition* (Minneapolis: Fortress, 2018). Heschel's treatment of the wrath of God is a must-read. See also Ellen F. Davis, *Biblical Prophecy:*

Perspectives for Christian Theology, Discipleship, and Ministry (Louisville: Westminster John Knox, 2014); David L. Petersen, *The Prophetic Literature: An Introduction* (Louisville: Westminster John Knox, 2002); and Donald E. Gowan, *Theology of the Prophetic Books: The Death and Resurrection of Israel* (Louisville: Westminster John Knox, 1998).

The classic study on the prophetic call texts is N. Habel, "The Form and Significance of the Call Narratives," *Zeitschrift für die alttestamentliche Wissenschaft* 77 (1965): 297–323. For the significance of Isaiah in Christian tradition, see John F. A. Sawyer, *The Fifth Gospel: Isaiah in the History of Christianity* (Cambridge: Cambridge University Press, 1996). For female prophets in Israel, see Wilda Gafney, *Daughters of Miriam: Women Prophets in Ancient Israel* (Minneapolis: Fortress, 2008); and Esther J. Hamori, *Women's Divination in Biblical Literature: Prophecy, Necromancy, and Other Arts of Knowledge* (New Haven: Yale University Press, 2015) For the marriage metaphor in the prophets, see Renita Weems, *Battered Love: Marriage, Sex, and Violence in the Hebrew Prophets* (Minneapolis: Fortress, 1995).

The citation from Wendell Berry is from "The Responsibility of the Poet," in his *What Are People For? Essays* (San Francisco: North Point, 1990), 90. The comment that the prophets were often "tall, spare, and nervous" is from W. C. Klein, *The Psychological Pattern of Old Testament Prophecy* (Evanston: Seabury-Western, 1956), 75. The citation about the prediction of Cyrus being unparalleled is from Brevard S. Childs, *Introduction to the Old Testament as Scripture* (Philadelphia: Fortress, 1979), 317. The language from Franz Kafka is taken from a letter he wrote to Oskar Pollack dated January 27, 1904.

THE WRITINGS (*KETUVIM*)

The third and final section of the Hebrew Bible, the Writings or *Ketuvim*, is by far the most disparate of the three. There is no dominant genre like law is (arguably) for the Torah or as prophecy is for the Latter Prophets. Neither is there an overarching narrative that runs from Creation to Canaan, as in the case of the Pentateuch, or from the taking of the land to its losing, per the Former Prophets. Instead, the Writings feel like more like a miscellany of somewhat randomly collected and unrelated compositions. The *Ketuvim* includes everything from the great religious poetry of the Psalms, to the profound ruminations on suffering in Job, to short stories like Ruth and Esther, to erotic love poetry (Song of Songs), even an apocalyptic text is included (Daniel)—and there's yet still more!

The varied nature of the Writings means it is much harder to discuss this division by means of the two stories that have guided the present introduction. There have been no grand unifying theories for the books of the *Ketuvim* like there is for the composition of the Pentateuch or the Deuteronomistic History. The story scholars have told *about* the Writings, therefore, has tended to be focused on individual books—not unlike the study of individual prophetic books discussed in the preceding chapter. Even so, there are scholarly theories about some smaller groupings of books within the *Ketuvim* that seem to be related in some way by genre, liturgical use, maybe even common authorship.

If there are no theories for the Writings as a whole, it is simply because the entire collection is so obviously diverse: in genre, liturgical use, and *non*-common authorship. The diversity found within the *Ketuvim* also complicates the other story pursued in the present introduction: the story the Bible itself tells. The previous chapters on the Torah and Prophets have occasionally shown that the usefulness of the "story" category might be questioned when it comes to these sections of the Bible. With the Writings, though, the category comes close to being downright irrelevant. To be sure, there are quite a few narratives in the *Ketuvim*, but much here is decidedly *not* narrative. Of course the same holds true for much of the Latter Prophets. The "story" notion will be discussed further in Chapter 5. For now, it suffices to say that, in the Writings, more than anywhere else in the Hebrew Bible, it is probably best to speak of the *stories* (plural) that this section tells, and it probably wouldn't hurt to put that word in scare quotes—"stories"—since much here is not story at all.

In light of these factors, the present chapter discusses scholarly theories about specific books in the Writings within the treatment of those books' own stories—their content. So, unlike Chapters 2 and 3, the stories *about* the Bible and *within* the Bible are intertwined here. Even so, a few general comments about scholarly study of the *Ketuvim* can be offered and are an appropriate place to begin.

THE SCHOLARLY STORY OF THE WRITINGS

The varied nature of the Writings has led scholars to the opinion that this section of the Hebrew Bible was the latest and last to be finalized and canonized. This might explain why some of the books included in the *Ketuvim* are here when they might reasonably have been located elsewhere in the Hebrew Bible. Their location in the Writings would be due, in this view, to the fact that they were likely written down and/or gained authority later than the books collected in the Pentateuch and Prophets. Even if the books in the Writings do not all date to the latest stages of Israelite history, it seems likely that they nevertheless reached their current form at a later period if only because they are now found in the last and latest division of the Hebrew Bible.

The possible fit of these books elsewhere is probably what led some versions of the Old Testament to reorder them (see Chart 1.1). A few examples from the order that is found in most English Bibles (dependent on Greek and Latin traditions) show that this alternative placement often makes good sense of the books in question:

1. The Book of Ruth is found between Judges and Samuel. Since Ruth 1:1 indicates that this book takes place during the time period of the judges, it is reasonable to read it alongside the Book of Judges. Ruth 4 concludes with a genealogy that culminates in the birth of David (vv. 18–22). This leads directly, and nicely, into the Book of Samuel, which pays great attention to David but lacks a genealogy for that great king. Ruth's placement with Judges and Samuel is related to a larger difference that was discussed in Chapter 2: the separation of the Latter Prophets from the Former Prophets in non-Hebrew versions of the Old Testament. This separation makes the Latter Prophets the sole prophetic collection and simultaneously creates a new category for the Former Prophets: they are now considered the Historical Books. Ruth, Chronicles, Ezra-Nehemiah, and Esther are then included in this new unit. Sequenced in this way, the Historical Books run from the taking of the land in the Book of Joshua well into the Persian Period in the Books of Ezra-Nehemiah and Esther.

2. The Book of Lamentations follows the Book of Jeremiah. This association is partly due to thematic reasons, given the profound grief that is articulated in both compositions, but it may also trade on a detail like the one found in 2 Chr 35:25, which states that Jeremiah wrote a lament for Josiah after that king died prematurely.

3. The Book of Daniel is placed with the prophetic books, either as the last in the collection (Septuagint) or between Ezekiel and the Minor Prophets (Vulgate).

While each of these "relocations" makes a certain amount of sense, each also creates some interpretive problems—or, at least, has an effect on how these books are subsequently understood. So, for example, associating Lamentations with Jeremiah may suggest that the prophet was responsible for authoring that book. Indeed, the Septuagint contains an additional, introductory verse not found in the Hebrew that makes this possibility explicit: "And it happened, after Israel was taken captive and Jerusalem was laid waste, Jeremiah sat weeping and gave this lament over Jerusalem and said ...." The Hebrew version of Lamentations, however, says nothing about its author. The English ordering also interrupts the prophetic sequence of Isaiah → Jeremiah → Ezekiel.

Or, as another example, Daniel should not be easily lumped in with the prophetic books. Daniel is an instance of apocalyptic literature, which shouldn't be confused with prophetic literature—or vice versa—since each is distinctive (see further below).

Within the Hebrew tradition there is some variation in the order of the Writings. This, too, is probably proof that this section (and these books) didn't have as long to "cook" when compared to the books of the Torah, which show no variation, and the Prophets, which show only very slight variation. In some Hebrew manuscripts, for example, Ruth begins the *Ketuvim*, perhaps reflecting the idea that it is the oldest book, or, at least, that it narrates the earliest period found in the collection. A similar chronological understanding may have been what led some manuscripts to begin the Writings with Chronicles since the first chapter of that book contains a genealogy that starts with Adam. But by far the most frequent order of the Writings puts the Book of Psalms first, probably because it is the longest. The typical placement of Psalms as the head of the *Ketuvim* may suggest that in some references, "Psalms" is a shorthand way to refer to the Writings as a whole (see, e.g., Luke 24:44).

A closer examination reveals that the *Ketuvim* isn't an entirely random collection since it seems to fall into four parts:

- First are Psalms, Proverbs, and Job, which in later Jewish tradition are called the books of truth. "Truth," in Hebrew, is *'emet*, which in this case serves as an acronym for the first Hebrew letter of each of these books. Each of these books is quite lengthy and concerns crucial arenas of life: the worship of God, the problem of suffering, and wise living. These three books are also united by a special punctuation system that differs from the other books of the Hebrew Bible.
- Next are five short books that are frequently called the *Megillot*, which means "scrolls" in Hebrew: Song of Songs, Ruth, Lamentations, Ecclesiastes, and Esther (though the order can vary). Each of these is associated with a particular liturgical celebration in the course of a year.
- Next is Daniel, an apocalyptic composition that begins with six chapters recounting stories about Daniel and his friends. The narrative quality of the first half of the book might warrant its combination with what follows.

- Finally come Ezra-Nehemiah, originally a single composition, and Chronicles, also one book but split into two, like Samuel and Kings due to length. These last books in the Writings retell the story of Israel, especially Judah (Chronicles), before narrating life in the postexilic period, after the edict of Cyrus allowed the Judean exiles to return from Babylon (Ezra-Nehemiah).

Whatever variations might be present in different traditions, the present chapter adopts the order now commonly found in the Hebrew Bible. This ordering seems to reflect some intentionality; at the very least it has certain effects. To cite an example: Ezra-Nehemiah tells of the time period *after* Chronicles but the Hebrew Bible ends with Chronicles, not Ezra-Nehemiah. This inverted sequence demonstrates that, despite modern obsession with history, chronology is *not* the primary interpretive key to understanding the Writings. The effect of this particular inverted sequence is probably best taken up in the course of the story or stories or "stories" the *Ketuvim* tells, to which we now may turn.

THE STORY/STORIES/"STORIES" THE WRITINGS TELL

PSALMS (*TEHILLIM*)

There are now 150 psalms that make up the Book of Psalms, which is also often called the Psalter. "Psalm" comes from the Greek term *psalmos*, which means "song." "Psalter" comes from Greek *psalterion*, "lyre," one of the instruments, presumably, that was used to play these psalm-songs. Interestingly enough, the earliest Hebrew manuscript to number the psalms (the Leningrad Codex) has only 149 psalms because Psalms 114–115 are counted as a single composition. Earlier Hebrew manuscripts used other means (e.g., blank lines) to signal where one psalm ended and another began. Most of these manuscripts basically had all of the psalms as we now know them, in the same order, but they differed with regard to which psalm was which—sometimes with good reason. Psalms 9 and 10, for instance, are typically set as two psalms in English Bibles, but they may well be one single composition since they seem to follow an acrostic pattern in which successive lines begin with sequential letters of the alphabet. (There are several acrostic poems in the Bible—e.g., Psalms 25, 34, 37, 111, 112, 119, 145; Lamentations 1–4; Prov 31:10–31.) The Septuagint, in fact, treats Psalms 9–10 as just one psalm and does the same with Psalms 114–115 (= Psalm 113 in Greek). In order to achieve a total of 150, the Septuagint divides Psalms 116 and 147 into two poems each: Ps 116:1–9 and Ps 116:10–19; Ps 147:1–11 and Ps 147:12–20. Variations like these explain why the numbering of the psalms frequently differs between the Hebrew Bible and other versions, including English Bibles. And the same is true for verse numbers: in Hebrew, the first line of a psalm is given a verse number no matter what. In English Bibles, if the first part is a superscription that provides various types of information *about* the psalm and not the content proper (see further below) it is *not* given a verse number. To add even more to the confusion, the Septuagint has one additional psalm (Psalm 151) and the Syriac tradition has no less than 155 psalms! These additional Greek and Syriac psalms may have once existed in Hebrew (especially Psalm 151, a version of which was found among the Dead Sea Scrolls), but they are typically treated as Apocryphal or deuterocanonical texts, outside the standard 150 that are found in all editions of the Bible.

Although the Psalter contains (at least) 150 psalms, there is a much smaller number of psalm-types (see Box 4.1). In fact, ever since the pioneering work of Hermann Gunkel (1862–1932) most scholars identify three main types of psalms:

BOX 4.1. TYPES OF PSALMS*

Main Types (total: 105)

Laments (63)

- *Individual Laments (48)*—Psalms 3, 4, 5, 6, 7, 9–10, 13, 14, 17, 22, 25, 26, 27, 28, 31, 35, 38, 39, 40, 41, 42–43, 51, 52, 53, 54, 55, 56, 57, 59, 61, 64, 69, 70, 71, 77, 86, 88, 102, 109, 120, 130, 139, 140, 141, 142, 143
- *Communal Laments (15)*—Psalms 12, 44, 58, 60, 74, 79, 80, 83, 85, 90, 94, 123, 126 (?), 129 (?), 137

Thanksgiving Songs (14)

- *Individual Thanksgiving Songs (9)*—Psalms 18, 30, 32, 34, 66, 92, 116, 118, 138
- *Communal Thanksgiving Songs (5)*—Psalms 65, 67, 75, 107, 124

Hymns/Praise Songs (28)—Psalms 8, 29, 33, 46, 47, 48, 76, 84, 87, 93, 95, 96, 97, 98, 99, 100, 103, 104, 111, 113, 114, 117, 145, 146, 147, 148, 149, 150

Minor Types (total: 45)

Historical Psalms (5)—Psalms 78, 105, 106, 135, 136
Liturgies (8)—Psalms 15, 24, 50, 68 (?), 81, 82 (?), 115, 134
Mixed-Type Psalms (2)—Psalms 36, 108
Royal Psalms (10)—Psalms 2, 20, 21, 45, 72, 89, 101, 110, 132, 144
Songs of Trust (9)—Psalms 11, 16, 23, 62, 63, 91, 121, 125, 131
Song of Zion (1)—Psalm 122 (some hymns, like Psalms 46 and 48, are also considered Songs of Zion)
Torah Psalms (3)—Psalms 1, 19, 119
Wisdom Psalms (7)—Psalms 37, 49, 73, 112, 127, 128, 133

*For convenience, this listing is adapted from Bernard W. Anderson with Steven Bishop, *Out of the Depths: The Psalms Speak for Us Today* (3rd ed.; Louisville: Westminster John Knox, 2000), 219–224. Different categories or terms, and the assignment of various psalms to different types can be easily found in works by different scholars, and so other lists should be consulted.

- *Hymns* or *Praise Songs.* These psalms offer praise for God's deeds or because of God's qualities, inviting others who hear (or read) the psalm to do the same. The familiar word "Hallelujah," sometimes anglicized as "Alleluia," is actually a Hebrew imperative directed to a plural audience: "you (plural) praise Yah!" ("Yah" is a short form of the divine name Yhwh; see Box 2.1.) Although this is not the most frequent type of psalm, it is nevertheless a well-known and favorite type especially in communal worship settings to this day. The popularity of this psalm-type may explain the title of the Book of Psalms in Hebrew: *Tehillim*, which means "Praises." For other examples of hymns/praise songs, see Box 4.1.

- *Lament Psalms*, often called *Prayers for Help* or *Petitions*, which captures their content nicely. These psalms come in two forms: *individual laments*, where a singular speaker ("I") prays for help (e.g., Psalms 3–7), and *communal laments*, where the community as a whole ("we") prays (e.g., Psalm 83, 85). The lament psalms follow a set literary pattern that moves from initial complaint to an ending in praise, with one rather notable exception (Psalm 88). There are more lament psalms in the Psalter than any other type, leading some to call these prayers for help "the backbone of the Psalter." Additional examples of laments can be found in Box 4.1.
- *Thanksgiving Songs:* These songs also come in *individual* and *communal* variations (see, e.g., Psalms 32 and 75, respectively). In the laments, the psalmists frequently promise to praise God once their difficult situations have been rectified; in the thanksgiving songs, they make good on those promises since these psalms look back on past problems that have been resolved in some way (e.g., Ps 30:11–12). Other examples of thanksgiving songs are listed in Box 4.1.

There are additional psalm-types, though none occur with the same frequency as these three major ones. So, for example, there are psalms that center on the king (e.g., Psalms 2, 45), others that discuss the Lord's law (*torah*; Psalms 1, 19, 119), and others that recount key elements in Israel's faith and history (Psalms 78, 105, 106, 135, 136). These (sub)types tend to be identified by *similar content*—they don't follow similar literary patterns or contain the same formal elements like praise songs, laments, and thanksgiving songs do.

Calling the 150 poems in the Psalter "songs" (cf. *psalmos*) suggests that the psalms are connected to oral performance and music (cf. *psalterion*). In fact, many of the psalms have introductory superscriptions that contain technical musical terms referring to either the instruments that were used, the musicians that were involved, perhaps even the tunes that were played (see, e.g., Psalm 4–6, 8–9, 22, 57–59, 75). Many of the psalms also contain the word *selah*, a term that occurs 71 times in the Psalter (e.g., Pss 3:5; 4:3; 7:6; etc.; elsewhere only in Hab 3:3, 9, 13). *Selah* is typically left untranslated because its exact meaning is uncertain. Most scholars believe *selah* is related to musicality in some way, indicating a pause or interlude, an occasion to change pitch, or that a section of the psalm and/or its music should be repeated.

Unfortunately, the music of the psalms is now almost entirely lost. What survives of that, outside the musical terms in the superscriptions, resides entirely in the language itself, in the fact that the psalms are poetry. Indeed, the Psalter is the poetic repository par excellence in the Hebrew Bible. Poetry is found elsewhere in the Old Testament. It figures prominently in the Latter Prophets, for instance, but it abounds in the Writings. The psalms, with the exception of the prosaic superscriptions, are entirely poetic.

Hebrew poetry shares qualities with other poetries known from around the world. It is spare, terse speech employing dense use of figurative language like imagery and metaphor amidst certain formal elements like the use of word-pairs, occasional rhyme or near rhyme, rhythm, assonance, consonance, and so forth—above all else, the setting of the language in verse (poetic lines). The primary formal element of Hebrew poetry, which assists in determining the nature and extent of the poetic line, is called parallelism. Parallelism is how two or occasionally three lines of Hebrew poetry relate to each other in some fashion. Psalm 24:1 provides a useful example:

> The earth is the LORD's and all that is in it
> the world, and those that live in it. (NRSV)

In this verse, "the earth" corresponds to "the world," as does "and all that is in it" with "and those that live in it." The only element in the first line that is not found in the second is "the LORD's." This absence is called *gapping*, and it is common within parallelism because it isn't necessary for the lines to correspond in a one-to-one fashion.

The lines of Ps 24:1 are closely related or "in parallel," with the sentiment of the two virtually identical. This sort of situation is called *synonymous* or *affirming parallelism*. But there are other kinds of parallelism. In *antithetical* or *opposing parallelism*, for example, the two lines offer contrasting sentiments. Consider Ps 1:6:

> For the LORD watches over the way of the righteous,
> but the way of the wicked will perish. (NRSV)

Many different kinds of parallelism could be mentioned with dozens posited by prior researchers. More recent scholarship has stressed that the fundamental point of parallelism is that there is a dynamic relationship of some sort between the poetic lines—a movement or advancement—that, together, makes the sentiment stronger than if it had occurred in just one line alone. As one scholar memorably put it: "A, and what's more, B"—the first line asserts something and the second adds to that, developing it in some dynamic fashion. This basic insight holds true for all instances of Hebrew parallelism, in the Latter Prophets as much as the Psalter, and in Proverbs as well as Job or Song of Songs.

In its present form, the Psalter is comprised of five "books" or collections: Psalms 1–41, Psalms 42–72, Psalms 73–89, Psalms 90–106, and Psalms 107–150. Each ends with a concluding doxology—Pss 41:13; 72:18–19; 89:52; 106:48, with Psalm 150 functioning as the conclusion to Book 5 and the Psalter as a whole. This fivefold structure may be meant to somehow correspond to the five-part Torah (Pentateuch).

While this last point remains uncertain, there is no doubt whatsoever that the Book of Psalms is especially associated with David. The connection is made explicit in later texts like the New Testament (see, e.g., Acts 4:25). Within the Psalter itself, the association with David is mostly found in the superscriptions, like the one found in Psalm 3: "A Psalm of David, when he fled from his son Absalom." There are actually only a handful of superscriptions like this one, which associate specific psalms with particular moments in David's life (see, e.g., Psalms 18, 34). There is a large number of psalms, however, that employ the phrase "of David" (*le-David*) in their superscriptions, though the precise significance of that phrase is uncertain (see Chapter 1 and further below). It is intriguing that Ps 72:20, at the end of Book 2, asserts that "the prayers of David, Jesse's son, are ended." Despite that claim, we are only a few psalms into Book 3 when we encounter another psalm (Psalm 86) containing the superscription "A prayer *le-David*." Three psalms in Book 1 (Psalms 1, 2, and 33) and a decent number in Book 2 *lack* Davidic superscriptions.

These observations show that the Psalter's relationship to David is complicated. What is clear, regardless, is that many of the psalms are *not* ascribed to David. Several other individuals are mentioned in the superscriptions: the Korahites, for example (Psalms 44–49, 83–88; cf. 1 Chr 9:19; 2 Chr 20:19); Asaph, one of Korah's sons (Psalms 50, 73–83; cf. 1 Chr 16:5, 7; 25:1–2; Ezra 3:10); Heman, another of Korah's sons (Psalm 88); even Solomon (Psalms 72, 127) and Moses (Psalm 90). These attributions reveal that the traditional association of the Psalter with David is stereotypical, honorific in some way, a literary trope. It is like ascribing the Torah to Moses or the books of Proverbs, Ecclesiastes, and Song of Songs to Solomon (see below). It is obvious from the Psalter itself, however, that other people besides David are associated with numerous psalms. Indeed, it is far from certain that the phrase *le-David*, "of David," means "written by David." It could just as well mean something like "dedicated to David" or "in Davidic mode" or something to similar effect. A number of royal seals have been found in ancient Israel/Palestine with a similar phrase, *le-melek*, "of the king." These seals were certainly *not* written by the monarch but instead simply designate the jars that bear these stamps as "royal." So, while some scholars believe that a few of the psalms are quite ancient, perhaps going back to David's time if not David himself, most believe that the majority of the psalms come from periods long after David. A few psalms are aware of the exile, for instance (e.g., Psalms 79, 137). But, if the psalms are tight-lipped with regard to exactly *who* wrote them, they are also not forthcoming about precisely *when* they were written. Only a precious few—Psalm 137 above all others—give clear indication of that. And yet, in the history of Jewish and Christian use of the psalms, this lack of historical specificity has been a virtue rather than a vice. The *timelessness* of the psalms has made them always potentially *timely* for the faithful who have prayed them ever since.

The Book of Psalms cannot be easily summarized but there have been numerous attempts to read its "story" from start to finish. If the Psalter tells a "story," it is not a typical one since the psalms are poetry not prose. Any "story" the Book of Psalms tells, or "argument" it makes, must be understood in lyrical categories, not narrative or philosophical ones: there will be much tension to go along with any cohesion, and much will be left unsaid and remain unconcluded.

Earlier scholars, like Gunkel, worked hard at assigning the different psalm-types to particular settings in the life of ancient Israelite worship and practice. Since much of that work is speculative, more recent scholarship has paid more attention to where specific psalms come within the book as a whole, and how they relate to the psalms that precede and follow. Not unlike recent work done on the Prophets, especially the Book of the Twelve (see Chapter 3), this is a shift from the *psalms-in-history* to the *Psalter-as-a-book*. So, according to many scholars, the first two psalms are an intentional editorial introduction to the book, with Psalms 146–150 (especially 150) as its conclusion. Psalms 15–24 are an example of an intentionally structured sub-collection. Another would be the pilgrimage-song collection found in Psalms 120–134 ("The Songs of Ascent").

The present form of the Book of Psalms moves from a beginning in obedience and *torah*-piety (Psalm 1) to a conclusion that ends in boundless praise (Psalm 150). How one moves from Psalm 1 to 150 is precisely through 148 intervening psalms. These psalms are full of many other kinds of things, very little of which concerns *torah* and only some of which is hymnic. Much that intervenes involves profound grief, deep disappointment with God, vehement anger over enemies, and gut-wrenching struggle with sickness and other setbacks. The movement from Psalm 1 to 150 is thus not easy. If that movement is a kind of "story," then it is a truly difficult and non-linear one—one that is as real and as gritty as the stories religious people live out all over the world on a daily basis.

PROVERBS (*MISHLEY SHELOMO*)

The opening verse of the Book of Proverbs attributes what follows to Solomon: "The proverbs of Solomon (*mishley Shelomo*), David's son, Israel's king" (1:1). With this notice, we encounter the third patron saint of the Hebrew Bible and its literature: Moses for Torah, David for Psalms, and Solomon for Proverbs and what appear to be the related texts of Ecclesiastes and the Song of Songs. As with Moses and the Pentateuch and David and the Psalter, however, the ascription of this material to Solomon mustn't be confused with modern notions of authorship. Proverbs, no less than Psalms with its mention of various non-David personnel (Asaph, Korahites, etc.), makes explicit that a decent bit of the material collected in the book comes from sources other than Solomon's wisdom. "The words of the wise" is the heading for Prov 22:17–24:22 (see also 24:23–34), without further description of who these wise people are. Proverbs 30:1–33 is attributed to Agur, Jaqeh's son, while Prov 31:1–9 is said to be the words of Lemuel, king of Massa, which his mother taught him. The majority of the book's proverbs, though, are associated with Solomon (see Prov 1:1; 10:1), even if some of these are said to have been copied down by later officials under King Hezekiah (25:1).

It is hard to know how accurate the attribution to Solomon really is. Like the association of Torah with Moses and psalmody with David, it is likely to be mostly traditional, or, better yet, *literary*: influenced by motifs like Solomon's legendary wisdom (e.g., 1 Kgs 3:1–28; 10:1–13). Indeed, according to 1 Kgs 4:32, Solomon composed 3,000 proverbs and 1,005 songs. He is said to have been well versed in flora and fauna and to have been renowned for his wisdom (1 Kgs 4:33–34). Ascribing texts concerned with wisdom to "Solomon the Wise" makes excellent sense, therefore. And that is exactly the kind of text Proverbs is. It begins by stating that the purpose of "the proverbs of Solomon"

> is to teach wisdom and discipline,
>> to help one understand wise sayings.
> They provide insightful instruction,
>> which is righteous, just, and full of integrity.
> They make the naive mature,
>> the young knowledgeable and discreet.
> The wise hear them and grow in wisdom;
>> those with understanding gain guidance.
> They help one understand proverbs and difficult sayings,
>> the words of the wise, and their puzzles. (Prov 1:2–6; CEB)

But what, exactly, is "wisdom"? The very next verse begins to offer a definition: "Wisdom begins with the fear of the LORD, but fools despise wisdom and instruction" (Prov 1:7; CEB). This verse—especially its notion of the fear or reverence of God—is a kind of motto that is repeated elsewhere with variation (4:7; 9:10; cf. Job 28:28; Prov 2:5; 8:13; 10:27; 14:2, 26–27; 15:16; 16:6; 31:30). In other places in Proverbs, wisdom is less religious than the recurring motto might imply. Wisdom, it seems, is mundane and practical: it includes insight, understanding, knowledge, and so forth. Folly, wisdom's opposite, is marked by ignorance, lack of good sense, arrogance, stubbornness, and the like. Folly frequently stems from or leads to moral culpability; wisdom, on the other hand, has positive ethical outcomes. Perhaps more than anything else, those who are wise are prudent, knowing what to do and when to do it. Prudence is what makes sense of an otherwise logically contradictory and insoluble piece of advice found in Proverbs:

> Do not answer fools according to their folly, or you will be a fool yourself.
>
> Answer fools according to their folly, or they will be wise in their own eyes. (26:4–5; NRSV)

Which one is it? Answer a fool or refuse to answer? Those who are wise will know!

Wisdom material like that preserved in the Book of Proverbs comes from more than one place. The *royal court* is one point of origin. Solomon was a king, after all, Hezekiah's officials copy some of Solomon's proverbs much later (25:1), and Lemuel was king of Massa (31:1). Beyond these explicit connections to named kings, proverbs relating to monarchs and proper behavior among royalty are not infrequent (e.g., 14:28; 16:10; 20:2, 8, 26, 28; cf. Eccl 8:4; 10:20). Another point of origin is the *home*. From the get go, Proverbs enjoins its readers to pay attention to their father's instruction and to their mother's teaching (Prov 1:8; cf. 6:20). Indeed, the first major section of Proverbs is set up as a sequence of addresses from a father to his child: the reader of the book is placed in this role, as the father's "son" who listens to his advice (1:8, 10, 15; 2:1; 3:1, 11, 21; 4:10, 20; 5:1, 20; 6:1, 3, 20; 7:1). Finally, wisdom is also an *international phenomenon*. Proverb collections are found throughout the ancient Near East. One such collection from Egypt, the *Instruction of Amenemope* (thirteenth or twelfth century BCE), was used as a source by the author of Prov 22:17–24:22.

After the opening collection of parent-child instructions (Prov 1:1–9:18), the large middle of the book (10:1–31:9) is made up of two-line proverbs that operate per the canons of Hebrew poetry, especially parallelism. Proverbs concludes with an acrostic poem celebrating the woman of substance (31:10–31).

Like the Psalter, it is not easy to read a "story" from the Book of Proverbs, though it, no less than the Psalms, can be assessed on larger levels than just an individual proverb or two. Such an approach applies to subunits like "the proverbs of Solomon" (10:1–22:16) or "the words of the wise" (22:17–24:22), but it can also be performed on the book as a literary whole—as a grand poetic sequence that is more than just the sum of its parts. In this latter mode, Proverbs tells of a "son" who begins at home, learning life lessons at his father's knee (1:1–9:18) before he makes his way into the wider world where wisdom is tested and tried amidst a mind-boggling number of scenarios (10:1–31:9). In the end, the boy—now a full-grown man—marries a woman of significant means and wisdom (31:10–31). Indeed, the similarities between this spouse and Wisdom, personified as a woman earlier in the book (see, e.g., 1:20–33; 8:1–36), are unmistakable. Read in this way, the Book of Proverbs tells a success story of one young person's path to and attainment of Wisdom, a wisdom that is rooted in godly reverence and includes one's dearest spouse (cf. Eccl 9:9). In the play of the literature—and the play of Wisdom (Prov 8:30–31)—that person ends up being none other than the reader of the book.

JOB (*'IYOV*)

The Book of Job takes its name from its primary character. Job's Hebrew name (*'Iyov*) means something like "the enemy, attacked one" or "where is the (divine) father?" Either suits the composition and the protagonist quite well since Job is subjected to intense misfortune in the book and, throughout it, seeks audience with "God the Father Almighty" (to cite from a much later, Christian creed). When Job finally gets it ... well, it isn't all it's cracked up to be!

Several critical issues in the Book of Job have long confounded scholars. The book begins and ends with a prose framework about Job and, eventually, his friends (1:1–2:13; 42:7–17); in between these prose bookends, there is a lengthy poetic dialogue in which Job and his friends speak to each other directly (3:1–31:40), which is followed by additional poetry from Elihu, God, and Job (chaps. 32:1–42:6). The relationship of the prose frame and poetic middle is debated: is one earlier than the other and, if so, which is which? The figure of "Job" may be a traditional one in light of texts like Ezek 14:14, 20—maybe even James 5:11, which many New Testament scholars believe refers, not to the biblical book of Job, but to a later, pseudepigraphical composition known as the *Testament of Job*. If the

Job character is a traditional one, it would be easy to imagine a prose tale or a poetic dialogue—or even both—growing up around it. Again, it is hard to know which would be earlier than the other if they were, in fact, originally discrete.

The prose framework itself may not be a unified piece since a key character in the prologue, "the Adversary" (CEB), does not recur in the epilogue. "The Adversary" is *ha-satan* in Hebrew but is not yet the fully developed "Satan" familiar from later texts in the New Testament. In the Book of Job, this term appears with the definite article, which indicates that it is a title not a proper name. The title refers to the particular, adversarial role played by one member of the divine entourage (1:6–7; 2:1–2).

Within the poetic sections of the book, there are three cycles of speeches in which Job and his friends take turns addressing themselves to the vexed matters at hand. The first two cycles (chaps. 3–14, 15–21) follow a set order with Job speaking first, then Eliphaz, Job, Bildad, Job, Zophar, and Job again. The cycle then repeats. The third cycle is different (chaps. 22–28). Bildad's third speech is very short (25:1–6) and Zophar does not speak at all, though some scholars have wondered if part of what Job says in his very long speeches in the third cycle may have once belonged to a now missing speech by Zophar. Whatever the case, the third cycle seems to be in disarray. Perhaps this is a compositional issue: a speech from Zophar has been lost or misattributed. Or perhaps this is a literary device that shows how the friends have run out of arguments and how all of the interlocutors are now talking past one another. Whatever the case, Job is quite clear that his friends are of little help. He calls them "plasterers of lies" and "ineffective healers" (13:4; CEB). And so, in the end, Job can do nothing but sum up his final defense and take it directly to God (29:1–31:40).

At this point in the book, another critical question arises. We are suddenly introduced to a new character, Elihu, who doesn't appear earlier in the book and is not mentioned in the prose ending either. Elihu is said to be very angry with Job and with the three friends since they had no good answer for him (32:2–3). Elihu is younger than the others, which explains his previous deferential silence (32:4, 6). But once he bursts on the scene, he gives an extended speech or series of speeches (32:1–37:24). Scholars debate the Elihu materials: is it a secondary addition or is it original to the book? Is it another failed "friendly" response to Job or is it to be understood as superior to the discourse of the three friends, maybe even the author's own take on the difficult problem of suffering?

At the very least the Elihu materials form an interlude between Job's final summation that calls God to account and the divine response that comes, finally, in 38:1–42:6. There are two divine speeches with Job offering a brief reply to each. The issues here are not compositional but interpretive. God is said to "answer" Job from the whirlwind (38:1; 40:6), but there is almost nothing in the divine speeches that speaks directly to Job's own suffering. Instead, God seems to direct Job to the wild, even chaotic nature of creation, culminating in extended passages praising the two frightening beasts known as Behemoth and Leviathan (40:15–41:34). Perhaps God is overwhelming Job; after the first divine speech, Job says he is "of little worth" (40:4) and after the second admits that he had "spoken about things I didn't understand" (42:3). But maybe the divine speeches are not meant to intimidate Job so much as reorient him, showing him that there can be no adequate answer for any one individual's suffering, especially from a cosmic perspective. A cosmic perspective may even reframe what does and does not count as suffering. Whatever the case, God gives no specific answer to Job's specific suffering, perhaps because an individualized response would not be meaningful to future readers of the book—all of whom share in the problem of suffering, in one form or another, but few of whom share in Job's particular brand of it. Furthermore, even if the cosmic answer of God out of the whirlwind is not exactly built to Job's smaller, human scale, it is nevertheless the case that Job got, in the end, what he wanted: audience with Almighty God. It may not be all that it's cracked up to be, but Job got it nevertheless. And he got it exactly where he wanted it and, evidently, when he needed it most: on the ash heap at the very end of his rope.

The book ends with a prose epilogue that, according to some readers, is an overly facile "happy ending." God doubles Job's earlier possessions (42:11) and is said to bless his later days more than his former ones (42:12). Job also has more children: seven sons and three daughters and, notably, gives his daughters names that relate to the beauty of life. Also noteworthy is that Job gives his daughters an inheritance along with their brothers (cf. Num 27:1–8, discussed in Chapter 2). Upon closer inspection, this is not a happy ending—at least not of the simplistic or syrupy-sweet variety. Job does not receive his first children back from the dead, nor his lost servants. They remain dead forever. But Job himself is restored—to his community and his family, who care for him (42:11), and even to some degree to his friends, since they learn directly from God that it is Job, not they, who spoke "correctly" of God (42:7, 8).

It is possible that this divine testimony about Job's right speech is better translated not as speaking correctly *about* God but *to* God—Job is the only interlocutor who addresses himself directly to the Lord. If so, the Book of Job is not only a profoundly theological book but also a profound book about how to do theology. How to do theology correctly, according to Job (and the God of Job), is by direct address *to* God, not by simply talking *about* God. If so, Job's preferred way of doing theology finds deep resonance with the Book of Psalms.

THE SONG OF SONGS (*SHIR HA-SHIRIM*)

The opening verse of the Song of Songs gives the book its title: "The song of songs, which is for Solomon" (1:1; CEB). Even after just one verse, several things require comment. First, the construction "the song of songs" (*shir ha-shirim*) is probably a superlative construction in Hebrew meaning "the best song," just like "king of kings" means "the greatest king" and "lord of lords" means "the ultimate lord" (cf. Ezra 7:12; Ezek 26:7; Dan 2:37; 1 Tim 6:15; Rev 17:14; 19:16). Greek and Latin Bibles have the same title as the Hebrew, though "The Song of Songs" is often abbreviated to simply "The Song."

Second, the mention of Solomon in v. 1 of the book has led to another common name for it: "The Song of Solomon." Some English translations suggest this connection by how they translate the opening verse: "The Song of Songs, which is Solomon's" (NRSV) or "The Song of Songs, by Solomon" (NJPSV). But the part that mentions Solomon in 1:1 is identical to the phrasing about David in the Psalms (see above): *le-Shelomo*. And so, here in the Song, as there in the Psalms, this particular construction does not necessarily designate who authored the book. Indeed, Solomon is spoken of in the book only in the third person (1:5; 3:7, 9, 11; 8:11–12), whereas the dominant male voice speaks in the first person. Furthermore, while

Solomon is (in)famous for his many wives and concubines (1 Kgs 11:3), the Song is resolutely focused on the love of *just one* man and one woman. Indeed, the end of the book may even poke fun at Solomon: while the great king had a famous vineyard (8:11; perhaps a veiled reference to his harem?), the man in the Song cares only for his beloved—Solomon can have his thousand, the speaker wants only his one and only (8:12; cf. 6:9)! Even so, like *le-David* in the Psalms, *le-Shelomo* is at least a dedication of some sort, perhaps because Solomon was known to be a composer (1 Kgs 4:32), an expert in botany and biology (1 Kgs 4:33), and, evidently, a capacious lover (1 Kgs 11:3). The rabbis went so far as to track the books associated with Solomon onto his lifecycle. Song of Songs, they said, was written by Solomon as a young, virile man; Proverbs was written at the height of his maturity; he composed Ecclesiastes when he was old and embittered (see below).

One final option for the title is that it might mean something like "a song (made) of songs," which is to say, "an anthology." An anthology of sorts is exactly what many scholars have thought the Song to be: a collection of much smaller, originally independent poems that were only later combined. If so, the various poems likely stem from different authors if not also different time periods. But others think the Song is one poem, or at least a lyric sequence that, now, has its own literary integrity. Others have understood the composition to be a drama of sorts. This last option seems unlikely: while the male and female voices are identifiable and distinguishable, it is not easy to trace a plot in the book, and some of the other "roles" and who plays them remain murky.

Most contemporary scholars treat the Song of Songs as a collection of secular love poetry, some of which may have been used in weddings. The book's structure is not straightforward and, as such, seems more indicative of an anthology or of a lyric sequence than any sort of narrative or drama. The overall sense of the book seems clear, however. The Song celebrates the love between a man and a woman. The love these two share is noteworthy, not only because it is frequently erotic but also because it is marked by equality and mutuality. The prominence of the woman, in particular, is striking amidst the patriarchy that dominates so much of the Hebrew Bible. Of the two lovers, she has both the first word (Song 1:2–7) and the last (8:14). She also speaks more than the man. These factors have led some interpreters to wonder if the Song of Songs was authored by a woman.

While that point remains uncertain, the erotic aspects of the book are unmistakable and unavoidable. Equally manifest, however, is how these aspects are carefully, even delicately presented. Once the mind is attuned to sexual connotations, it is easy to find them everywhere in the Song, but the Song itself, while allusive, is a long way from pornography. Instead, one finds sensuality and sexuality portrayed with a healthy dose of poetic reticence. The lovers' secret garden may be full of double entendre—it most certainly is!—but it remains a garden nonetheless: perhaps more, but certainly not less than that.

We learn about love in the Song by what the lovers say about it and about each other. In Hebrew, the two voices can be distinguished given certain grammatical features in the language. He likes to call her "my dearest" (CEB; 1:9, 15; 2:2, 10, 13; 4:1, 7; 5:2; 6:4), while she calls him "my love" (CEB; 1:13, 14, 16; 2:3, 8, 9, 10, 16, 17; 4:16; 5:2, 4, 6, 8, 10, 16; 6:2; 7:11, 13; 8:14). The typical content of their speeches also differs. She might be said to be lovesick over the man (see 2:5; 5:8), and she tells stories about him (2:8–17; 3:1–5; 5:2–8). He, on the other hand, could be said to be awestruck by the woman (see 4:9; 6:5), and he praises her physique in great detail in three distinct poems, the details of which, if depicted woodenly, are rather bemusing (see 4:1–15; 6:4–10; 7:1–9). The woman, too, praises the man's physical beauty (5:10–16). While the man and woman are each distinct and unique, the two are nevertheless united and equal in their love. In one place, the woman finishes the sentence begun by the man (7:9)—exactly what those in love so often do!

The Song never once mentions God. An unusual word in 8:6, *shalhebetyah* (CEB: "a divine flame") is sometimes thought to contain an abbreviated reference to the divine name (the *yah* part; see Box 2.1). But this is far from certain and, even if true, it would be highly oblique if not downright opaque. The absence of God coupled with the book's focus on real, even erotic love has led many to wonder how and why the Song made it into the biblical canon. Perhaps as a way to justify that canonization, or as a side effect of its canonization, the Song has long been interpreted as a religious allegory. In this view, which is commonly enountered in classical Jewish and Christian sources, the Song is not only or merely about two human lovers; instead, or additionally, the two lovers somehow represent God's love for Israel or Christ's love for the church (and vice versa). In more spiritual perspectives, this line of interpretation extends to God's love for the individual believer's soul (and vice versa).

It is very hard to say if allegorical meanings were intended by the original author(s) of the Song. Many modern scholars vigorously reject allegorical interpretation. But with the exception of Esther, every other book of the Old Testament mentions God—often extensively—and so it is understandable if God is "on the brain" when one comes to the Song as well, especially given the prominence of the marriage metaphor to describe the God-Israel relationship elsewhere in the Hebrew Bible. In this regard, it is worth noting that only one medieval Jewish commentary has survived that does not engage in allegorical interpretation. The allegorical approach was dominant and pervasive for a very long time within both Christianity and Judaism. Moreover, even if one resists allegory proper but wishes to read the Song as somehow pertinent for or representative of all lovers or the best of human love, that is still a kind of expansive reading that is not too far off from more developed allegorical approaches. Whatever the case, within the Bible proper, the Song can be seen as offering an inner-biblical response to Genesis 2–3. Both texts concern a man and a woman in a garden of delight, but in the Song, in contrast to Genesis, the story ends not in curse, distance, and domination (Gen 3:16–19) but in mutual, egalitarian love. It is perhaps for reasons like these that the great Rabbi Akiva in the first century CE said that, while all Scripture is holy, the Song of Songs is the most holy of all.

Last but not least, the Song of Songs is considered one of the five scrolls or *Megillot*, a special sub-collection within the Writings (see above). These five compositions can all fit on one scroll together, and each is associated with an important liturgical celebration. Collecting five books relating to five key religious holidays may reflect a desire to have yet another pentad to accompany the five books of Psalms and the five books of the Torah (a few Hebrew manuscripts actually place the *Megillot* immediately after the Torah!). Be that as it may, the Song of Songs is the scroll that is read at Passover, which, in Judaism, is often thought to be the beginning of the courtship between God and Israel. The book is also read at the onset of Sabbath, a marriage of sorts between Israel and that holy day. Either use suggests that the Song of Songs—no less than other books of the Bible—is about far more than what it seems to be about.

RUTH

The Book of Ruth is a beautiful short story, widely praised for its literary art. Appearing where it does in English Bibles (see above), it prepares for the Book of Samuel by ending with David's genealogy, but it is also a blessed respite after the terrible violence—especially violence done against women—in the Book of Judges.

Ruth is a story involving not one but two female protagonists, an unparalleled situation in the Hebrew Bible. These two women, the immigrant Moabite Ruth and her Israelite mother-in-law Naomi, both of whom are widows, must make their way amidst loss, famine, and socio-economic insecurity. And that is exactly what they do. Ruth ends up married to a pillar in the Bethlehem community, Boaz, who provides for her and Naomi. The son born to Ruth and Boaz, Obed, will end up as David's grandfather (Ruth 4:17–22). Naomi is also given credit for Obed and she plays a role in his care (4:14–16). She who was once full, then empty in grief (1:20–21), is full once again.

The story is an idyllic one, quite literally so since much takes place in the fields of Bethlehem during barley harvest (1:22; 2:1–23). There is a notable lack of villains in the account; instead, the community is marked by mutual care and attention. People frequently greet each other in the name of the Lord and bless one another in God's name (2:4, 12, 20; 3:10; 4:11, 14). A central motif in the book is the key Hebrew term *ḥesed*. This word has proven notoriously difficult to translate, but it is a rich term that encompasses loyalty, faithfulness, even kindness. The term appears three times in Ruth. In 1:8 and 2:20, it is God's *ḥesed* that is mentioned; in 3:10, it is Ruth's *ḥesed* that is the focus. These two types of *ḥesed* are related somehow, or so it would seem. There are points of connection here between the Book of Ruth and other books in the *Megillot*, like Esther, which never mentions God but abounds in what might be understood as divine coincidence (see below). Another connection is with the Song of Songs. Reading Ruth after the Song gives one even more reason (if more were needed) to see the encounter at the threshing floor in Ruth 3 as intimate in some way—though that encounter, no less than the Song, is told discreetly with a good bit of reticence.

Ruth is traditionally read during Shavu'ot, the Festival of Weeks (see Exod 34:22; Num 28:26; Deut 16:10–12), which is associated with receiving and accepting the Torah at Sinai. The connection works well because Ruth appears to cover the weeks from the beginning of barley harvest to the end of wheat harvest. The connection to Sinai and Torah is evocative since the book suggests that, Deut 23:3 notwithstanding, a foreigner actually *can* be incorporated into Israel, affirming both that people and their God (Ruth 1:16). Indeed, according to Ruth, such a foreigner might even end up as great-grandmother to Israel's most famous king. *Ḥesed*, says the Book of Ruth—in both divine and human varieties—is far more important than ethnicity.

LAMENTATIONS (*EYKAH*)

The Book of Lamentations derives its English name from the Talmud's reference to the book as *qinot*, "elegies" or "lamentations." The Greek title is *Threnoi*, "dirges," which comes into Latin as *Threni*. In Hebrew, the title is *Eykah*, the first word of the first verse (1:1; see also 2:1; 4:1). *Eykah* is an interjection: "Alas!" (NJPSV), "Oh no!" (CEB), or "How …!" as in "How lonely sits the city that was once full of people!" (1:1; NRSV). As noted earlier, the Septuagint adds a superscription to Lamentations that attributes the book's authorship to Jeremiah. It also places Lamentations after that prophetic book. In the *Ketuvim*, however, Lamentations is one of the *Megillot*, read on the ninth day of the month of Av, the day that commemorates the destructions of the first and second temples in 587 BCE and 70 CE, respectively. This liturgical use is more than appropriate since Lamentations is a compelling and disturbing collection of poems about the destruction of Jerusalem at the hand of the Babylonian Empire.

The five chapters of the Book of Lamentations correspond to five discrete poems, the first four of which are acrostics, with chapter 3 a triple-acrostic: three successive lines use the same letter of the alphabet before moving to the next letter in the next three lines. Why this form should be adopted in chapters 1–4 is unclear. Perhaps the acrostic form indicates that Lamentations contains the "A to Z" of grief, with the alphabet providing a structure to signify the totality of Jerusalem's destruction and the vastness of the pain associated with that. Alternatively (or additionally), the acrostic form might be a means to comprehend what is otherwise incomprehensible, a way to bring order to a chaotic situation and form to an experience that was profoundly form*less* if not also *de*forming. It is intriguing that, after chapter 1, the acrostic form is somewhat imperfectly used. Chapters 2–4 each have two letters out of order (2:16–17; 3:46–51; 4:16–17). Is this a sign that even a structure as secure as the alphabet cannot contain the sorrow of these poems and the suffering of Jerusalem? Chapter 5 also suggests the ultimate failure of this poetic form: this chapter is not an acrostic at all, though the 22-letter Hebrew alphabet may leave its trace in the 22 verses of this last poem.

The significance of the triple-acrostic in chapter 3 is hard to determine. On the one hand, its particularly developed form and its placement in the center of the composition suggest a certain kind of importance—not to mention poetic skill (only Psalm 119 surpasses it with its eight-line acrostic form). It is perhaps for these reasons that some interpreters have placed special emphasis on Lamentations 3, which also contains some of the more hopeful sentiments found within the book:

> Certainly the faithful love of the LORD hasn't ended;
>> certainly God's compassion isn't through!
> They are renewed every morning.
>> Great is your faithfulness.
> I think: The LORD is my portion! Therefore, I'll wait for him.
> The LORD is good to those who hope in him,
>> to the person who seeks him. (3:22–25; CEB)
>
> …
>
> My Lord definitely won't reject forever.
> Although he has caused grief,
>> he will show compassion in measure with his covenant loyalty.
> He definitely doesn't enjoy affliction, making humans suffer. (3:31–33; CEB)

The other chapters of Lamentations aren't nearly so positive, however, and in some instances offer sentiments that are quite opposite to those found in chapter 3 (see, e.g., 1:15; 2:1–8, 17; 4:11, 16; 5:20). Moreover, since chapter 3 is smack-dab in the middle of the book, not at the end, it is hard to know how significant these hopeful moments are, coming, as they do, in mid-stream. At the very least, given the lyrical nature of the poems in Lamentations and in the book as a whole, these positive elements must be held in poetic tension with other, less hopeful moments. The hopeful sentiments do not eclipse the others—though the reverse is also true.

What Lamentations offers, therefore, is a complicated take on the destruction of Jerusalem and the various roles—human and divine—that were part of that tragedy. In this way, the messiness of the poetry reflects the messiness of life, especially life confronted by death. Lamentations is thus not for the faint-hearted nor for the weak of stomach (see 2:20; 4:10 and cf. Deut 28:53–57; note also Lam 2:11–12, 19; 4:2–4). Indeed, the sheer brutality of the book is no doubt what led to the Jewish practice of repeating 5:21 after 5:22 when Lamentations is read liturgically so as to not end on a dire note (see NJPSV). Perhaps that is unnecessary, however, if only because the last verse of the book seems to end rather elliptically: "*unless* you have rejected us completely, become far too angry with us …" (5:22; cf. CEB, NRSV). This "unless" leaves the door of Lamentations open. Perhaps the Lord *has not* rejected Israel, despite and in spite of the tragedy of Jerusalem's brutal destruction. It is the burden of the Latter Prophets, especially, but also several other texts in the Bible, including in the Writings, to demonstrate exactly that.

ECCLESIASTES (QOHELET)

The Book of Ecclesiastes is something of an enigma. Even the Hebrew designation of the book, Qohelet, is curious. Qohelet is evidently a name or perhaps a title of some sort since it occurs with the definite article in Eccl 12:8: "*the* Qohelet." The grammatical form of this word is feminine but the speaker in the book—who goes by "Qohelet" (or "the Qohelet")—is referred to as male. The meaning of Qohelet is also unclear. It is usually thought to mean something like "Gatherer" and, by extension, "Teacher"—one who gathers proverbs, for instance, or one who gathers the community together for instruction (cf. 12:9–10). The German reformer, Martin Luther (1483–1546), famously translated the term "Preacher," perhaps because the Greek title of the book, *Ecclesiastes*, is related to the word used in the New Testament for "church" (*ekklesia*), though the same translation works for *Qohelet*, which is related to the Hebrew word for "assembly."

As noted above, the rabbis posited that Solomon wrote Ecclesiastes when he was old and dour. That seems about right: according to one modern scholar, "Qoheleth is crabby." There is no discernible structure to the book, which complicates its reading, as does the fact that it seems riddled with contradictions. Maybe both qualities are further evidence of the author's disagreeable disposition. Though the book frequently mentions God, the relationship between the speaker and the Deity is, at best, cool. As another scholar put it, when the notion of the fear or reverence of God occurs in Qohelet it means "be on guard against Elohim"! (see Box 2.1 for the divine name *Elohim*).

Attributing the book to Solomonic authorship may be traditional, but it is unlikely. The opening chapter definitely evokes Solomon: only one of David's immediate sons was king over all Israel in Jerusalem (1:1, 12). The book then proceeds to talk about this king's wisdom and riches, all of which are familiar tropes from Solomon's reign (see 1 Kings 3–11). But this literary persona—the speaker in the guise of King Solomon—is dropped after Eccl 2:12. When the book speaks of kings later, it speaks of them in the third person, as entities that the speaker and his audience must submit to and respect (8:4; 10:20; cf. 4:13, 15; 5:9; 9:14; 10:16–17). The Hebrew that is used in Ecclesiastes also reveals that it dates from an era long after Solomon. Among other things, the book contains two Persian loan words (*pardes*, "park," in 2:5; and *pitgam*, "sentence, condemnation," in 8:11) which means that it must date from sometime after the start of the Persian period (538 BCE). In fact, most scholars would put the book even later, sometime in the Hellenistic period (after 332 BCE). Whatever the case, careful readers will note that Qohelet is actually not the author of the book. Instead, an anonymous narrator introduces the book (1:1–2) and concludes it (12:8–14) with remarks *about* "the Teacher" (cf. also 7:27, which also speaks of Qohelet in the third person).

The theme of Ecclesiastes is announced in the book's opening verse: "Perfectly pointless, says the Teacher, perfectly pointless. Everything is pointless" (1:2; CEB). The Hebrew word translated as "pointless" is *hevel*. It is a key term in Ecclesiastes, used more than 30 times in the book. Various translations include "vanity" (NRSV) or "futility" (NJPSV). This word is also the name of Cain's brother, way back in Genesis 4. In that story, "Abel" (*Hevel*) is present one minute and gone the next; he doesn't even get a speaking part! In Ecclesiastes, *hevel* refers to something similarly ephemeral, elusive—like chasing after wind, to use another of Qohelet's favorite phrases (1:14, 17; 2:11, 17, 26; 4:4, 6, 16; 6:9), or like herding cats, to use a modern idiom. Even if some particular thing isn't entirely meaningless, the use of *hevel* in Ecclesiastes indicates that the meaning in question can't be grasped. And that, Qohelet says, is exactly how God intended it (see 3:11; 7:14; 8:17; cf. also 1:15 with 7:13). In fact, as he goes on to assert, even those who are wise are unable to grasp what is really going on (8:17)—a stunning critique of the entire pursuit of wisdom. (Of course, if accurate, that critique undercuts Qohelet's own authority on these matters!)

Readers hoping for some development or an uptick in Qohelet's mood at the end of the book will be disappointed. Qohelet ends where he began: "Perfectly pointless, says the Teacher, everything is pointless" (12:8; CEB). And yet, despite the fact that he seems thoroughly unreformed, the narrator immediately commends Qohelet for being wise in addition to being a skillful, knowledgeable, truthful, and rhetorically savvy teacher of the people (12:9–10).

The epilogue continues by sounding some notes that many interpreters have found a wee bit too orthodox for crabby ole' Qohelet. For many scholars, the sentiment in 12:13–14 sounds more like Deuteronomy than something Qohelet would say. For this reason, scholars have often deemed this epilogue a secondary addition, one that sought to somehow save or baptize Qohelet by making it more palatable, thereby facilitating its inclusion in the canon of Scripture. Other interpreters are not so sure, thinking that there is real resonance between the epilogue and Qohelet's general disposition elsewhere in the book. If the epilogue is brief and leaves some aspects of the book underdeveloped, how could it be otherwise? Summations are, by definition, reductive—including any summary of what Qohelet "is all about."

Despite Qohelet's crabby temperament and realistic (if not pessimistic) outlook on life, he nevertheless commends enjoyment in seven important passages in the book (2:24–26; 3:12–13, 22; 5:18–20; 7:14; 8:15; 9:7–10; 11:7–10). It might be going slightly too far to call Qohelet a "preacher of joy," but there is no reason to downplay these passages or treat them as less important or serious than any others in the book. It is worth noting that, within the *Megillot*, Ecclesiastes is the scroll associated with Sukkoth, the Festival of Booths, which was a joyous celebration (see Lev 23:33–36; Deut 16:13–17). Reading Qohelet in that kind of setting could, of course, provide a sobering effect. It seems far more likely, however, given its commendation of joy, that reading the book during Sukkoth is a means to encourage people to enjoy the festival—and all of life—to the maximum extent possible. To borrow from the words of the Teacher: "Go, eat your food joyfully and drink your wine happily because God has already accepted what you do" (9:7; CEB).

ESTHER

The title of the Book of Esther, named after its primary protagonist, first appears in the Septuagint. Esther's name may be related to that of the Mesopotamian goddess Ishtar or the Persian word *stareh* ("star"). Her Hebrew name was Hadassah, which means "myrtle" (Esth 2:7). Esther's two names are related to her dual identity: she was, first, a Jew who, second, lived in the non-Jewish world of Persia. Dual names and renaming were common in such contexts (cf. Gen 41:45; Dan 1:6–7).

The world Esther lives in is fraught—and on more than one level. The book begins with the Persian Queen Vashti's refusal to come when King Ahasuerus summoned her. This displeased the king who disciplined her, and all insubordinate wives in the kingdom, in response. Orders went out across the empire that "each husband should rule over his own house" (Esth 1:22; CEB). To be a woman in such an empire is to be in a threatening situation; Esther's own situation is further complicated by the fact that she is an orphan, under the protection of her cousin, Mordecai (2:7). Esther is included in the beauty contest to replace Vashti and wins—a dubious distinction given the unfortunate turn of events with the previous queen.

The narrative notes that Esther was not forthcoming about her race or family background because Mordecai had instructed her to keep both secret (2:10, 20). This hint that anti-Semitism is in the air of Ahasuerus' kingdom becomes a major theme in the chapters that follow. Chapter 3 introduces us to a villain named Haman, who is said to be an Agagite, a descendent of the Amalekite king

Agag (see 1 Samuel 15). Mordecai is a Benjaminite, from the line of Kish (Esth 2:5), just as King Saul was (1 Sam 9:1–2). The ancient conflict between Saul and Agag is thus renewed in Mordecai and Haman. Haman is incensed when Mordecai refuses to bow down to him (3:5). Upon learning he is a Jew (3:6), Haman uses Mordecai's independence as irrational pretense to kill all of the Jewish people throughout the kingdom (3:6, 8–9). Equally absurdly, the king agrees (3:10–15).

This, then, is the main problem that drives the book's plot. Haman wishes to wipe out all of the Jews, but Esther, now in the palace as the king's favorite (2:17), has the chance to save them, but will she? Mordecai puts the matter to Esther directly, pointing out that she, too, is likely to die due to this decree; furthermore, she may have come to power for just such an opportune moment as this (4:12–14). But things aren't so straightforward. The matter is complicated because the queen is not to go to the king without being summoned under pain of death (4:11). Yes, Esther's world is fraught—and on more than one level.

Esther courageously decides to act on behalf of her people (5:1–8; 7:1–4). This leads to the ironic honoring of Mordecai (6:1–13; 8:1–2) and the demise of Haman (7:5–8) who is quite literally hoisted on his own petard (7:9–10; cf. 5:14). Unexpectedly, the story indicates that the king's previous law enacted under Haman still stands: it is one of the proverbial "laws of the Medes and Persians" which cannot be undone (cf. 1:19; Dan 5:28; 6:8, 12, 15). A new law must be written and distributed. This one does not repeal Haman's, but it does allow the Jews to defend themselves (Esth 8:7–17). When the fateful day set by Haman arrives, the Jews turn the tables on their enemies and roundly defeat them (9:1–19). This event is celebrated in the festival of Purim (9:26), and the Book of Esther is read during Purim to this day. (Purim means "lots," which is how the date was decided [3:7; 9:24].)

Some have seen in the Book of Esther a model for Jewish life in the Gentile world, not unlike the stories of Joseph in Egypt or Daniel and his friends in Babylon. Aspects of Esther resonate with such an interpretation: among other things, the book shows how it is often costly to be faithful in a hostile world. In other ways, this interpretation seems to falter. The non-Jewish characters seem caricatured, for one thing. They are irrational, absurd, and profoundly hostile—Gentiles are not always portrayed in such ways elsewhere in the Old Testament. For another thing, the Jews' response to their enemies is equally hostile. If this is a model for life in the Gentile world, it is a violent one, though admittedly in a self-defensive mode.

Another complicating factor for seeing the book as a kind of ideal presentation is that there is no mention of God in the Hebrew version of Esther. We encountered the same situation in the Song of Songs. There, the presence of God in so many other parts of the Bible may be seen to exercise pressure to somehow "find the divine" in the Song, which led to allegorical and other types of religious readings. The same might hold true for the Book of Esther, though not with reference to allegory. Esther too, amidst the many books of the Bible that mention God, may also be read as revealing traces of the divine presence. There is a good bit more to go on, in this regard, in Esther than in the Song of Songs. The book mentions fasting and mourning rituals like sackcloth and ashes (4:1, 3, 16; 9:31). Some interpreters have seen in Mordecai's mention of help "from another place" a veiled reference to God (4:14). If so, it is an understated one, and this interpretation may have more to do with Esther's canonical neighbors, which talk a lot about God, than it does with what the book itself says.

Whatever the case, it seems unlikely that Esther should be seen as an entirely secular composition. Instead, human initiative combines with poetic justice in ways that seem to imply divine providence. Things are far more religiously explicit in the Greek version of the book, which adds more than 100 verses that aren't found in the Hebrew version. These verses are spread across six passages known as the Additions to Esther, which are part and parcel of the book of Esther in Catholic and Orthodox traditions (see Chart 1.1). These additions are chocked full of references to "God" and to "the Lord" (24 times in 22 verses and 23 times in 18 verses, respectively). They also showcase Mordechai and Esther praying—something that the Hebrew version never does (but cf. 4:1).

According to some scholars, it is possible that the Hebrew version of Esther that we now have was derived from a more religious version like the one preserved in Greek. If that is true, it would mean that religious aspects were edited *out* of the current Hebrew version, making it less religious and more (though still not entirely) secular. Why that would have been done is unclear, but one possibility might be because some of what happens in the book is, in fact, *not* exemplary—the retaliatory violence, for instance. Removing references to God in such presentations makes it harder to use God as a justification for other types of violence (cf. the discussion of Judges 17–21 in Chapter 3).

Whatever the case, the Book of Esther—or perhaps better, the *Books* of Esther (Greek and Hebrew versions)—remains an excellent example of the biblical short story or historical novella (cf. Genesis 37–50, Ruth, Jonah). While many of the literary details in Esther seem to have some authenticity about them, scholars have identified enough that is inaccurate in the book to lead most to deem Esther a piece of historical fiction—an account that either led to the holiday of Purim or provided an explanation for its existence and origin.

DANIEL

The Book of Daniel is an apocalypse, a Greek word that has to do with the unveiling, revealing, or disclosure of future realities (*apocalypsis*; cf. Rev 1:1). Parts of the Latter Prophets, too, relate to future realities, but these are typically far more immediate, less specific in their predictions, and less fantastically symbolical. Because of such factors, these bits of the prophets are typically seen as *eschatological* or, at most, *proto-apocalyptic*, but not yet full-blown *apocalyptic*.

In later periods, apocalyptic is a distinct literary genre, attested in the Christian Bible only in Daniel in the Old Testament and Revelation in the New but found in a large number of non-biblical texts. Daniel's status as something more or other than biblical prophecy is signaled by its inclusion in the Writings, rather than the Latter Prophets, within the Hebrew Bible. As previously discussed, most English Bibles, following the Septuagint, place Daniel with the Prophets, after Ezekiel and before the Book of the Twelve. This creates a very different set of expectations about the book—that its futuristic aspects are identical to what is found in the prophetic books. But this is not accurate if only because apocalyptic is not prophecy, nor vice versa. It is true that early Christian interpretation preferred a prophetic connotation for Daniel in light of the relationship of texts like Dan 7:13–14 ("one like a son of man") or 12:2 (which mentions resurrection) to various texts in the New Testament. But rabbinic interpretation, partly in response to this Christian tendency, preferred to think of Daniel as a visionary, not a prophet (*b. Meg.* 3a; *b. Sanh.* 94a).

The origins of apocalyptic literature are debated. Some scholars relate it to prophecy, especially eschatological and proto-apocalyptic aspects; others relate apocalyptic to certain tendencies in wisdom circles; still others find evidence of foreign influence, especially the strong dualism that marked Persian religion. Apocalyptic is probably some combination of all of these options.

One common element across biblical and non-biblical apocalyptic texts is (not surprisingly) their "revelation" of future events. This revelation is usually given by an angelic intermediary to a famous individual (see Ezek 14:14, 20; 28:3 for references to a character named Daniel). Apocalypses are also made up of different genres, which seems to explain why chapters 1–6 of the Book of Daniel contain tales about Daniel and his friends, but chapters 7–12 contain apocalyptic visions. In the New Testament, the Book of Revelation is called an apocalypse (Rev 1:1) but also a prophecy (1:3), and contains, among other things, letters to various churches (2:1–3:22); it, too, is a hybrid.

The Book of Daniel is bipartite in a second way, too: the book is written in both Hebrew and Aramaic. The book begins in Hebrew, but shifts, in Dan 2:4a, to Aramaic, precisely when the Chaldeans answer Nebuchadnezzar "in Aramaic." And they really do! The Aramaic section continues through 7:28, crossing the boundary between the court tales (chaps. 1–6) and the visions (chaps. 7–12). But then, in 8:1, the book shifts back to Hebrew and continues in that language through the end of the book. Scholars continue to debate the meaning and significance of Daniel's bilingualism.

The theme of God's sovereignty unites the different parts of the book. God has sovereignty over the Gentile rulers who, in chapters 1–6 at least, aren't all bad. Sure, they are often slow on the uptake, but they are also willing to take instruction and learn from their mistakes. They frequently end up promoting Daniel or his fellow Judean exiles to prominent positions, recognizing the power of their God in the process (see 2:46–49; 3:28–30; 4:34–37; 6:25–28). In this sense, the first half of the book strikes a fairly positive note with regard to the purposes of God in history. Daniel 1–6 offers a model for how faithful Jews may survive and thrive in the court of the foreign king that is more like Joseph in Egypt than Esther in Persia.

In the second half of the book, however, God is still sovereign, but the picture of human kingship is decidedly more negative. The visions here are fantastic with the imagery occasionally disturbing (cf. Dan 7:15). Human rulers are likened to terrifying, hybrid beasts. They are arrogant and violent, with one waging war against the holy ones, even defeating them (7:21)—"until," Daniel continues, "the Ancient One came" (7:22). At that point, things change decidedly and for the better for these "holy ones." This shift—from all seems lost to all is not lost—captures the hope that apocalyptic literature holds for those oppressed by more dominant imperial regimes. While scholars have shown that the functions of apocalyptic are several, most agree that at least one of those functions is to encourage those who suffer, offering them hope—indeed the firm belief—that God will soon set the world aright.

There are enough historical details in Daniel 7–12 to confidently date this material to the Hellenistic period. These details culminate in allusions to the Seleucid ruler Antiochus IV Epiphanes, who oppressed the Jewish people to such a degree that it led to the Maccabean revolt (see the Book of 1 Maccabees in the Apocrypha [Chart 1.1]) and the eventual reclaiming of the temple and its rededication (celebrated today in Hanukkah). These allusions do not accurately reflect the details of Antiochus' death in 164 BCE, however, or events thereafter, and that means that the Book of Daniel must have been completed sometime before that date. This timeframe likely makes Daniel the latest book included in the Old Testament canon.

Not unlike Esther, the historical details in Daniel 1–6 often go awry, which indicates that, even if these court tales are from an earlier period than chapters 7–12, they, like Esther, are likely another instance of historical fiction. It is even possible that historical errors (like identifying Belshazzar's successor as Darius, rather than Cyrus of Persia [5:31]) are intentional, purposeful hints the author left toward a proper understanding of the material. According to most scholars, the Book of Daniel comes from circles known for their wisdom—the importance of wise teachers in the book is revealing in this regard (e.g., 1:4; 11:33, 35; 12:3, 10). If so, that kind of authorship would have been fully able to leave genre clues in the book; and that kind of audience would have been fully able to discern them.

The Greek form of the Book of Daniel, like Esther, contains several additions that are not found in the Hebrew version (see Chart 1.1). These include a two-part section located between 3:23 and 3:24, which is called the *Prayer of Azariah and the Hymn of the Three Young Men*. This addition recounts what Shadrach, Meshach, and Abednego said when they were in the fiery furnace and thus fills a gap that most readers would definitely like to know about. Another addition called *Susanna* is sometimes placed at the end of the book in the manuscript tradition but belongs, conceptually, prior to chapter 1. It showcases Daniel's skill as he is able to rescue a young Jewish woman from unjust accusation by sequestering the witnesses. Finally, *Bel and the Dragon* demonstrates Daniel's wisdom in seeing through the false nature of Babylonian religion, especially its worship of idols.

EZRA-NEHEMIAH

The two Books of Ezra and Nehemiah were originally one composition. Their division was evidently first proposed by the early Christian writer, Origen (184–253 CE). When considered alongside the Book of Chronicles, Ezra-Nehemiah gives a good deal of information about postexilic life, especially since the other biblical books that cover similar ground, like Esther and Daniel, contain some historical inaccuracies (see above), and the prophets that date to this period are either brief or not descriptive in quite the same way (e.g., Haggai, Zechariah).

But using Ezra-Nehemiah for historical reconstruction of the postexilic period has proven difficult for a number of reasons. One question concerns the relationship of this material to the Book of Chronicles. According to one influential theory, the same author was responsible for all of this material which can thus be seen as a kind of "Chronicler's History" (abbreviated as ChrH). This history begins with Adam in 1 Chr 1:1 and continues through Nehemiah 13. It is thus a parallel, maybe even an alternative or rival account to what is found in the Deuteronomistic History, if not the entire Primary History that spans the Enneateuch from Genesis through Kings (see Chapter 3). More recent scholarship has argued that, even if Ezra-Nehemiah is a kind of sequel to Chronicles, there are too many differences between them to ascribe these works to a single author. They have different emphases that draw from distinct traditions. Chronicles, for instance, cares deeply about the temple and the Davidic monarchy. Ezra-Nehemiah is far more interested in the Torah of Moses. Ezra-Nehemiah is exclusivist when it comes to understanding the people of God, going so far as to require divorce of foreign wives (see Ezra 9–10; Neh 10:30; 13:23–30). Chronicles seems to reflect a more inclusive vision of Israel (see below). In fact, some scholars believe that the Books of Jonah and Ruth date from the same period and offer a critical corrective to the nationalistic view found in Ezra-Nehemiah. The more exclusive vision that is encountered in Ezra-Nehemiah, especially the concerns over exogamy (marriage outside an ethnic group), shouldn't be too quickly or easily condemned, however. According to Ezra-Nehemiah, the people who return from the Babylonian exile are a small and beleaguered minority. It is common in situations like that for groups to pay careful attention to boundaries and membership for the sake of the long-term survival of their communities.

Another question facing the use of Ezra-Nehemiah in understanding the postexilic period is its precise historical information. There is more than one Persian king named Artaxerxes: which is the one mentioned in Ezra-Nehemiah? Most scholars think it is Artaxerxes I (465–424 BCE) rather than the slightly later Artaxerxes II (404–358 BCE). Whichever choice is made impacts the dating of the careers of Ezra and Nehemiah. Related to this question is another: who came first, Ezra or Nehemiah? Most scholars put Ezra first, with Nehemiah following him. The (separated) Book of Ezra would thus cover the period of 538–457 BCE. Nehemiah's account would begin around 445 BCE. These dates place both figures solidly in the mid-fifth century.

Ezra-Nehemiah, like other books in the Old Testament, reflects a complicated literary history. Like Daniel, portions of the book are preserved in Aramaic (Ezra 4:6–6:18; 7:12–26). Some of this material purportedly reflects official correspondence with Persian rulers, a good bit of which concerns the construction of the second temple. Whether such correspondence is authentic is vigorously debated by scholars. What is not debated is that various sources were used in the composition of Ezra-Nehemiah. These sources would include, for example, lists of the exiles who returned (Ezra 2:1–67; 8:14) and what is frequently called "The Nehemiah Memoir" (Neh 1:1–7:73a; 11:1–2; 12:31–43; 13:4–31).

A final compositional matter is to consider how Ezra-Nehemiah fares in Greek and other translations of the Old Testament (cf. Chart 1.1). In the Septuagint, 1 Esdras is a combination of 2 Chronicles 35–Nehemiah 8 with some additional material. It is considered an apocryphal work by Protestants. 2 Esdras is the Greek translation of Ezra-Nehemiah. The Vulgate uses different nomenclature for these various compositions: 1 Esdras in the Septuagint is 3 Esdras in the Vulgate; Greek 2 Esdras is the Vulgate's 1–2 Esdras. As if that wasn't confusing enough, the Latin tradition has its own 2 Esdras, which is sometimes included in English versions in the Apocrypha and which is sometimes divided into three parts: 4, 5, and 6 Ezra! The largest block, 4 Ezra, is an early Jewish apocalyptic text like Daniel.

Despite the complexities surrounding Ezra-Nehemiah's compositional history, the book begins by reporting how the Judean exiles were allowed to return under the decree of King Cyrus (Ezra 1:1–4) before recounting various waves of returnees and their adventures (and misadventures) in restoring the city, the temple, and, finally, the city walls. Just as important—if not, in fact, more important— is the fact that in Ezra-Nehemiah, the people are reconstituted as people of the book, with the book in question none other than "the book of the law (*torah*) of Moses" (see Nehemiah 8–9; cf. Ezra 3:2; 7:10; 10:3; Neh 10:29, 30, 35, 37; 12:44; 13:3). When he is first introduced, Ezra is described as "a scribe skilled in the law (*torah*) of Moses that the LORD the God of Israel had given" (Ezra 7:6; NRSV) and someone who "had set his heart to study the law (*torah*) of the LORD, and to do it, and to teach the statutes and ordinances in Israel" (7:10; NRSV). The resonances with Deuteronomy are unmistakable. These connections led later Jewish tradition to view Ezra as an authoritative interpreter of the Torah, and some scholars have gone so far as to wonder if he didn't play an important role in the Pentateuch's early formulation and promulgation—perhaps even as an author or editor.

CHRONICLES (*DIVREI HA-YAMIM*)

The Hebrew name for the Book of Chronicles is "daily events" (*divrei ha-yamim*). This phrase, preceded by the word for "book" or "scroll" (*sefer*), is frequently used in the Book of Kings to refer to the royal annals of the kings of Israel and Judah (e.g., 1 Kgs 14:19, 29).

In 1 Chr 27:24, the phrase refers to official records of King David. Books of annals or official records are also mentioned in Neh 12:23; and Esth 2:23; 6:1; 10:2. Though none of these references has the Book of Chronicles specifically in mind, Jerome's (347–420 CE) reference to this composition as a chronicle made good sense and stuck. In Greek, Chronicles is known as *Paraleipomena*, "things left out," a designation that seems to draw attention to the unique material found in Chronicles that is not found in the parallel accounts of Samuel and Kings. Like Samuel and Kings, Chronicles should be considered a single composition, divided for convenience into two parts so as to fit on reasonably sized scrolls.

The theory that Chronicles and Ezra-Nehemiah came from the same author was discussed above; this view is no longer widely held. The double presentation of Cyrus' edict that is found in 2 Chr 36:22–23 and Ezra 1:1–4 is thus not the result of separating a composition that was originally unified. Instead, it is more likely a secondary attempt to join the two compositions somewhat artificially into a prequel-sequel kind of relationship. If so, Ezra-Nehemiah may be considered alongside Chronicles—regardless of authorship questions—which, together, provide alternative and additional information to the other historical narratives in the Old Testament.

The relationship of Chronicles to those other historical narratives is a curious one. On the one hand, there is much that is similar to, parallel with, or repeated in Chronicles from Samuel and Kings—even Genesis-Judges, given the opening genealogies in 1 Chronicles 1–2. Most scholars believe that the author of Chronicles had access to Samuel-Kings, though probably in a slightly different (shorter) version than how they are presently preserved in the Hebrew Bible. Chronicles also includes a decent amount of material that is *not* found in Samuel-Kings, a good bit of which concerns Hezekiah. Scholars are divided as to the historical reliability of this unique material—the "things left out" of Samuel and Kings. Many scholars think this additional information is unlikely to be of much use, since the Book of Chronicles probably dates from the late Persian period in the fourth century BCE, far removed from the events it describes. Other scholars are willing to grant this material some credence, especially if it is corroborated by other sources or by archaeological findings.

There can be no doubt that some of the additional material found in Chronicles is present for theological reasons. For example, the book appears to support a fairly straightforward notion of retribution when it comes to royal behavior. The fact that one of the religiously worst kings, Manasseh, has a very long life and rule must, therefore, be accounted for in some fashion. In 2 Chr 33:10–13, it is explained by a story that is not found in Kings, in which Manasseh is captured and taken into exile in Babylon. There, Chronicles reports, he entreated the Lord, humbled himself before God, and prayed. God listened to Manasseh's prayer, Chronicles continues, and subsequently restores him to his rule in Jerusalem, after which point Manasseh is a reformed (and reforming!) man (33:14–20). A text preserved in the Apocrypha, the Prayer of Manasseh, purportedly recounts what the king prayed while in Babylon: it repeatedly confesses his sin and begs for God's mercy.

Manasseh's isn't the only portrait to get cleaned up in Chronicles. Chronicles apparently skipped 2 Samuel 9–20 which means that the stories about David's wrongdoings with Bathsheba and Uriah go unmentioned in the book. This sanitization of David—or censorship of his bad actions—correlates with Chronicles' intense focus on the Davidic dynasty and Judah. The book is concentrated solely on the south, omitting the parallel history of the Northern Kingdom found in Kings. After an extensive genealogy (1 Chronicles 1–9), Chronicles treats the reigns of Saul (1 Chronicles 10), David (1 Chronicles 11–29), and Solomon (2 Chronicles 1–9), before covering the remaining Judean monarchs until the Babylonian exile (2 Chr 10:1–36:16). The very end of the book narrates the destruction of the temple, the exile, and the edict of Cyrus (2 Chr 36:17–23).

Despite cleaning up David's portrait more than a little, Chronicles makes clear something the Book of Samuel does not: that David is not permitted to build the temple because he is a warrior who has spilled blood (1 Chr 28:3). Chronicles nevertheless goes to great lengths to show how important David is in the preparations for the temple's construction—another part of David's career that is not found in Samuel or Kings. And, while Chronicles does not contain the history of the northern kingdom—its apostasy is probably too offensive for the book's author—it does evidence some interest in the north. The northern tribes appear to be included in what Chronicles calls "all Israel"; also, Hezekiah and Josiah are both reported to have conducted reforming activities in the north as well as the south (2 Chr 30:6–9; 35:18). And so, as already noted, Chronicles seems more inclusive than Ezra-Nehemiah.

In brief, Chronicles provides a highly theologized account of Israel's history that differs at some points from the Enneateuch (Primary History), more broadly, or the Deuteronomistic History, more narrowly. The account in Chronicles should not be thought of as biased fabrication so much as revisionist history—or, perhaps better, a kind of edifying exegesis which supplements the other "histories" in the Old Testament, especially in the current form of the canon. Each of these compositions provides a window or perspective that is valuable for what it includes and for what it excludes. An especially important difference from the Primary History and DtrH is how Chronicles ends on a very high point: the edict of Cyrus that allowed the exiles to return to Jerusalem and to a rebuilt temple for "the LORD, the God of heaven" (2 Chr 36:23). Although the content of Ezra-Nehemiah properly *follows* 2 Chronicles 36, the present order of the Hebrew Bible reverses that order so as to end in this way: with an unexpected but most hoped-for homecoming.

The ending of Chronicles, which is also the ending of the Hebrew Bible, deserves further comment because it is one of the major differences between the order of the Hebrew Bible and Christian versions of the Old Testament. By concluding with Chronicles, the Hebrew Bible has a very different feeling than the Old Testament's ending with the Prophets, especially Malachi, in the Christian Bible. As noted in Chapter 3, it seems like a very short hop, skip, and jump from Malachi, with its mention of the Lord's messenger who will prepare the way (Mal 3:1) and Elijah's return (4:5), to the Gospel of St. Matthew, the first book of the New Testament, with its mention of John the Baptist, who is explicitly likened to Elijah and preaches in both word and deed like the Old Testament prophets (see Matt 3:1–12; 11:14; cf. also John 1:21).

Ending with Chronicles, especially 2 Chronicles 36, creates a very different effect. The Hebrew Bible ends, that is, not with words that can easily be taken up and applied to John the Baptist, let alone Jesus Christ, but with Cyrus' edict about homecoming. This ending takes the reader, not forward, to the New Testament (or any other corpus) but *backward*, squarely—or so it would seem—to the middle of Israel's history: to Jerusalem and its temple, perhaps even to a restored monarchy (cf. 2 Kgs 25:27–30). This might suggest that readers who finish Chronicles ought to go back and start reading again, if not from the very start of the Old Testament, then at least from the middle of its story.

WHAT THE WRITINGS ARE ALL ABOUT: TWO THINGS

If it was difficult to summarize what the Torah and the Prophets are all about (see Chapters 2 and 3), the task seems even more daunting when it comes to the Writings, the most diverse and least cohesive of the three parts of the Hebrew Bible. The sheer diversity of the material found in the *Ketuvim*, its irreducible pluralism, means by definition that it lacks consensus and that this rich collection cannot be captured in a few pithy statements. Even so, as in the case of the Pentateuch and the Prophets, a summary statement remains a worthwhile endeavor for pedagogical purposes, providing, if nothing else, points of entry for further probes of the riches contained in the *Ketuvim*. So, while the two things that summarize "what the Writings are all about" are no less reductionist than those found in Chapters 2 and 3, a special effort has been made to make these two items as capacious as possible to reflect the wideness of the Writings themselves.

LIFE ...

The Writings, first, are about *life*—the fullness of life in all its great, glorious heights and in its worst, most despairing lows. The Psalms alone are proof of this point, or, rather of both points: the highs and the lows that mark human existence. So also is Chronicles, a book of occasionally mundane "daily events." Or consider Proverbs, replete with hundreds of maxims for wise living in the real world(s) of family, commerce, and politics. Then there is Job, which, like the darkest of the psalms, is a book about what happens when life happens *to you*, and in the worst possible way. Lamentations adds to the somberness in its sad elegy over disaster, destruction, loss, and the troubling presence—and absence—of God in all that. Then there's Ecclesiastes, which couldn't be more sober about life. Qohelet's spirituality, if it may be called that, is edgy to say the least; "crabby" is probably more accurate. The Writings (and so also the entire Old Testament) have room for a truly wide range of religious affects and how they encounter and cope (or don't) with life.

The Writings capture the full, often painful reality of human life, and do so with unblinking eyes. But there is more to life than pain—so says the *Ketuvim*. Even Qohelet, as dour as he appears to be (and is!), repeatedly commends joy and pleasure. The Song of Songs agrees, including within such goods a healthy dose of (discreet) erotic-but-somehow-also religious love. And while life often deals the worst to human beings by means of famine, death, enemies, and the like … well, it is also the case in life that sometimes famines end and babies are born (Ruth). Sometimes enemies get what they deserve (Psalms, Esther). Sometimes the faithful thrive in difficult—even the worst of circumstances (Psalms, Ruth, Daniel, Ezra-Nehemiah). At the very least, they survive (Job, Esther). And surviving is no small thing when it comes to life.

… AND LIFE WITH GOD

Second, the Writings are about *life with God*. There are compositions in the *Ketuvim* that seem ambivalent about God (Ecclesiastes, certain psalms) or that don't mention God at all (Song of Songs, Esther). But these are mostly exceptions that prove the rule: if the Writings are about life, then that life is resolutely, fundamentally, and finally *life with God*. Even the relatively speaking "godless" bits of the *Ketuvim* can be seen as tracks on an album that is otherwise so heavily "God-full" that they, too, can be read as somehow pertaining to God and life with God, even when they are rather tight-lipped about that. The long-standing tradition, in both Jewish and Christian circles, to read the Song of Songs in allegorical fashion, relating to God and Israel or Christ and the Church, makes perfect sense in this (canonical) context. And there is an even older tradition that read the Book of Esther as having to do with God and life with God. That tradition didn't interpret Esther that way, by means of allegory or the like, it *translated* Esther that way in the Septuagint. As noted above, Greek Esther is full of explicit references to God, with both Esther and Mordecai uttering prayers to God. There can be no doubt that Greek Esther is a very different book than Hebrew Esther. In a very real sense, however, Greek Esther can be seen as having rightly understood Hebrew Esther within its native context in the Hebrew Bible, generally, and amidst the Writings, more specifically—both of which overflow with references to God and which are everywhere about life under, with, and before God.

Other books in the *Ketuvim* underscore the point. The Psalms, Lamentations, and Job show that even at life's lowest points, one still has to do with God. The wise life, not just the faithful life, begins with proper reverence for the Lord according to the sages of Proverbs. Daily matters, including those of institutional maintenance, construction, reconstruction, and repair, too, are done before God and with God's help (Ezra-Nehemiah, Chronicles). Even one who is agnostic about the meaning of God's doings knows that they are still God's doings (Ecclesiastes). Everyday human concerns from love and sex (Song of Songs) to food for immigrants and refugees (Ruth)—these, too, are part of the life with God. And life with God includes the future, even when that future is uncertain and not a bit frightening (Daniel).

If the Writings are about life, they are also about the entirety of that life under, with, and before God. At the end of the day, "books about life and about life with God" is a good summary, not only of the *Ketuvim* but also of the entire Old Testament.

SUGGESTIONS FOR FURTHER READING

For an informative collection of essays that deal with how the Writings achieved their current shape, see Julius Steinberg and Timothy J. Stone with Rachel Stone, eds., *The Shape of the Writings* (Siphrut 16; Winona Lake: Eisenbrauns, 2015). For a book length treatment of the Writings by a single author, see Donn F. Morgan, *Between Text and Community: The "Writings" in Canonical Interpretation* (Minneapolis: Fortress, 1990).

The phrase that the laments comprise the "backbone of the Psalter" comes from James Crenshaw, "Foreword: The Book of Psalms and Its Interpreters," in Sigmund Mowinckel, *The Psalms in Israel's Worship* (Grand Rapids: Eerdmans, 2004), xxvi. Hermann Gunkel's pioneering work on the various types of psalms, completed by Joachim Begrich, is translated into English as *Introduction to Psalms: The Genres of the Religious Lyric of Israel* (Macon: Mercer University Pres, 1998). For a study of the overall shape of the Book of Psalms, from torah obedience to unfettered praise, see Walter Brueggemann, "Bounded by Obedience and Praise: The Psalms as Canon," in *The Psalms and the Life of Faith* (ed. Patrick D. Miller;

Minneapolis: Fortress, 1995), 189–213 (this entire volume, from one of the best contemporary Psalm interpreters, is worthwhile). On biblical poetry, see, briefly, Brent A. Strawn, "Hebrew Poetry," in *The New Interpreter's Bible One Volume Commentary* (eds. Beverly Roberts Gaventa and David L. Petersen et al.; Nashville: Abingdon, 2010), 959–960. The major studies are by James L. Kugel, *The Idea of Biblical Poetry: Parallelism and Its History* (New Haven: Yale University Press, 1981); Robert Alter, *The Art of Biblical Poetry* (rev. ed.; New York: Basic, 2011); and F. W. Dobbs-Allsopp, *On Biblical Poetry* (New York: Oxford University Press, 2015). The description of parallelism as "A, and what's more, B," is Kugel's (*The Idea*, 1, and passim).

For wisdom texts like Proverbs, Job, and Ecclesiastes, see James L. Crenshaw, *Old Testament Wisdom: An Introduction* (3rd ed.; Louisville: Westminster John Knox, 2010); and Samuel E. Balentine, *Wisdom Literature* (Nashville: Abingdon, 2018). More recently, Will Kynes, *An Obituary for "Wisdom Literature": The Birth, Death, and Intertextual Reintegration of a Biblical Corpus* (Oxford: Oxford University Press, 2019), has questioned the usefulness of the category. For the narrative reading of the Book of Proverbs recounted in this chapter, see William P. Brown, *Character in Crisis: A Fresh Approach to the Wisdom Literature of the Old Testament* (Grand Rapids: Eerdmans, 1996), 22–49, revised in *Wisdom's Wonder: Character, Creation, and Crisis in the Bible's Wisdom Literature* (Grand Rapids: Eerdmans, 2014), 29–66. For the God-speeches in Job as a kind of reorientation, see Kathleen O'Connor, "Wild, Raging Creativity: The Scene in the Whirlwind (Job 38–41)," in *A God So Near: Essays on Old Testament Theology in Honor of Patrick D. Miller* (eds. Brent A. Strawn and Nancy R. Bowen; Winona Lake: Eisenbrauns, 2003), 171–179.

For the *Megillot*, see Robert Williamson, Jr., *The Forgotten Books of the Bible: Recovering the Five Scrolls for Today* (Minneapolis: Fortress, 2018). The description of the two lovers' views of love and of each other in the Song of Songs follows J. Cheryl Exum, *Song of Songs* (Louisville: Westminster John Knox, 2005), 14–17. For allegorical readings of the Song in both Judaism and Christianity, see, respectively, Michael Fishbane, *Song of Songs* (Philadelphia: Jewish Publication Society, 2015); and Edmée Kingsmill, *The Song of Songs and the Eros of God: A Study in Biblical Intertextuality* (Oxford: Oxford University Press, 2009). See Phyllis Trible, *God and the Rhetoric of Sexuality* (Philadelphia: Fortress, 1978), 144–165, for a treatment of the Song of Songs and its relationship to Genesis 2–3. The comments on the Passover as the courtship of God and Israel, and the Sabbath as a marriage come from Carl S. Ehrlich, "Hebrew/Israelite Literature," in *From an Antique Land: An Introduction to Ancient Near Eastern Literature* (ed. Carl S. Ehrlich; Lanham: Rowan & Littlefield,

2009), 390 n. 49. For Ruth and the notion of *ḥesed*, see Katharine Doob Sakenfeld, *Ruth* (Louisville: John Knox, 1999). For insightful treatments of Lamentations, see Kathleen M. O'Connor, *Lamentations and the Tears of the World* (Maryknoll: Orbis, 2004); and F. W. Dobbs-Allsopp, *Lamentations* (Louisville: John Knox, 2002). It was Michael Fox who wrote that "Qoheleth is crabby"—see his *A Time to Tear Down and a Time to Build Up: A Rereading of Ecclesiastes* (Grand Rapids: Eerdmans, 1999), 267. Elias Bickerman is the one who said that the fear of God in Ecclesiastes meant to be on guard against Elohim: *Four Strange Books of the Bible: Jonah, Daniel, Koheleth, Esther* (New York: Schocken, 1967), 149. For the joy passages in Qohelet, see R. N. Whybray, "Qohelet, Preacher of Joy," *Journal for the Study of the Old Testament* 23 (1982): 87–98; as well as Eunny P. Lee, *The Vitality of Enjoyment in Qohelet's Theological Rhetoric* (Berlin: Walter de Gruyter, 2005).

For apocalyptic literature, see Greg Carey, *Ultimate Things: An Introduction to Jewish and Christian Apocalyptic Literature* (St. Louis: Chalice, 2005); idem, *Apocalyptic Literature in the New Testament* (Nashville: Abingdon, 2016); and John J. Collins, *The Apocalyptic Imagination: An Introduction to Jewish Apocalyptic Literature* (3rd ed.; Grand Rapids: Eerdmans, 2016). A collection of non-biblical apocalyptic material can be found in James H. Charlesworth, ed. *The Old Testament Pseudepigrapha*, Vol. 1: *Apocalyptic Literature and Testaments* (New York: Doubleday, 1983).

FROM STORY TO SONG

Despite the concision of the present introduction, much ground has been covered since Chapter 1, let alone since Genesis 1. The scholarly story about the Old Testament as well as the Old Testament's own, mostly literary story have been overviewed and sketched out—not nearly with the detail that each deserves, but with enough color that readers should now feel oriented to the Old Testament "forest" and the lay of its land in light of some of its distinguishing landforms and according to some of its more notable cartographers. With this big picture in place, readers should be better prepared to appreciate the native fauna, constituent sub-regions, and the beauty of the individual "trees" that make up the Hebrew Bible. This concluding chapter summarizes these two stories of the Old Testament before returning to some of the problems raised in Chapter 1 about reading the Old Testament "as if" it were a story.

SUMMARIZING THE OLD TESTAMENT'S "STORIES"

THE SCHOLARLY STORY ABOUT THE OLD TESTAMENT

The story that scholars tell about the Old Testament is a long and complicated one. Claus Westermann, an important biblical scholar of the mid-twentieth century, wrote an introduction to the Old Testament called *A Thousand Years and a Day* because the Old Testament spanned 1,000 years and because 1,000 years contributed to its development (by contrast, what took place in the New Testament, according to Westermann, could be compressed into a single day!). The gist of scholarship on the Bible for the past few centuries indicates that Westermann is actually understating things. The Old Testament's own internal storyline spans far more than 1,000 years since it goes back all the way to creation itself. On the academic side, the scholarly story of Old Testament's formation and development, interpretation and reception is longer than just one millennium. Even scholars who date the earliest biblical materials quite late, in the exilic or postexilic periods, would agree that the academic story of the Old Testament winds through the centuries, into the common era, and up to the present day in the virtually infinite ways it has been understood, practiced, and interpreted in art, music, film, literature, religious experience, and so on and so forth.

The present introduction has offered only a small sampling of scholarly opinion on only some of these matters—the proverbial tip of the iceberg. With a history of interpretation that spans more than 2,000 years, one is hard pressed to find another artifact of human history that is as long or as thoroughly studied as the Old Testament. Given the vast scope of that interpretive history, it comes with its fair share of wrong moves, dead ends, oddities, curiosities, and rabbit trails. Be that as it may, two takeaways from the academic story scholars tell *about* the Old Testament must not be missed.

First, as stated already in the first sentence of Chapter 1, a good bit of this story about the Old Testament's history remains unknowable. We are on solid ground in some cases, but not in all, and so much remains speculative, especially when it comes to early forms or preexistent layers of the text that lie *behind* what we now have. Composition criticism, especially when it deals with conjectural, non-extant "sources," or when it deals with hypothetical editions or additions, is a highly technical enterprise that is both sophisticated and learned. But despite any and all such sophistication and learning, the cold hard fact is that composition-critical reconstructions often fail to convince anyone other than the scholar who conceived them. So, first and foremost, much about the origin(s) and growth of the Old Testament—its own history—remains uncertain.

Second, despite the first point, there is still a good bit that can be and that is known. Some of the best minds in human history have devoted extensive attention to the Bible and its story. So, while much remains uncertain and unknowable about this story, much *can* be known and much *is* known—even if much remains debated and under discussion.

The largest point of agreement among scholars in the story they tell about the Old Testament is that the Hebrew Bible is the end result of a long process—or better, as the present introduction has repeatedly shown, *a long set of processes*. The Bible does not self-present as something that fell out of heaven straight from God fully intact, even if some religious adherents might like to think as much. Instead, the Bible self-presents as something that has been mediated through various individuals, some of whom are named (e.g., Moses, the prophets, Qohelet) but a goodly number of whom are not (e.g., the narrator of Ecclesiastes, many of the psalmists, "Second Isaiah"). And so the history of the Old Testament also includes countless unnamed individuals who transmitted the biblical text through telling and retelling, copying and recopying over centuries and millennia. No wonder it is hard to be definitive about the (singular) "story" of, say, a book like Isaiah. *Which* Isaiah? The eighth-century prophet active in Jerusalem or the prophet of the exile or of the postexilic period? The Isaiah of the Hebrew text or the Greek text? The Isaiah of the Leningrad Codex or of the various Isaiah scrolls found among the Dead Sea Scrolls that differ among themselves at various points? The Isaiah of the Septuagint or Isaiah as cited within the pages of the New Testament or as known from compositions in the Middle Ages? The complexities are real and manifold—overwhelming, if we are honest. And yet that is exactly what should be expected when studying a life story that spans more than 2,000 years.

In the end, academic accounts of the Old Testament—at least in their most complicated forms—are of less importance for the immediate reading and enjoyment of the Bible than the "story" the Old Testament itself tells. *Origin*, that is, is not the same as *meaning*. Where someone comes from originally, while important and often intriguing, is usually just the beginning of their story and often not determinative for who they are later in life. And so the story the Old Testament itself tells—its content—is as important as if not more important than the story scholars tell about its origin and development.

THE OLD TESTAMENT'S (OWN) STORY

Meaning may be different from origin, but meaning is no less vexed than origin. The millennia-long history of the interpretation of the Bible is not only about the complex set of processes that gave us the Old Testament. That history of interpretation is equally a story of the Bible's *complex set of meanings*. Summarizing the story the Old Testament tells, therefore, is no more straightforward than, and often as complicated as, the scholarly story about the Old Testament. Numerous interpretations—some contradictory—have been offered for virtually every verse in the Bible. Contemporary interpretive approaches vary widely, with some self-consciously contrarian, intentionally reading against the grain of the text.

With the difficulties surrounding method and the Bible's meaning duly noted, the present introduction has dared to identify two key points for each of the three parts of the Hebrew Bible. Encapsulating the Torah, Prophets, and Writings in just two points is obviously to oversimplify matters—*greatly*. But the attempt is not a futile one since the goal has been pedagogical: to offer a few handholds on what is an intimidating amount of material. The points identified were the following:

- Torah: *Divine Creation(s)* and *Divine Command(s)*
- Prophets: *God's Mirror* and *God's Mishpat-and-Tzedekah*
- Writings: *Life … and Life with God.*

While somewhat reductive, these points are intentionally roomy. With them in mind, one can go back to the Pentateuch, say, and ponder how some part of the Torah contributes, even if not obviously at first, to the notions of divine creation or divine command or, somehow, to both. Reading and rereading will thicken up what "creation" means or what "command" signifies or, more likely, what both connote—perhaps even together. Reading and rereading will add color, nuance, and richness. Nuance will be added to these points of emphasis and entirely new emphases, some equally important, will be revealed. How best to approach this kind of revealing rereading leads me to revisit the idea of the Old Testament as "story."

REVISITING THE OLD TESTAMENT AS "STORY"

Despite the intuitive, almost commonsensical nature of the category "story" when applied to both the story *of* the Old Testament and the story *in* the Old Testament, there are also problems using it, especially in the case of the second "story." Some of these problems were identified in Chapter 1. Others became clear in the course of Chapters 3–4. To repeat some of the most important considerations:

1. Parts of the Old Testament don't fit "the story" because they do not belong to a linear plot progression that supposedly starts in Genesis and proceeds straightforwardly thereafter. It is fairly easy to trace a story of sorts from Genesis–Deuteronomy (Torah) and even into the Former Prophets (the Enneateuch). But the Latter Prophets tell, at best, a "story" (in scare quotes) since they are anthologies, full of poetry, and not always chronologically arranged. Where, then, does "the story" begun in Genesis end? Thereafter, with the Writings, all bets are off. There might be a continuation of "the story" in the *Ketuvim*, but only in some of its books (Chronicles, Ezra-Nehemiah, Esther). Others, like Job, tell different "stories" (plural) altogether, with still others, like the Psalms and Ecclesiastes, not interested in stories much at all—at least not the ones found in the Torah or the Former Prophets.

2. The tripartite form of the Hebrew Bible complicates reading it as a story that leads seamlessly into the New Testament or into later rabbinic literature. The Hebrew Bible ends with the Book of Chronicles, which seems to return us to the center of Israel's story in the land without pointing anywhere beyond that central locus (see Chapter 4).

3. A number of biblical compositions (e.g., the Psalms, most of the Latter Prophets, Ecclesiastes, Song of Songs, etc.) are manifestly not "stories" at all. Many of these are poetic compositions. Both reasons make it unclear how these books relate to "the story."

Factors like these demonstrate that "the story that the Old Testament tells" is actually *not* self-evidently a story at all. If someone says the Old Testament is a story, they have made it so by asserting as much. They have "narrativized" the Old Testament, *constructing* or *construing* it as a story even when its overall form and constituent parts resist the category. That is what Chapter 1 meant by reading the Old Testament "as if" it were a story. "As if" is not "is."

A story construal of the Hebrew Bible is well and good as far as it goes, but upon closer inspection it doesn't appear to go very far because of the factors listed above. A story construal of the Old Testament in the order found in most English Bibles doesn't fare much better. Thanks to the creation of the Historical Books category (see Chapter 3), this order runs from Genesis through Esther (not without problems), but at that point the non-story elements found in the Poetic and Prophetic Books intrude, frustrating a linear, narrative reading. And so, again, reading the Old Testament "as if" it were a story is very much an operation readers perform on the Old Testament. A closer look at the whole and its parts reveals that much of what is found here is definitely *not* story.

There are other things to worry about when it comes to "narrativizing" the Hebrew Bible as (only) a story. One of these is that such a construal might do damage to the Old Testament by privileging its story parts over its non-story parts. "Reading for plot" or "expecting a story" makes a lot of sense—appears natural—but it could also mislead readers by creating an expectation that what they will find in the Old Testament is a story like others: one with background, character development, rising action, climax, and falling action (denouement) that wraps everything up nicely. But, once again, that is exactly *not* what one experiences in the "story" of the Old Testament. If someone reads with that kind of expectation, therefore, they are sure to be quickly if not fully frustrated since much of the Old Testament simply does not fit that formula. To force it into that formula—reading it "as if" it were a story—can help in some ways but hurt in others. At the very least, reading the Old Testament as if it were a story requires a generous (re)definition of the category "story." But at that point, why insist on calling it a "story" at all?

The above leads to a simple question: Is there another way to read the Old Testament "as if"—one that isn't limited to "story" and that might avoid some of its problems?

THE OLD TESTAMENT AS "POETRY"

The answer to this question is positive. In truth, there are a number of ways that people can and have read the Old Testament "as if." Some read it *as if* it is a kind of self-help book, others *as if* it is a dictionary or encyclopedia to consult on hot-button topics, still others *as if* it is an instruction manual for life. In addition to proponents, each of these approaches has problems. In my own opinion, a particularly helpful model is to think of the Bible as poetry, reading it *as if* it were a poem.

Here is not the place to explore this idea in detail. But a few remarks might be useful to show how a poetic model is helpful, perhaps even better than the story approach. For starters, all of the parts of the Old Testament that resist a straightforward, linear reading as story—above all others, the poetic sections of the Hebrew Bible—are exactly those parts that make the Old Testament feel more like a poem or a song than a story. Admittedly, the Old Testament is *not* one big poem. But neither is it one big story. A poetic reading, like a narrative one, is certainly reading "as if," but even then, for the analogy to work, the Old Testament has to be considered as if it were *an anthology of poems* put together in a certain way to make *a lyric sequence*. Poets use lyric sequences to make larger arguments or more extensive plots beyond what any one, fairly short poem can achieve. But poetic "arguments" or "plots" are very different from what one finds in a philosophical treatise or a novel. Poetry follows different rules than the logic of philosophy or the workings of narrative. Among other characteristics that could be identified, poetry is spare and terse even while it is simultaneously dense, especially in its use of figurative language (see Chapter 4).

Poetry, especially lyric poetry, has a powerful immediacy: it is a kind of event, a happening, a mode of address—one that is often not descriptive or narratival in character. A single poem, let alone a poetic sequence, can be highly tensive within itself while still maintaining its own integrity and cohesion. Poetry is also remarkably open-ended, subject to interpretation, and intentionally so. Poetry's spare-and-yet-overfull imagistic language means that more than one reading of a poem is possible—even required. Poetry must be read slowly to be appreciated, and it must be reread to be appreciated fully. But when a good poem is read well and rightly appreciated, it can be a transforming experience for a reader. Poems can even transform the same reader again, differently, in the future, with subsequent readings.

If the Old Testament can be read "as if" it were a grand story—as many believe—it is equally possible to read it "as if" it were a grand poem or a lengthy lyric sequence. And the poetic analogue fits in many ways. For example, if the Old Testament leaves many questions unanswered (and it does), that is less like a narrative, with plot resolution, than it is like poetry. Poetry rarely answers all of our questions but, rather, seems to invite every kind of interpretive question. Or, if parts of the Old Testament exist in profound tension with others, that, too, seems less like a story than like poetry with its often rough juxtaposition of images and metaphors within particular poems and across a number of poems within a poetic sequence. And if the Old Testament is forever open to interpretation, susceptible to more than one understanding, that, too, sounds like poetry which yields its many meanings slowly, after patient reading and rereading, all the while remaining elusive (and allusive!).

Reading the Old Testament, like reading poetry, is rarely easy and is not something to be done quickly. Poetry is a demanding kind of literature. The proper approach to reading poetry is an unhurried and luxurious savoring of its language, with the best possible result being that the reader is captivated, captured, maybe even changed in the process. Poetry, it seems, is another, quite excellent and commendable way to read the Old Testament *as if*.

THE OLD TESTAMENT: AN OPEN BOOK

What someone expects to find when they being reading a piece of literature makes a difference in how it is read and what emerges from such reading. The present introduction has read the Old Testament's content (mostly) *as if* that were a story. The story category is helpful in various ways even if isn't a perfect analogy. The same holds true for reading the Old Testament *as if* it were a poem. Poetry, too, isn't a perfect analogy for the Old Testament. Much in the Hebrew Bible is most certainly *not* poetry, much *really is* story, and there is a good bit that is neither (law, for instance). Even so, reading the Old Testament as if it were poetry has two results that suggest it may be superior to the idea that the Old Testament is a story.

First, reading the Bible as if it were a poem demands close, painstaking attention to its language. The Russian linguist Roman Jakobson (1896–1982) said poetry trafficked in "the poetic function"—his term for how poetry calls attention to itself by means of its unusual and highly artful diction. The poetic function mandates that every line, word, and syllable in a poem must be attended to with the greatest of care because nothing is in poetry by accident; instead, even the smallest, most minute part contributes to the meaning(s) of the poem. If the "poem" in question is the Hebrew Bible, the same careful attention is required.

Second, reading the Bible as if it were poetry means that one should expect to find in the Old Testament the same sort of profundity, artistry, playfulness, seriousness, terseness-with-density, and every other quality that marks the best poetry. This may mean, once again, that many a reader's questions will go unanswered since this is not a philosophical tract nor a neatly arranged story nor a self-help book. It is, instead, grand, deep, even opaque poetry. But it also means that the Old Testament may end up having a kind of immediacy, becoming a kind of experience that is missing from even the best narratives.

Other benefits of the poetic model could be mentioned, but these two results combine to suggest that the Old Testament is an open book—an open-ended story, perhaps, to return to that genre, or an unfinished drama, to use another. But also, if not instead (and better), the Old Testament remains an open book *of poetry*: a very long and open-ended poem made up of many other, shorter poems along the way.

As noted, reading the Old Testament *as* poetry requires that one pay exceedingly close attention to *what* is there: the words, the diction, the images, and so forth and so on. At the same time, *how* this language is there is of equal if not greater importance when it comes to poetry. *What* is found in the Old Testament—its basic content or "story"—is, in the poetic sense, only part of the story. *How* it is found is just as significant. In the case of the Old Testament, much of that *how* is *as poetry*, in poetic form, not only in the Psalms or Latter Prophets but perhaps also, analogically, in the overall form, shape, and sense of the Hebrew Bible.

The Old Testament cannot say everything because everything cannot be said—certainly not in just one poem, not even in a very long, multi-poem sequence. Reading the Old Testament as if it were poetry leads one to expect language that is dense and demanding, poignant and beautiful, but also language that is full of imagery, metaphor, figure—that evokes more than it explains, that connotes more than it denotes, because it is very difficult to say the most important things, and it's even harder to get those important things said right. In the case of the poetry of the Old Testament, it could be said that it is very difficult to get God said right.

The Old Testament is about more than just God, of course, though God is a major preoccupation. The fact that the divine name *Yhwh* (see Box 2.1) occurs over 5,000 times in the Hebrew Bible is proof enough of that. Further proof might be that the summary points identified for the Pentateuch, Prophets, and Writings in the present introduction all had to do with God in some way: *divine* creation(s) and command(s), *God's* mirror and *mishpat*-and-*tzedekah*, life *with God*. God's ways in the world, the world's ways with God, and the interaction of the divine and non-divine realms that takes place in the pages of the Bible only make the difficulties of getting things said right that much harder, if not altogether impossible. Like the prophet Ezekiel by the river Chebar in Babylon, the various texts of the Old Testament are trying to describe something that is indescribable, to express something that is inexpressible. And so they struggle with and against language even though they must depend on it and deploy it as the only tool available at hand. Once again and once more, it is hard to get important things said just right.

Contemporary readers of the Old Testament should recognize how this struggle to say things right is at work on every page of the Bible. It will not do to reify any one particular text as if it could capture the essence of its author(s), let alone the subjects (and Divine Subject!), it treats. No, like Ezekiel, this is just "the *appearance* of the *likeness* of the *glory* …"—at least three-times removed from the reality! At the same time, the poetic function demands that readers attend to each text and its words and way of putting things with the greatest of care—these texts matter in profound ways because they are all that we have, all that we have access to, in the Old Testament's quest to say important things and say them well.

The brevity and episodic nature of poetry means that there is always more that can be said, always more *than* can be said, because a poem can never be as encompassing or as exhaustive as it might otherwise appear. One day a poet may write a poem capturing the world and the imagination and then … tomorrow … write another, very different one. The two poems can be at profound odds. Why that would be the case may be due to the complexity of the topic at hand or due to the complexity of the poet who is writing about it. The Old Testament and its topics: God, Israel, the nations, and so forth—not to mention its authors!—is every bit as complex and certainly no more simple.

So, again, the Old Testament, whether understood as story or as song, must remain an open book. Someone can finish reading it, but they will not then be done with it, nor it with them, thereafter. We could read, for example, the Book of Jonah quickly, in a matter of minutes, and come up with a rather decent summation of its "point." Something like the following:

> Jonah refutes a narrow mindset in the Persian period (evidenced, for example, by Ezra-Nehemiah) by demonstrating that God cares about more in the world than just Israel, that God is capable of saving even the worst of Israel's enemies (Assyria!), and that God can show up a falsely pious prophet in the process.

Such a short recapitulation might even be *right*. But, regardless, the Book of Jonah remains stubbornly *there*. Once summarized and paraphrased, the Book of Jonah still lives on—*un*-summarized and *not* paraphrased. It refuses to disappear but remains in the Bible in its four-chaptered form (despite our brilliant summations), waiting to be read and reread, even and perhaps especially after we think we have it all figured out and said just right.

As with Jonah, so also for the Old Testament as a whole. It is a very complex and long poem, after all. Poetry ought not be read quickly, and poetry must often be read more than once to reveal its deepest meanings. Poetry repays that kind of (re)reading. And, so even at the end of reading the Old Testament, if we are tempted to think we've "got" it somehow, the Old Testament refuses to disappear. It keeps on living its life, in its many-chaptered, many-booked, many-poemed form, waiting to be read, and reread, and reread yet again.

But that is a story—or, rather, *a poem*—for another time.

★★★

The grass withers, the flower fades,
   but the word of our God will stand forever. (Isa 40:8; NRSV)

SUGGESTIONS FOR FURTHER READING

The history of biblical interpretation begins within the pages of the Bible itself. See Michael Fishbane, *Biblical Interpretation in Ancient Israel* (Oxford: Oxford University Press, 1985). See Chapter 1 for suggested readings on interpretive method. For biblical narrative, see Adele Berlin, *Poetics and Interpretation of Biblical Narrative* (Winona Lake: Eisenbrauns, 1994), and the classic treatment by Robert Alter, *The Art of Biblical Narrative* (rev. ed.; New York: Basic, 2011). See Chapter 4 for works on biblical poetry, especially those by Robert Alter and F. W. Dobbs-Allsopp. For lyric poetry and lyric sequences in the Old Testament, see Brent A. Strawn, "Lyric Poetry," in *Dictionary of the Old Testament: Wisdom, Poetry and Writings* (eds. Tremper Longman III and Peter Enns; Downers Grove: IVP Academic, 2008), 437–446. For the Old Testament itself as poetry, see that same essay as well as Brent A. Strawn, "The Triumph of Life: Towards a Biblical Theology of Happiness," in *The Bible and the Pursuit of Happiness: What the Old and New Testaments Teach Us about the Good Life* (ed. Brent A. Strawn; Oxford: Oxford University Press, 2012), 287–322; and the TheoEd talk, "The Greatest Story Never Told: Re-Thinking the Bible as Poetry" (available online at: https://vimeo.com/238641255; accessed 4/28/19). I am presently working on a book-length treatment of this idea.

Claus Westermann's book is *A Thousand Years and a Day: Our Time in the Old Testament* (Philadelphia: Fortress, 1962). The passage about getting God said right is indebted to Walter Brueggemann, "Preaching a Subversion," *Theology Today* 55 (1998): 199: "But it is this quality that pushes the Psalmists to the extremity of their imagination, and it is this quality that evokes in the prophets daring images and affrontive metaphors, because no easy language will ever get this God said right."

For the importance of reading the Bible slowly, see Ellen F. Davis, *Wondrous Depth: Preaching the Old Testament* (Louisville: Westminster John Knox, 2005), and Gerhard von Rad, *God at Work in Israel* (Nashville: Abingdon, 1980), 10: "Whatever one wrote in ancient Israel, it was not for speed-reading"; and 18: "Reading the Bible has always demanded that one be prepared for contemplation." For Roman Jakobson, see Linda R. Waugh, "The Poetic Function in the Theory of Roman Jakobson," *Poetics Today* 2/1a (1980): 57–82.

For the Bible as a library of questions, see the book by Timothy Beal, *The Rise and Fall of the Bible: The Unexpected History of an Accidental Book* (Boston: Houghton Mifflin Harcourt, 2011) which is both delightful and instructive in a vast number of ways.

LIST OF INTRODUCTIONS TO THE OLD TESTAMENT AND OTHER USEFUL WORKS

The list here is limited almost exclusively to introductions, categorized into small to mid-range introductions (generally under 300 pages), large-scale introductions (usually over 300 pages and/or marked by extensive coverage of preexisting scholarly literature), and state-of-the-question overviews of the field. The latter are typically edited collections comprised of essays on various sections or books of the Hebrew Bible and/or topics relating to the Old Testament that are composed by different authors. I have arranged this category in chronological order so that one can trace the development of the field. I have also appended a short list of useful reference works. In each category, the sampling provided is truly small (especially as I have limited the list with but one exception to English language publications), selecting works that I have personal familiarity with, that I deem particularly helpful in one way or another, and that may be profitably consulted for future study. Of course, new publications appear almost every day. There is also much that is available on the web, though online material sometimes lacks the careful vetting that continues to mark publication with established presses. The most important book to read next, however, before any other, is the Old Testament itself!

SMALL TO MID-RANGE INTRODUCTIONS

Barstad, Hans M. *A Brief Guide to the Hebrew Bible*. Louisville: Westminster John Knox, 2010. A relatively concise treatment of the three parts of the Hebrew Bible.

Barton, John. *The Bible: The Basics*. 2nd ed. Abingdon: Routledge, 2018. Barton covers the Bible in the modern world, its nature, major genres, religious themes, relationship to history, its social world, and biblical interpretation today.

Beal, Timothy. *Biblical Literacy: The Essential Bible Studies Everyone Needs to Know*. New York: HarperOne, 2009. Covering both Old and New Testaments, Beal gathers some of the most famous selections from the Bible with brief commentary. Helpful introductory information is peppered throughout.

Burnette-Bletsch, Rhonda. *Studying the Old Testament: A Companion*. Nashville: Abingdon, 2007. This volume is organized, like the present book, with chapters on the Torah, Prophets, and Writings.

Ceresko, Anthony R. *Introduction to the Old Testament: A Liberation Perspective*. Rev. ed. Maryknoll, NY: Orbis, 2001. Influenced by the work of Norman Gottwald (see, e.g., his large introduction in the next section), this book understands the Old Testament as emerging from the struggle for liberation and social equality.

Collins, John J. *A Short Introduction to the Hebrew Bible*. 3rd ed. Minneapolis: Fortress, 2018. An abbreviated version of Collins' well-established large introduction (see the next section).

Coogan, Michael D. *The Old Testament: A Very Short Introduction*. Oxford: Oxford University Press, 2008. A concise and insightful probing of several aspects of the Old Testament and its study, including historical probes of the exodus from Egypt and the Assyrian siege of Jerusalem.

Coogan, Michael D. and Cynthia R. Chapman. *A Brief Introduction to the Old Testament: The Hebrew Bible in Its Context*. 4th ed. Oxford: Oxford University Press, 2019. An abbreviated version of the authors' standard introduction (see the next section).

Davis, Ellen F. *Getting Involved with God: Rediscovering the Old Testament*. Cambridge: Cowley, 2001. An elegant treatment of the Psalms, Proverbs, Ecclesiastes, Job, Song of Solomon, a half-dozen other selected texts, and particular issues from the Old Testament. Not a comprehensive introduction but beautifully written and remarkably insightful.

Dell, Katharine. *Opening the Old Testament*. Malden, MA: Blackwell, 2008. A thematic approach that helps readers "open" the Old Testament in terms of history, literature, theology, and ethics.

Goldingay, John. *An Introduction to the Old Testament: Exploring Text, Approaches and Issues.* Downers Grove, IL: IVP Academic, 2015. Following the ordering of the Hebrew Bible, Goldingay offers a host of small chapters of two to four pages in length that helpfully digest a great deal of learning in bite-sized portions.

Kaltner, John. *Reading the Old Testament Anew: Biblical Perspectives on Today's Issues.* Winona, MN: Anselm Academic, 2017. A thoughtful introduction that focuses on creation, covenant, liberation, the human condition, the other, and social justice.

Kaltner, John and Steven L. McKenzie. *The Back Door Introduction to the Bible.* Winona, MN: Anselm Academic, 2012. A lively and humorous introduction to both the Old and New Testaments.

Kaminsky, Joel S. and Joel N. Lohr. *The Hebrew Bible for Beginners: A Jewish and Christian Introduction.* Nashville: Abingdon, 2015. Co-authored by a team of Jewish (Kaminsky) and Christian (Lohr) scholars, this is a book-by-book treatment that includes, for each composition, discussion of the book's use in Judaism and Christianity. See also their earlier treatment of the Pentateuch alone: Joel S. Kaminsky and Joel N. Lohr, *The Torah: A Beginner's Guide* (Oxford: Oneworld, 2011).

Laffey, Alice L. *An Introduction to the Old Testament: A Feminist Perspective.* Philadelphia: Fortress, 1988. Each chapter (on the Pentateuch, Deuteronomistic History, Prophets, and Writings) includes treatments of both themes and texts from a feminist perspective. More extensive and recent works are now widely available but are not introductions. See, for example, the commentary edited by Newsom, Ringe, and Lapsley (under Other Useful Works below).

Levenson, Jon D. *Sinai and Zion: An Entry into the Jewish Bible.* New York: Harper and Row, 1987. A popular, readable, and highly useful introduction from a Jewish perspective.

Levin, Christoph. *The Old Testament: A Brief Introduction.* Princeton: Princeton University Press, 2005. A short and accessible introduction that is focused primarily on matters of composition history.

Linafelt, Tod. *The Hebrew Bible as Literature: A Very Short Introduction.* Oxford: Oxford University Press, 2016. True to its title, Linafelt focuses a keen eye on biblical narrative and poetry and their interaction.

Longman, Tremper III. *Introducing the Old Testament: A Short Guide to Its History and Message.* Grand Rapids: Zondervan, 2012. A brief book-by-book treatment that covers similar issues for each composition including content, authorship and date, genre, and connections to the New Testament.

Magonet, Jonathan. *A Rabbi Reads the Bible*. New ed. London: SCM, 2004. A thematic approach by a gifted literary interpreter.

McConville, Gordon. *The Old Testament*. World Faiths; Teach Yourself Books. London: Hodder & Stoughton, 1996. A remarkably thorough treatment that covers the world of the Old Testament, Old Testament history, contents and composition, criticism and canon, and Jewish and Christian interpretations—all in brief compass.

Novick, Tzvi. *An Introduction to the Scriptures of Israel: History and Theology*. Grand Rapids: Eerdmans, 2018. This volume is organized thematically, rather than chronologically, while still paying attention (per the subtitle) to matters of history and theology, as well as literary convention.

Rendtorff, Rolf. *The Old Testament: An Introduction*. Philadelphia: Fortress, 1986. Originally published in German in 1983, the author of this book is famous for his work on the composition of the Pentateuch. The volume is organized into three parts: The Old Testament as a source of the history of Israel, the literature of the Old Testament in the life of ancient Israel, and the books of the Old Testament. Rendtorff includes an extensive and helpful cross-referencing system in the margins.

Schmid, Konrad. *The Old Testament: A Literary History*. Minneapolis: Fortress, 2012. Although the size of this volume (published in German in 2008) warrants its inclusion here, it is a thorough treatment of the composition history (often called "literary history" in European circles) of the Bible and its constituent parts from the tenth through the second centuries BCE, in which Schmid basically arranges the pieces of the Old Testament in what he deems to be their chronological order.

Sinclair, Celia Brewer. *A Guide Through the Old Testament*. Louisville: Westminster John Knox, 1989. This is a workbook designed to accompany and facilitate reading of the Old Testament on one's own, replete with questions.

Wall, Robert W. and David R. Nienhuis, eds. *A Compact Guide to the Whole Bible: Learning to Read Scripture's Story*. Grand Rapids: Baker Academic, 2015. This volume begins with two chapters on reading the Bible as Scripture and as Story. Four chapters cover the Old Testament, one chapter the intertestamental period, and three cover the New Testament.

Westermann, Claus. *Handbook to the Old Testament*. Minneapolis: Augsburg, 1967. While now quite dated, this book is still useful for its summaries of the biblical books and because its author was one of the greatest biblical scholars of the twentieth century.

Wolff, Hans Walter. *The Old Testament: A Guide to Its Writings*. Philadelphia: Fortress, 1973. Offers a three-fold arrangement around historical books (the past), prophetic books (the future), and the books of teaching (the present).

LARGE-SCALE INTRODUCTIONS

Arnold, Bill T. *Introduction to the Old Testament*. Cambridge: Cambridge University Press, 2014. A handsomely produced volume that adopts a literary approach that nevertheless pays extensive attention to the historical development of monotheism.

Barth, Christoph. *God with Us: A Theological Introduction to the Old Testament*, ed. Geoffrey W. Bromiley. Grand Rapids: Eerdmans, 1991. A thematic treatment of nine key theological topics, written by the second son of the great theologian Karl Barth.

Birch, Bruce C., Walter Brueggemann, Terence E. Fretheim, and David L. Petersen. *A Theological Introduction to the Old Testament*. 2nd ed. Nashville: Abingdon, 2005. A very insightful treatment by a quartet of luminaries.

Boadt, Lawrence. *Reading the Old Testament: An Introduction*. 2nd ed., revised by Richard Clifford and Daniel Harrington. New York: Paulist, 2012. A well-tested introduction by a leading Catholic scholar.

Brettler, Marc Zvi. *How to Read the Bible*. Philadelphia: Jewish Publication Society, 5766/2005. Also published as *How to Read the Jewish Bible* (Oxford: Oxford University Press, 2007). An excellent treatment by one of the best Jewish biblical scholars active in the field today.

Brueggemann, Walter and Tod Linafelt. *An Introduction to the Old Testament: The Canon and Christian Imagination*. 2nd ed. Louisville: Westminster John Knox, 2012. A lucid treatment, organized around the three parts of the Tanakh.

Carvalho, Corrine L. *Encountering Ancient Voices: A Guide to Reading the Old Testament*. 2nd ed. Winona: Anselm Academic, 2010. A thorough treatment, mostly organized canonically, by a leading Roman Catholic scholar.

Childs, Brevard S. *Introduction to the Old Testament as Scripture.* Philadelphia: Fortress, 1979. A breakthrough work when it appeared because it offers a "canonical" (final-form) reading of each book of the Old Testament which assumes the standard historical- and composition-critical reconstructions but attempts to move beyond them to assess the meaning (and theology) of the book as it now stands.

Collins, John J. *Introduction to the Hebrew Bible.* 3rd ed. Minneapolis: Fortress, 2018. A thoroughly historical treatment with some attention to ethical ramifications. Note the helpful companion volume compiled and edited by Ryan P. Bonfiglio with contributions by Ingrid E. Lilly and Michael J. Chan, *A Study Companion to Introduction to the Hebrew Bible.* 2nd ed. Minneapolis: Fortress, 2014.

Coogan, Michael D. and Cynthia R. Chapman. *The Old Testament: A Historical and Literary Introduction to the Hebrew Scriptures.* 4th ed. Oxford: Oxford University Press, 2017. Aptly subtitled, this is a standard textbook in many introductory classrooms.

Driver, S. R. *An Introduction to the Literature of the Old Testament.* Repr. of 9th ed. Gloucester, MA: Peter Smith, 1972. Written by one of the greatest British scholars of the late nineteenth century (1846–1914), this volume remains useful for its rich collection of data and for its superb presentation of the field at the time it was first written (1891; 9th edition = 1919).

Eissfeldt, Otto. *The Old Testament: An Introduction including the Apocrypha and Pseudepigrapha, and also Works of Similar Type from Qumran: The History of the Formation of the Old Testament.* New York: Harper and Row, 1965. A classic work from a giant among mid-twentieth century German scholars. The extended subtitle is revealing of the massive scope and primary focus of this introduction. For many years this was the standard critical introduction to the field and it still retains great usefulness, much like the early work by S. R. Driver (see above).

Gertz, Jan Christian, Angelika Berlejung, Konrad Schmid, and Markus Witte. *T&T Clark Handbook of the Old Testament: An Introduction to the Literature, Religion and History of the Old Testament.* London: T&T Clark International, 2012. A translation of a German original (3rd ed., 2008), this volume, like Zenger et al.'s below, is a thorough and accessible collection of the best in European scholarship on the Old Testament.

Gravett, Sandra L., Karla G. Bohmbach, F. V. Griefenhagen, and Donald C. Polaski. *An Introduction to the Hebrew Bible: A Thematic Approach*. Louisville: Westminster John Knox, 2008. The subtitle is determinative: this introduction includes chapters on space and time, identity, family, gender, the body, ethnicity, class, ideology, media, and deity—among others—before concluding with a chapter that considers the Book of Job. An innovative and intriguing approach.

Gottwald, Norman K. *The Hebrew Bible: A Socio-Literary Introduction*. Philadelphia: Fortress, 1985. For many years a standard introduction, Gottwald's volume—also available in an abbreviated form (*The Hebrew Bible: A Brief Socio-Literary Introduction*. Minneapolis: Fortress, 2008)—is still unique in its heavy attention to sociopolitical matters.

Hamilton, Mark W. *A Theological Introduction to the Old Testament*. Oxford: Oxford University Press, 2018. A theological treatment, mostly oriented around the books in the order of the Christian Bible.

Hayes, Christine. *Introduction to the Bible*. New Haven: Yale University Press, 2012. This accessible treatment is based on the author's popular introductory course at Yale University.

Hess, Richard S. *The Old Testament: A Historical, Theological, and Critical Introduction*. Grand Rapids: Baker Academic, 2016. A lengthy volume that attempts coverage of the full range of comparative, critical, and confessional issues; written by an acknowledged expert in ancient Near Eastern studies.

Hubbard, Robert L. and J. Andrew Dearman. *Introducing the Old Testament*. Grand Rapids: Eerdmans, 2018. A thorough, recent volume that is organized according to Torah, Historical Books, Prophets, and Poetry with an introductory chapter to each of these four divisions.

Knight, Douglas A. and Amy-Jill Levine. *The Meaning of the Bible: What the Jewish Scriptures and Christian Old Testament Can Teach Us*. New York: HarperOne, 2011. A thematic introduction arranged around topics like law and justice, the divine, self and other, sexuality, critique and reform, and so forth.

Kugel, James L. *How to Read the Bible: A Guide to Scripture, Then and Now*. New York: Free Press, 2007. A volume that is noteworthy for its engagement with the history of interpretation, one of the author's primary specialties. See further his amazing treatment of the Pentateuch's history of interpretation in *Traditions of the Bible: A*

Guide to the Bible as It Was at the Start of the Common Era (Cambridge: Harvard University Press, 1998).

Rofé, Alexander. *Introduction to the Literature of the Hebrew Bible.* Jerusalem Biblical Studies 9. Jerusalem: Simor, 2009. A literary treatment by a great Israeli biblical scholar.

Schmid, Konrad. *A Historical Theology of the Hebrew Bible.* Grand Rapids: Eerdmans, 2019. Written by one of the leading biblical scholars alive today, this volume is a lengthy study of the three parts of the Hebrew Bible, assessing the theology of each within a diachronic framework.

Schmidt, Werner H. *Old Testament Introduction.* 2nd ed. New York: Walter de Gruyter and Louisville: Westminster John Knox, 1999. A fully critical introduction but executed on a slightly smaller scale. Includes a helpful section devoted to theology and hermeneutics.

Sellin, Ernst and Georg Fohrer. *Introduction to the Old Testament.* Nashville: Abingdon, 1968. A classic in the tradition of Otto Eissfeldt (see above), which is updated now in the more recent works by Gertz et al. (see above) and Zenger et al. (see below).

Soggin, J. Alberto. *Introduction to the Old Testament from Its Origins to the Closing of the Alexandrian Canon.* Old Testament Library. Louisville: Westminster John Knox, 1989. A standard, full-scale treatment in a renowned series.

Sweeney, Marvin A. *Tanak: A Theological and Critical Introduction to the Jewish Bible.* Minneapolis: Fortress, 2012. A thorough treatment of each book (the Torah is treated together) of the Hebrew Bible by a leading Jewish scholar.

Telushkin, Joseph. *Biblical Literacy: The Most Important People, Events, and Ideas of the Hebrew Bible.* New York: HarperCollins, 1997. A thorough treatment by a popular rabbi. The Torah is treated in the first part of the book (people and events) in 150 pages and is covered again in a second part (laws and ideas) in another 100 pages. The third part helpfully gathers together the 613 laws of the Torah in order of appearance.

Zenger, Erich et al. *Einleitung in das Alte Testament.* 9th ed., ed., Christian Frevel. Studienbücher Theologie 1, 1. Stuttgart: Kohlhammer, 2015. A multi-authored introduction that comes in at over 700 pages. Now in a 9th edition, this is a tried and true repository of some of the best in German scholarship.

STATE-OF-THE-QUESTION OVERVIEWS OF THE FIELD

Peake, Arthur S., ed. *The People and the Book: Essays on the Old Testament*. Oxford: Clarendon, 1925.

Robinson, H. Wheeler, ed. *Record and Revelation: Essays on the Old Testament*. Oxford: Clarendon Press, 1938.

Rowley, H. H., ed. *The Old Testament and Modern Study: A Generation of Discovery and Research: Essays by Members of the Society for Old Testament Study*. Oxford: Clarendon, 1951.

Anderson, G. W., ed. *Tradition and Interpretation: Essays by Members of the Society for Old Testament Study*. Oxford: Clarendon, 1979.

Clements, R. E., ed. *The World of Ancient Israel: Sociological, Anthropological and Political Perspectives: Essays by Members of the Society for Old Testament Study*. Cambridge: Cambridge University Press, 1989.

Knight, Douglas A. and Gene M. Tucker, eds. *The Hebrew Bible and Its Modern Interpreters*. Minneapolis: Fortress and Atlanta: Scholars Press, 1989.

Mays, James Luther, David L. Petersen, and Kent Harold Richards, eds. *Old Testament interpretation: Past, Present, and Future: Essays in Honor of Gene M. Tucker*. Nashville: Abingdon, 1995.

McKenzie, Steven L. and M. Patrick Graham, eds. *The Hebrew Bible Today: An Introduction to Critical Issues*. Louisville: Westminster John Knox, 1998.

Baker, David W. and Bill T. Arnold, eds. *The Face of Old Testament Studies: A Survey of Contemporary Approaches*. Grand Rapids: Baker, 1999.

Mayes, A. D. H., ed. *Text in Context: Essays by Members of the Society for Old Testament Study*. Oxford: Oxford University Press, 2000.

Perdue, Leo G., ed. *The Blackwell Companion to the Hebrew Bible*. Oxford: Blackwell, 2001.

Greenspahn, Frederick. *The Hebrew Bible: New Insights and Scholarship*. New York: New York University Press, 2007.

Barton, John, ed. *The Hebrew Bible: A Critical Companion*. Princeton: Princeton University Press, 2016.

Chapman, Stephen B. and Marvin A. Sweeney, eds. *The Cambridge Companion to the Hebrew Bible / Old Testament*. Cambridge: Cambridge University Press, 2016.

OTHER USEFUL WORKS

Barton, John and John Muddiman, eds. *The Oxford Bible Commentary*. Oxford: Oxford University Press, 2001.

Brueggemann, Walter. *Theology of the Old Testament: Testimony, Dispute, Advocacy*. Minneapolis: Fortress, 1997.

Coggins, R. J. and J. L. Houlden, eds. *The SCM Dictionary of Biblical Interpretation*. London: SCM, 1990.

Ehrlich, Carl S., ed. *From an Antique Land: An Introduction to Ancient Near Eastern Literature*. Lanham: Rowan & Littlefield, 2009.

Freedman, David Noel, ed. *The Anchor Bible Dictionary*. 6 vols. New York: Doubleday, 1992.

Gorman, Michael J., ed., *Scripture and Its Interpretation: A Global, Ecumenical Introduction to the Bible*. Grand Rapids: Baker Academic, 2017.

Hayes, John H., ed. *Dcitionary of Biblical Interpretation*. 2 vols. Nashville: Abingdon, 1999.

Newsom, Carol A., Sharon H. Ringe, and Jacquelyn E. Lapsley, eds. *Women's Bible Commentary*. 3rd. ed. Louisville: Westminster John Knox, 2012.

O'Day, Gail R. and David L. Petersen, eds. *Theological Bible Commentary*. Louisville: Westminster John Knox, 2009.

Patte, Daniel, ed. *Global Bible Commentary*. Nashville: Abingdon, 2004.

Powell, Mark Allan, ed. *HarperCollins Bible Dictionary*. Rev. ed. New York: HarperOne, 2011.

Roncace, Mark and Joseph Weaver, eds., *Global Perspectives on the Bible*. Boston: Pearson, 2014.

Roncace, Mark and Joseph Weaver, eds. *Global Perspectives on the Old Testament*. Boston: Pearson, 2014.

Sakenfeld, Katharine Doob, ed. *The New Interpreter's Dictionary of the Bible*. 5 vols. Nashville: Abingdon, 2006–2009.

Soulen, Richard N. and R. Kendall Soulen. *Handbook of Biblical Criticism*. 4th ed. Louisville: Westminster John Knox, 2011.

Vanhoozer, Kevin J., ed. *Dictionary for Theological Interpretation of the Bible*. Grand Rapids: Baker Academic, 2005.

SCRIPTURE AND ANCIENT SOURCE INDEX

SUBJECT AND AUTHOR INDEX

Note: **Bold** page numbers refer to charts.

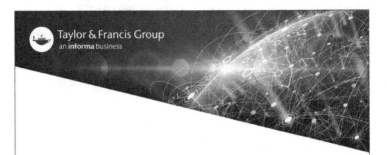